Social Engineering

Hacking Systems, Nations, and Societies

Social Engineering
Hacking Systems, Nations, and Societies

Michael Erbschloe

CRC Press
Taylor & Francis Group
Boca Raton London New York

CRC Press is an imprint of the
Taylor & Francis Group, an **informa** business

CRC Press
Taylor & Francis Group
6000 Broken Sound Parkway NW, Suite 300
Boca Raton, FL 33487-2742

© 2020 by Taylor & Francis Group, LLC
CRC Press is an imprint of Taylor & Francis Group, an informa business

No claim to original U.S. Government works

Printed on acid-free paper

International Standard Book Number-13: 978-0-367-31337-1 (paperback)

Visit the Taylor & Francis website at
http://www.taylorandfrancis.com

and the CRC Press website at
http://www.crcpress.com

Contents

Author

Michael Erbschloe has worked for over 30 years performing analysis of the economics of information technology, public policy relating to technology, and utilizing technology in reengineering organization processes. He has authored several books on social and management issues of information technology, most of which cover some aspects of information or corporate security. He has also taught at several universities and developed technology-related curricula. His career has focused on several interrelated areas: technology strategy, analysis, and forecasting; teaching and curriculum development; writing books and articles; speaking at conferences and industry events; publishing and editing; and public policy analysis and program evaluation. He has authored books and articles addressing the use of the Internet and social media in social engineering efforts.

1

INTRODUCTION TO SOCIAL ENGINEERING USE BY BAD GUYS

Social engineering is an incredibly effective process of attack with more than 80% of cyber attacks, and over 70% of those from nation-states, being initiated and executed by exploiting humans rather than computer or network security flaws. Thus to build secure cyber systems, it is not only necessary to protect the computers and networks that make up these systems but also to educate and train their human users about security procedures as well.

Attacks on humans are called social engineering because they manipulate or engineer users into performing desired actions or divulging sensitive information. The most general social engineering attacks simply attempt to get unsuspecting Internet users to click on **malicious links**. More focused attacks attempt to elicit sensitive information, such as passwords or private information from organizations or steal things of value from particular individuals by earning unwarranted trust.

These attacks generally ask people to perform the desired behavior that the attacker wants to induce from the victim. To do this, they need the victim's trust, which is typically earned through interaction or co-opted via a copied or stolen identity. Depending on the level of sophistication, these attacks will go after individuals, organizations, or wide swathes of the population. Scammers often use familiar company names or pretend to be someone known to the victim. A 2018 real-world example exploited the name of Netflix when an email designed to steal personal information was sent to an unknown number of recipients. The email claimed the user's account was on hold because Netflix was having some trouble with their current billing information and invited the user to click on a link to update their payment method.[1]

One reason social engineering attacks work is that it is difficult for users to verify each and every communication they receive. Moreover, verification requires a level of technical expertise that most users lack. To compound the problem, the number of users that have access to privileged information is often large, creating a commensurately large attack surface.[2]

The act of convincing individuals to divulge sensitive information and using it for malicious endeavors is ages old. Social engineering attacks have occurred on the Internet since it came into existence. But before the growth of the Internet, criminals used the telephone, the postal service, or advertising to pose as a trusted agent to acquire information. Most people agree that the term **phishing** originated in the mid-1990s, when it was used to describe the acquisition of Internet service provider (ISP) account information. However, the term has evolved to encompass a variety of attacks that target personal or corporate information possessed by individuals, including by telephone, email, social media, in person observation, gaming platforms, theft of postal delivery letters or packages, and, an age-old favorite, dumpster diving or trash picking.

1.1 Understanding the Breadth of Social Engineering as a Weapon

Regardless of the social network, users continue to be fooled online by persons claiming to be somebody else. Unlike the physical world, individuals can misrepresent everything about themselves when they communicate online, ranging not only from their names and business affiliations (something that is fairly easy to do in person as well), but also extending to their gender, age, and location (identifiers that are far more difficult to fake in person). Years ago investigators called these types of people confidence or con men.

Perhaps as a result of the high-tech times, con artists are now referred to as being engaged in social engineering. It should come as no surprise to learn that the Federal Bureau of Investigation (FBI) is investigating classic investment fraud schemes, such as **Ponzi schemes**, that are now being carried out in virtual worlds. Other con artists are able to conduct identity theft crimes by misidentifying themselves on social networking sites and then tricking their victims into giving them their account names and passwords as well as other personally identifiable information.

In addition to **identity theft crimes,** child predators routinely use social networking sites to locate and communicate with future victims and other pedophiles. In at least one publicized case from 2018, an individual attempted to extort nude photos of teenage girls after he gained control of their email and social networking accounts. That particular FBI investigation led to an 18-year federal sentence for the offender, reflecting that these crimes are serious and will not be tolerated.[3]

Social engineering is the broad term for any attack that relies on fooling people into taking action or divulging information. Social engineering has been defined in several ways as is shown in Box 1.1.

BOX 1.1   DEFINITIONS OF SOCIAL ENGINEERING

The act of deceiving an individual into revealing sensitive information by associating with the individual to gain confidence and trust.

Source: NIST SP 800-63-2 under Social Engineering [superseded]

An attempt to trick someone into revealing information (e.g., a password) that can be used to attack systems or networks.

Source(s): CNSSI 4009-2015 (NIST SP 800-61 Rev. 2), NIST SP 800-61 Rev. 2 under Social Engineering, NIST SP 800-82 Rev. 2 under Social Engineering (NIST SP 800-61)

A general term for attackers trying to trick people into revealing sensitive information or performing certain actions, such as downloading and executing files that appear to be benign but are actually malicious.

Source: NIST SP 800-114 under Social Engineering [superseded]

The process of attempting to trick someone into revealing information (e.g., a password).

Source: NIST SP 800-115 under Social Engineering

The act of deceiving an individual into revealing sensitive information, obtaining unauthorized access, or committing fraud by associating with the individual to gain confidence and trust.

Source: NIST SP 800-63-3 under Social Engineering

Source: Glossary. Computer Security Resource Center. Accessed February 1, 2019. https://csrc.nist.gov/glossary/ term/social-engineering.

Today the term phishing has evolved to encompass a variety of attacks that target personal or corporate information. Originally, phishing was identified as the use of electronic mail messages, designed to look like messages from a trusted agent, such as a bank, auction site, or online commerce site. These messages usually implore the user to take some form of action, such as validating their account information. They often use a sense of urgency (such as the threat of account suspension) to motivate the user to take action. Recently, there have been several new social engineering approaches to deceive unsuspecting users. These include the offer to fill out a survey for an online banking site with a monetary reward if the user includes account information, and email messages claiming to be from hotel reward clubs, asking users to verify credit card information that a customer may store on the legitimate site for reservation purposes. Included in the message is a uniform resource locater (URL) for the victim to use, which then directs the user to a site to enter their personal information. This site is crafted to closely mimic the look and feel of the legitimate site. The information is then collected and used by the criminals. Over time, these fake emails and websites have evolved to become more technically deceiving to casual investigation.[4]

1.2 Social Engineering Fraud Schemes

There are a variety of Internet fraud schemes being used by cyber-criminals at any given time. By way of example, a recent fraud scheme involved a cybercriminal gaining access to an unsuspecting user's email account or social networking site. The fraudster, who claimed to be the account holder, then sent messages to the user's friends. In the message, the fraudster stated that he was on travel and had been robbed of his credit cards, passport, money, and cell phone, and was in need of money immediately. Without realizing that the message was from a criminal, the friends wired money to an overseas account without validating the claim.

Phishing schemes attempt to make Internet users believe that they are receiving email(s) from a trusted source even though that is not the case. Phishing attacks on social networking site users come in various formats, including messages within the social networking site either from strangers or compromised friend accounts; links or videos within a social networking site profile claiming to lead to something harmless that turns out to be harmful; or emails sent to users claiming to be from the social networking site itself. Social networking site users fall victim to the schemes due to the higher level of trust typically displayed while using social networking sites. Users often accept into their private sites people that they do not actually know, or sometimes fail to properly set privacy settings on their profile. This gives cyber thieves an advantage when trying to trick their victims through various phishing schemes.

Social networking sites, as well as corporate websites in general, provide criminals with enormous amounts of information to be able to create official-looking documents and send them to individual targets who have shown interest in specific subjects. The personal and detailed nature of the information erodes the victim's sense of caution, leading them to open the malicious email. Such an email will contain an attachment that holds malicious software designed to provide the email's sender with control over the victim's entire computer. By the time the **malware** infection is discovered, it is often too late to protect the data from compromise.

Cybercriminals design advanced malware to act with precision to infect, conceal access, steal, or modify data without detection. Coders of advanced malware are patient and have been known to test a network and its users to evaluate defensive responses. Malware, also known as malicious code, refers to a program that is covertly inserted into another program with the intent to destroy data, run destructive or intrusive programs, or otherwise compromise the confidentiality, integrity, or availability of the victim's data, applications, or operating system. Malware is the most common external threat to most hosts, causing widespread damage and disruption and necessitating extensive recovery efforts within most organizations. Advanced malware may use a layered approach to infect and gain elevated privileges on a system. Usually, these types of attacks are bundled with an additional cybercrime tactic, such as social engineering or zero day exploits. Malware is often employed to misappropriate information and data that can be readily used such as login credentials, credit card and bank account numbers, and, in some cases, trade secrets.

In the first phase of a malware infection, a user might receive a **spear phishing** email that obtains access to the user's information or gains entry into the system under the user's credentials. Once the cybercriminal initiates a connection to the user or system, they can further exploit it using other vectors that may give them deeper access to system resources. In the second phase, the hacker might install a backdoor to establish a persistent presence on the network that can no longer be discovered through the use of anti-virus software or firewalls.

Cyber thieves use data mining on social networking sites as a way to extract sensitive information about their victims. This can be done by criminal actors on either a large or small scale. For example, in a large-scale data mining scheme, a cybercriminal may send out a "getting to know you" quiz to a large list of social networking site users. While the answers to these questions do not appear to be malicious on the surface, they often mimic the same questions that are asked by financial institutions or email account providers when an individual has forgotten their password. Thus, an email address and the answers to the quiz questions can provide the cybercriminal with the tools to enter a bank account, email account, or credit card account in order to transfer money or siphon the account. Small-scale data mining may also be easy for cybercriminals if social networking site users have not properly guarded their profile or access to sensitive information. Indeed, some networking applications encourage users to post whether or not they are on vacation, simultaneously letting burglars know when nobody is home.[5]

Ransomware scams, which involve a type of malware that infects computers and restricts users' access to their files or threatens the permanent destruction of their information unless a ransom—anywhere from hundreds to thousands of dollars—is paid. Ransomware impacts home computers, businesses, financial institutions, government agencies, and academic institutions, and other organizations can and have become infected with it as well, resulting in the loss of sensitive or proprietary information, a disruption to regular operations, financial losses incurred to restore systems and files, and/or potential harm to an organization's reputation.

Ransomware has been around for several years, but there's been a definite uptick lately in its use by cybercriminals. The FBI, along with public and private-sector partners, is targeting these offenders and their scams. When ransomware first hit the scene, computers predominately became infected with it when users opened email attachments that contained the malware. But more recently, we are seeing an increasing number of incidents involving so-called drive-by ransomware, where users can infect their computers simply by clicking on a compromised website, often lured there by a deceptive email or pop-up window.

Another new trend involves the ransom payment method. While some of the earlier ransomware scams involved having victims pay ransom with pre-paid cards, victims are now increasingly asked to pay with Bitcoin, a decentralized virtual currency network that attracts criminals because of the anonymity the system offers. Another growing problem is ransomware that locks down mobile phones and demands payments to unlock them.

The FBI and federal, international, and private-sector partners have taken proactive steps to neutralize some of the more significant ransomware scams through law enforcement actions against major botnets that facilitated the distribution and operation of ransomware. For example, Reveton ransomware, delivered by a malware known as Citadel, falsely warned victims that their computers had

been identified by the FBI or Department of Justice as being associated with child pornography websites or other illegal online activity.
In June 2013, Microsoft, the FBI, and financial partners disrupted
a massive criminal botnet built on the Citadel malware, putting the
brakes on Reveton's distribution. Cryptolocker was a highly sophisticated ransomware that used cryptographic key pairs to encrypt the
computer files of its victims and demanded ransom for the encryption key. In June 2014, the FBI announced in conjunction with the
Gameover Zeus botnet disruption that the United States and international law enforcement officials had seized the Cryptolocker command and control servers.[6]

1.3 The Cyber Underground

The impact of cybercrime on individuals and commerce can be substantial, with the consequences ranging from a mere inconvenience
to financial ruin. The potential for considerable profits is enticing to
young criminals and has resulted in the creation of a large underground
economy known as the cyber underground. The cyber underground is a
pervasive market governed by rules and logic that closely mimic those
of the legitimate business world, including a unique language, a set of
expectations about its members' conduct, and a system of stratification
based on knowledge and skill, activities, and reputation.

One of the ways that cybercriminals communicate within the cyber
underground is on online forums. It is on these forums that cybercriminals buy and sell login credentials (such as those for email, social networking sites, or financial accounts); phishing kits, malicious software,
and access to botnets; and victim social security numbers (SSNs), credit
cards, and other sensitive information. These criminals are increasingly
professionalized, organized, and have unique or specialized skills.

In addition, cybercrime is increasingly transnational in nature,
with individuals living in different countries around the world working together on the same schemes. In late 2008, an international
hacking ring carried out one of the most complicated and organized
computer fraud attacks ever conducted. The crime group used sophisticated hacking techniques to compromise the encryption used to
protect data on 44 payroll debit cards, and then provided a network
of cashers to withdraw more than $9 million from over 2,100 ATMs
in at least 280 cities worldwide, including cities in the United States,

Russia, Ukraine, Estonia, Italy, Hong Kong, Japan, and Canada. The $9 million loss occurred within a span of less than 12 hours. The cyber underground facilitates the exchange of cybercrime services, tools, expertise, and resources, which enables this sort of transnational criminal operation to take place across multiple countries.

Apart from the cybercrime consequences associated with social networking sites, valuable information can be inadvertently exposed by military or government personnel via their social networking site profile. In a recently publicized case, an individual created a fake profile on multiple social networking sites posing as an attractive female intelligence analyst and extended friend requests to government contractors, military personnel, and other government personnel. Many of the friend requests were accepted, even though the profile was of a fictitious person. According to press accounts, the deception provided its creator with access to a fair amount of sensitive data, including a picture from a soldier taken on patrol in Afghanistan that contained embedded data identifying his exact location. The person who created the fake social networking profiles, when asked what he was trying to prove, responded: The first thing was the issue of trust and how easily it is given. The second thing was to show how much different information gets leaked out through various networks. He also noted that although some individuals recognized the sites as fake, they had no central place to warn others about the perceived fraud, thus helping to ensure 300 new connections in a month.

This last point is worth expanding upon. Some social networking sites have taken it upon themselves to be model corporate citizens by voluntarily providing functions for users to report acts of abuse. A number of sites have easy to use buttons or links that, with a single click, will send a message to the system administrator alerting them of potentially illegal or abusive content. Unfortunately though, many sites have not followed the lead. Some sites provide users with no ability to report abuse, while others either intentionally or unintentionally discourage reporting by requiring users to complete a series of onerous steps every time they want to report abuse.[3]

1.4 FBI and Strategic Partnerships

The Department of Justice (DOJ) leads the national effort to prosecute cybercrime, and the FBI, in collaboration with other federal law enforcement agencies, investigates cybercrime. The FBI's cybercrime mission is fourfold: First and foremost, to stop those behind the most serious computer intrusions and the spread of malicious code; second, to identify and thwart online sexual predators who use the Internet to meet and exploit children and to produce, possess, or share child pornography; third, to counteract operations that target US intellectual property, thus endangering national security and competitiveness; and fourth, to dismantle national and transnational organized criminal enterprises engaging in Internet fraud. To this end, the FBI has established cyber squads in each of their 56 field offices around the country, with more than 1,000 specially trained agents, analysts, and digital forensic examiners. However, the FBI cannot combat this threat alone.

Some of the best tools in the FBI's arsenal for combating any crime problem are its long-standing partnerships with federal, state, local, and international law enforcement agencies, as well as with the private sector and academia. At the federal level, and by presidential mandate, the FBI led the National Cyber Investigative Joint Task Force (NCIJTF) as a multi-agency national focal point for coordinating, integrating, and sharing pertinent information related to cyber threat investigations in order to determine the identity, location, intent, motivation, capabilities, alliances, funding, and methodologies of cyber threat groups and individuals. In doing so the partners of the NCIJTF supported the US government's full range of options across all elements of national power.

The FBI also partnered closely with not-for-profit organizations, including extensive partnerships with the National White Collar Crime Center (NW3C), in establishing the Internet Crime Complaint Center (IC3), the National Cyber-Forensic and Training Alliance (NCFTA), the InfraGard National Members Alliance in establishing InfraGard, the Financial Services Information Sharing & Analysis Center (FS-ISAC), and the National Center for Missing and Exploited Children (NCMEC).

Just one example of coordination highlights how effective we are when working within these closely established partnerships. In early 2019, Romanian police and prosecutors conducted one of Romania's largest police actions ever—an investigation of an organized crime group engaged in Internet fraud. The investigation deployed over

700 law enforcement officers who conducted searches at 103 locations, which led to the arrest of 34 people. Over 600 victims of this Romanian crime ring were US citizens. The success in bringing down this group was due in large part to the strength of the partnership between Romanian law enforcement and the US domestic federal, state, and local partners. Through extensive coordination by the FBI's legal attaché (legat) in Bucharest, the Internet Crime Complaint Center provided the Romanians with over 600 complaints it had compiled from submissions to the www.IC3.gov reporting portal. In addition, and again in close coordination with the FBI's legat, over 45 FBI field offices assisted in the investigation by conducting interviews to obtain victim statements on Romanian complaint forms, and by obtaining police reports and covering other investigative leads within their divisions.

Working closely with others, sharing information, and leveraging all available resources and expertise, the FBI and its partners have made significant strides in combating cybercrime. Clearly, there is more work to be done, but through a coordinated approach the United States has become more nimble and responsive in its efforts to bring justice to the most egregious offenders.[3]

1.5 The Basic Steps to Countering Phishing Attacks

Phishing is when a scammer uses fraudulent emails or texts, or copycat websites, to get you to share valuable personal information—such as account numbers, social security numbers, or login IDs and passwords. Scammers use this information to steal a person's money, or identity, or both. Scammers also use phishing emails to get access to computers or networks; then they install programs like ransomware that can lock users out of important files on their computer.

Phishing scammers lure their targets into a false sense of security by copying the familiar, trusted logos of established, legitimate companies. Or they pretend to be a friend or family member. Phishing scammers make it seem like they need your information or someone else's, quickly—or something bad will happen. They might say your account will be frozen, you'll fail to get a tax refund, or your boss will get mad, even that a family member will be hurt or you could be arrested. They tell lies to get to you to give them information.

There are several practices that computer users should employ to prevent phishing from being successful:

- Be cautious about opening attachments or clicking on links in emails. Even your friends' or family members' accounts could be hacked. Files and links can contain malware that can weaken your computer's security.
- Do your own typing. If a company or organization you know sends you a link or phone number, don't click. Use your favorite search engine to look up the website or phone number yourself. Even though a link or phone number in an email may look like the real deal, scammers can hide the true destination.
- Make the call if you're not sure. Do not respond to any emails that request personal or financial information. Phishers use pressure tactics and prey on fear. If you think a company, friend, or family member really does need personal information from you, pick up the phone and call them yourself using the number on their website or in your address book, not the one in the email.
- Turn on two-factor authentication. For accounts that support it, two-factor authentication requires both your password and an additional piece of information to log in to your account. The second piece could be a code sent to your phone or a random number generated by an app or a token. This protects your account even if your password is compromised.
- As an extra precaution, you may want to choose more than one type of second authentication (e.g., a PIN) in case your primary method (such as a phone) is unavailable.
- Back up your files to an external hard drive or cloud storage. Back up your files regularly to protect yourself against viruses or a ransomware attack.
- Keep your security up to date. Use security software you trust, and make sure you set it to update automatically.[7]
- Be suspicious of unsolicited phone calls, visits, or email messages from individuals asking about employees or other internal information. If an unknown individual claims to be from a legitimate organization, try to verify his or her identity directly with the company.
- Do not provide personal information or information about your organization, including its structure or networks,

unless you are certain of a person's authority to have the information.
- Do not reveal personal or financial information in an email, and do not respond to email solicitations for this information. This includes following links sent in emails.
- Do not send sensitive information over the Internet without checking a website's security.
- Pay attention to the Uniform Resource Locator of a website. Malicious websites may look identical to a legitimate site, but the URL may use a variation in spelling or a different domain (e.g., .com vs. .net).
- If you are unsure whether an email request is legitimate, try to verify it by contacting the company directly. Do not use contact information provided on a website connected to the request; instead, check previous statements for contact information.
- Install and maintain anti-virus software, firewalls, and email filters to reduce some of this traffic.
- Take advantage of any anti-phishing features offered by your email client and web browser.
- Report phishing emails and texts (Box 1.2).[8]

BOX 1.2   HOW TO REPORT PHISHING SCAMS

Forward phishing emails to spam@uce.gov—and to the organization impersonated in the email. Your report is most effective when you include the full email header, but most email programs hide this information. To ensure the header is included, search the name of your email service with "full email header" into your favorite search engine.

File a report with the Federal Trade Commission at FTC.gov/complaint.

Visit Identitytheft.gov. Victims of phishing could become victims of identity theft; there are steps you can take to minimize your risk.

You can also report phishing email to reportphishing@apwg.org. The Anti-Phishing Working Group—which includes ISPs, security vendors, financial institutions, and law enforcement agencies—uses these reports to fight phishing.

The Federal Trade Commission (FTC) and the National Association of Realtors® warned home buyers about an email and money wiring scam in 2016. Hackers had been breaking into some consumers' and real estate professionals' email accounts to get information about upcoming real estate transactions. After figuring out the closing dates, the hacker would send an email to the buyer, posing as the real estate professional or title company. The bogus email would say there had been a last minute change to the wiring instructions, and tell the buyer to wire closing costs to a different account. But it would be the scammer's account. If the buyer took the bait, their bank account could be cleared out in a matter of minutes. Often, that would be money the buyer would never see again.

At that time the FTC reiterated its recommendations to not email financial information and if users give financial information on the web, to make sure the site is secure. Look for a URL that begins with https (the "s" stands for secure). And, instead of clicking a link in an email to go to an organization's site, look up the real URL and type in the web address yourself. In addition be cautious about opening attachments and downloading files from emails, regardless of who sent them. These files can contain malware that can weaken a computer's security.[9]

Phishing attacks can also attempt to leverage recent events like when health insurer Anthem's data breach affected more than 80 million customers. Scam artists sent phony Anthem emails that pretended to help customers, but actually phished for their personal information. The phony email was designed to look as if it came from Anthem and asked customers to click on a link for free credit monitoring or credit card account protection. Anthem reported that it would contact current and former customers by postal mail with specific information on how to enroll in credit monitoring. Anthem also stated that it would not be calling customers about the data breach or asking for credit card information or social security numbers over the phone.[10]

1.6 A New Level of Social Engineering for the 21st Century

Russia has deployed hybrid forms of information and cyber warfare in ways that, until now, have been unfamiliar to most Americans.

By weaponizing stolen information and propagating **disinformation**, Russian intelligence services have worked to discredit the United States both at home and abroad, disrupt its foreign policy, and sow divisions internally. The most recent glaring example, of course, was Russia's intervention in the 2016 US presidential election, which the intelligence community confirmed was aimed at aiding the election of President Trump and undermining Americans' confidence in the electoral system.

Russian intervention in foreign elections to advance its interests is not a new phenomenon, and it is not confined to the United States. The governments of Germany and France have sounded alarm bells that Russia is currently conducting similar operations on their territory in advance of national elections in 2019, targeting candidates thought to be unfriendly to Russian interests.

Russia also spends significant resources on a vast network of propaganda outlets, including Russia Today (RT) in the United States, to disseminate disinformation that weakens democratic consensus and strengthens the political fringe. RT reportedly spends $400 million on its Washington bureau alone; and it has more YouTube subscribers than any other broadcaster, including the BBC. Russia oversees dozens of other news sources in tandem with RT, seeding salacious stories through one website that are picked up and amplified through others. Deep in the shadows, Russia employs hundreds of English-literate young people to operate a vast network of fake online identities to write blog posts and comments.

Russia's ability to wage information warfare has been greatly aided by its heavy investments in cyberspace, where the US remains ill-equipped to counter or deter its aggressive probing. Russia's activity in this domain reflects an updated national security strategy that emphasizes asymmetric tactics to exploit vulnerabilities in adversaries while weakening their ability and resolve to counter Russian policy. In recent public reports, the US intelligence community identified Russia as one of the most sophisticated nation-state actors in cyberspace.[11]

Russia's interference is covert as well as overt, where active measures are diverse, larger-scale, and more technologically sophisticated. They continually adapt and morph in accordance with changing technology and circumstances. By striking at Europe and the United States at the same time, the interference appears to be geared toward undermining the effectiveness and cohesion of the Western alliance as such and the legitimacy of the West as a normative force upholding a global order based on universal rules rather than might alone.[12]

In 2007, the Facebook Platform was expanded with more applications that enabled a user's calendar to be able to show your friends' birthdays, maps to show where the user's friends live, and address book to show their pictures. To do this, Facebook enabled people to log in to apps and share who their friends were and some information about them. Then, in 2013, a Cambridge University researcher named Aleksandr Kogan created a personality quiz app. It was installed by around 300,000 people who agreed to share some of their Facebook information as well as some information from their friends whose privacy settings allowed it. Given the way the platform worked at that time meant Kogan was able to access some information about tens of millions of friends. In 2014, to prevent abusive apps, Facebook announced that they were changing the entire platform to dramatically limit the Facebook information apps could access. Most importantly, apps like Kogan's could no longer ask for information about a person's friends unless their friends had also authorized the app. Facebook also required developers to get approval from Facebook before they could request any data beyond a user's public profile, friend list, and email address. These actions would prevent any app like Kogan's from being able to access as much Facebook data today.

In 2015, Facebook learned from journalists at *The Guardian* that Kogan had shared data from his app with Cambridge Analytica even though it is against Facebook policies for developers to share data without people's consent. Facebook immediately banned Kogan's app and demanded that Kogan and other entities he gave the data to, including Cambridge Analytica, formally certify that they had deleted all improperly acquired data. Later Facebook learned from *The Guardian*, *The New York Times*, and Channel 4 that Cambridge Analytica may not have deleted the data as they had certified. Facebook immediately banned them from using any Facebook services.

The Facebook security team had been aware of traditional Russian cyber threats like hacking and malware for years. Leading up to Election Day in November 2016, Facebook detected and dealt with several threats with ties to Russia. This included activity by a group called APT28 that the US government had publicly linked to Russian military intelligence services. But while the primary focus was on traditional threats, Facebook also saw some new behavior in the summer of 2016 when APT28-related accounts, under the banner of DC Leaks, created fake personas that were used to seed stolen information to journalists. Facebook shut these accounts down for violating policies. After the election, Facebook continued to investigate and learn more about these new threats and found that bad actors had used coordinated networks of fake accounts to interfere in the election: Promoting or attacking specific candidates and causes, creating distrust in political institutions, or simply spreading confusion. Some of these bad actors also used Facebook ad tools as phishing tools to draw people deeper into the myriad of misinformation and disinformation. Facebook also learned about a disinformation campaign run by the Internet Research Agency (IRA) a Russian agency that has repeatedly acted deceptively and tried to manipulate people in the United States, Europe, and Russia. Facebook found about 470 accounts and pages linked to the IRA, which generated around 80,000 Facebook posts over about a two-year period. The best estimate is that approximately 126 million people may have been served content from a Facebook page associated with the IRA at some point during that period. On Instagram, where data on reach is not as complete, about 120,000 pieces of content were found, and the estimate is that an additional 20 million people were likely served it. Over the same period, the IRA also spent approximately $100,000 on more than 3,000 ads on Facebook and Instagram, which were seen by an estimated 11 million people in the United States. Facebook shut down these IRA accounts in August 2017.[13]

In a white paper draft released by US Senator Mark R. Warner in 2018, he contended that, in the course of the US Congress investigating Russia's interference in the 2016 election, the extent to which many Internet technologies were exploited and their providers repeatedly caught wrong-footed has been unmistakable. More than illuminating the capacity of these technologies to be exploited by bad actors, the revelations of 2018 have revealed the dark underbelly of an entire ecosystem. The speed with which these products have grown and come to dominate nearly every aspect of our social, political, and economic lives has in many ways obscured the shortcomings of their creators in anticipating the harmful effects of their use. The Government has failed to adapt and has been incapable or unwilling to adequately address the impacts of these trends on privacy, competition, and public discourse.

Warner further contended that the size and reach of these platforms demand that we ensure proper oversight, transparency, and effective management of technologies that in large measure undergird our social lives, our economy, and our politics. Numerous opportunities exist to work with these companies, other stakeholders, and policymakers to make sure that we are adopting appropriate safeguards to ensure that this ecosystem no longer exists as "the Wild West"—unmanaged and not accountable to users or broader society—but instead operates to the broader advantage of society, competition, and broad-based innovation.

This is just the beginning of discovery as to how social media tools have been and are being used in social engineering campaigns. It is also just the beginning of what will be a long-term effort to regulate social media providers and require them to protect the public from social engineers using these tools to manipulate behavior and impact the outcome of elections and the functioning of social institutions.[14]

1.7 The Organization of this Book

This book is designed to save managers and cybersecurity foot soldiers time that it would otherwise take to research all aspects of social engineering approaches and mitigation methods. As a result, this book will better inform planners on setting goals and about defensible actions to take against social engineering attacks and better enable managers to deal with those that may victimize them.

To make this book helpful for graduate- or professional-level seminar classes, Seminar Discussion Topics are provided in each chapter as well as possible Seminar Group Projects that are expected to take no more than 30 minutes for the group to work, with time for groups to present their results. The chapters are arranged in a manner that provides for the analysis of social engineering use by different types of criminals or legitimate organizations and special interests groups.

Chapter 1 provides a brief introduction to social engineering, phishing, and the efforts of law enforcement in the United States to combat electronic crime.

Chapter 2 examines the continuum of social engineering approaches and tactics that scammers employ to exploit or steal information or money from victims including individuals and organizations. This includes fake emails and websites evolving to become more technically deceiving to casual investigation and the definition of phishing has grown to encompass a wider variety of electronic financial crimes.

Chapter 3 examines several approaches to phishing scams that have flourished in recent years due to favorable economic and technological conditions. The chapter also provides an overview of government agencies that combat the scams, identity theft, and online fraud in general including the Internet Crime Complaint Center (IC3), the Federal Trade Commission (FTC), which works to prevent fraudulent, deceptive, and unfair business practices in the marketplace, and the Securities and Exchange Commission (SEC), which protects against fraud in the securities market. Many of the complaints handled by the SEC are regarding crimes perpetrated through the use of social engineering. In addition, the chapter reviews several instances of social engineering being employed to commit criminal acts.

Chapter 4 focuses on securing organizations and protecting individuals against social engineering attacks. An organization's security culture contributes to the effectiveness of its information security program. The management team should understand and support information security and provide appropriate resources for developing, implementing, and maintaining the information security program. The result of this understanding and support is a program in which management and employees are committed to integrating the program into lines of business, support functions, and third-party management programs.

Chapter 5 analyzes how social engineering attacks are more effective when the bait or the ploy fits into a context that the recipient of a message relates to as routine or normal. The vast amount of **Personally Identifiable Information (PII)** available on the Internet makes it easy for social engineering attackers to find subject matter that can be relatable to individuals in their private lives and corporate employees in the pursuit of their business activities. Thus, the information that is publicly available about individuals or organizations has become a security issue because it can be used in socially engineered attacks on systems or attempts to defraud or steal identities. The chapter reviews many of the security issues surrounding PII.

Chapter 6 examines the debate and speculation regarding the exploitation of social media for foreign organizations to influence the outcome of elections in the United States and Europe during recent elections. There is little doubt that Russian organizations, and perhaps those of other nations, have indeed used social media to attempt to influence elections. This chapter provides a brief overview of testimony of social media executives before the US Congress. It then continues by examining the activity of foreign players as well as domestic organizations' and individuals' use of social engineering to influence election outcomes.

Chapter 7 examines social engineering attacks that were perpetrated by insiders who engineered their way into government agencies only to end up walking away with sensitive and classified materials. It is just not the government that is at risk—all organizations face some level of threat from insiders and the possibility that an insider may collaborate and conspire with an outsider to steal, sabotage, or humiliate their employees. In this chapter, we turn our attention to the efforts of insiders' social engineering attacks.

Chapter 8 examines the need for greater educational efforts about social engineering. When it comes to preventing social engineering attacks, the main defenses are preventing spam, requiring permissions for code to run a system, and a collection of tip sheets offered up by various organizations and government agencies. These efforts have certainly been helpful in reducing the number and the effectiveness of social engineering attacks, but the attacks continue and people continue to be victimized at the cost of billions of dollars every year. The education effort needs to be greatly expanded and, above all, it needs to include accurate information in order to fight against disinformation, misinformation, and fake news—and to be able to do this with unbiased and accurate information. This will require the use of all communication tools to inform people about inaccurate or malicious material being circulated through all media in which it is identified.

Chapter 9 draws conclusions from previous chapters and also focuses on the future of efforts to counter social engineering attacks.

1.8 Conclusion

Nothing is off limits to the cybercriminal whether they use phishing, ransomware, impersonation, or other forms of deception.

The inspector general for the Social Security Administration (SSA) has warned the public and social security beneficiaries in particular to be aware of fraud scams that target personal information. Scammers use phone calls, emails, and other methods to obtain personal information, then use it to commit identity theft. In recent scams, identity thieves posed as government officials in an attempt to convince people to provide personal and financial information. They may claim to be SSA employees—or Federal Emergency Management Agency (FEMA) employees, in the wake of Hurricane Sandy—and ask for social security numbers and bank information to make sure that people can receive their benefits. Scammers may also claim that a person has won a lottery or other prize, but they must send money to pay fees, taxes, or other expenses before they can claim their winnings.[15]

Tax identity theft is when someone uses a stolen SSN to get a tax refund or a job. People might find out it's happened when they get a letter from the Internal Revenue Service (IRS) saying that more than one tax return was filed with their SSN, or IRS records show that they earned income from an employer they don't know. Or, the IRS may reject their e-filed tax return as a duplicate filing. Tax scammers also use email and phone calls to try to convince taxpayers to provide personal information. The IRS has warned of these scams numerous times.[16]

1.9 Key Points

Key points covered in this chapter include:

- Social engineering is an incredibly effective process of attack with more than 80% of cyber attacks and over 70% of those from nation-states being initiated by exploiting humans rather than computer or network security flaws.
- Social engineering attacks generally ask people to perform a desired behavior that the attacker wants to induce from the victim.
- Social engineering is the broad term for any attack that relies on fooling people into taking action or divulging information.
- Phishing schemes attempt to make Internet users believe that they are receiving email from a trusted source when that is not the case.

- Social networking sites, as well as corporate websites in general, provide criminals with enormous amounts of information to send official-looking documents and send them to individual targets who have shown interest in specific subjects.
- In the first phase of a malware infection, a user might receive a spear phishing email that obtains access to the user's information or gains entry into the system under the user's credentials.
- The impact of cybercrime on individuals and commerce can be substantial, with the consequences ranging from a mere inconvenience to financial ruin.
- Cybercrime is increasingly transnational in nature, with individuals living in different countries around the world working together on the same schemes.
- There are several practices that computer users should employ to prevent phishing from being successful and even though those practices are widely publicized there are victims of social engineering schemes every day.
- Social media platforms have become a new tool for social engineers to exploit in pursuit of their criminal activities.
- The speed with which social media products have grown and come to dominate nearly every aspect of our social, political, and economic lives has in many ways obscured the shortcomings of their creators in anticipating the harmful effects of their use.

1.10 Seminar Discussion Topics

Discussion topics for graduate- or professional-level seminars:

- What experience have seminar participants had in situations where social engineering strategies or tactics were employed?
- Discuss any experience that participants have had with phishing attacks or that their relatives or friends have had with phishing attacks.
- Discuss what participants, their families, or their friends have done when they received phishing emails or phone calls. Why do they take that approach?
- Discuss how participants view law enforcement's efforts to deal with cybercrime.

1.11 Seminar Group Project

Divide participants into multiple groups, with each group taking 10 to 15 minutes to develop a list of how social engineering tactics are being employed and the many settings in which they are being employed. Upon completion, have groups exchange their lists of social engineering tactics, with groups taking 10 to 15 minutes to develop a checklist of things that help to quickly identify the social engineering tactics and the task involved in the tactic. Meet as a group and discuss the tactics selected and how they were identified.

Key Terms

Disinformation: is false and irrelevant information made available in order to deceive.

Identity theft crimes: identity theft and identity fraud are terms used to refer to all types of crime in which someone wrongfully obtains and uses another person's personal data in some way that involves fraud or deception, typically for economic gain.

Malicious links: are hyperlinks that lead users to websites that contain malicious code such as spyware, viruses, or Trojans that can infect computers that are used to visit those websites.

Malware: includes viruses, spyware, and other unwanted software that gets installed on your computer or mobile device without your consent. These programs can cause your device to crash and can be used to monitor and control your online activity. They also can make your computer vulnerable to viruses and deliver unwanted or inappropriate ads. Criminals use malware to steal personal information, send spam, and commit fraud.

Personally Identifiable Information (PII): is information that can be used to distinguish or trace an individual's identity, either alone or when combined with other personal or identifying information that is linked or linkable to a specific individual.

Phishing: phishing is when a scammer uses fraudulent emails or texts, or copycat websites, to get you to share valuable personal information—such as account numbers, social security numbers, or your login IDs and passwords. Scammers use your information to steal your money, or your identity, or both.

Ponzi schemes: are an investment fraud that pays existing investors with funds collected from new investors. Ponzi scheme organizers often promise to invest your money and generate high returns with little or no risk. But in many Ponzi schemes, the fraudsters do not invest the money. Instead, they use it to pay those who invested earlier and may keep some for themselves.

Ransomware scams: employ a type of malware that infects computers and restricts users' access to their files or threatens the permanent destruction of their information unless a ransom is paid, which is often required to be paid in Bitcoin.

Spear phishing: spear phishing attacks differ from regular phishing attempts because they target a specific recipient and appear to be from a trusted source.

References

1. Netflix Phishing Scam: Don't Take the Bait. Federal Trade Commission. Tressler, Colleen. December 26, 2018. Accessed February 2, 2019. https://www.consumer.ftc.gov/blog/2018/12/netflix-phishing-scam-dont-take-bait

2. Active Social Engineering Defense (ASED). Shen, Wade. Defense Advanced Research Projects Agency Program Information. Accessed February 1, 2019. https://www.darpa.mil/program/active-social-engineering-defense

3. Statement before the House Judiciary Subcommittee on Crime, Terrorism, and Homeland Security. Gordon M. Snow, Assistant Director Federal Bureau of Investigation. Washington, DC, July 28, 2010. Accessed February 1, 2019. https://archives.fbi.gov/archives/news/testimony/the-fbis-efforts-to-combat-cyber-crime-on-social-networking-sites

4. Technical Trends in Phishing Attacks. US-CERT. Milletary, Jason. Accessed February 2, 2019. www.us-cert.gov/sites/default/files/publications/phishing_trends0511.pdf

5. Guide to Malware Incident Prevention and Handling for Desktops and Laptops. National Institute of Standards and Technology, Information Technology Laboratory (ITL), Computer Security Division (CSD), Applied Cybersecurity Division (ACD). Murugiah Souppaya (NIST) and Karen Scarfone (Scarfone Cybersecurity). July 2013. Accessed February 2, 2019. https://csrc.nist.gov/publications/detail/sp/800-83/rev-1/final

6. Ransomware on the Rise: FBI and Partners Working to Combat this Cyber Threat. Federal Bureau of Investigation. January 20, 2015. Accessed February 2, 2019. https://www.fbi.gov/news/stories/ransomware-on-the-rise

7. Phishing. Federal Trade Commission. July 2017. Accessed February 2, 2019. https://www.consumer.ftc.gov/articles/0003-phishing

8. Security Tip (ST04-014) Avoiding Social Engineering and Phishing Attacks. U.S.-CERT. Original release date: October 22, 2009. Last revised: November 21, 2018. Accessed February 2, 2019. https://www.us-cert.gov/ncas/tips/ST04-014

9. Scammers Phish for Mortgage Closing Costs. Federal Trade Commission. Tressler, Colleen. March 18, 2016. Accessed February 2, 2019. https://www.consumer.ftc.gov/blog/2016/03/scammers-phish-mortgage-closing-costs

10. Anthem Hack Attack, Part 2: Phishing Scams. Federal Trade Commission. Tressler, Colleen. February 10, 2015. Accessed February 2, 2019. https://www.consumer.ftc.gov/blog/2015/02/anthem-hack-attack-part-2-phishing-scams

11. Testimony before the Senate Foreign Relations Committee. Julianne Smith, Senior Fellow and Director, Strategy and Statecraft Program, Center for a New American Security. February 9, 2017. Accessed February 2, 2019. www.foreign.senate.gov/download/smith-testimony-020917&download=1

12. The Impact of Russian Interference on Germany's 2017 Elections. Dr. Constanze Stelzenmüller and Robert Bosch, Senior Fellow, Center on the United States and Europe, Brookings Institution. Testimony before the U.S. Senate Select Committee on Intelligence. June 28, 2017. Accessed February 2, 2019. www.intelligence.senate.gov/sites/default/files/documents/sfr-cstelzenmuller-062817b.pdf

13. Facebook at the Hearing before the United States House of Representatives Committee on Energy and Commerce. Testimony of Mark Zuckerberg, Chairman and Chief Executive Officer. April 11, 2018. Accessed February 2, 2019. www.docs.house.gov/meetings/IF/IF00/20180411/108090/HHRG-115-IF00-20180411-SD002.pdf

14. Potential Policy Proposals for Regulation of Social Media and Technology Firms (DRAFT). U.S. Senator Mark R. Warner. Accessed February 3, 2019. https://www.warner.senate.gov/public/_cache/files/d/3/d32c2f17-cc76-4e11-8aa9-897eb3c90d16/65A7C5D983F899DAAE5AA21F57BAD944.social-media-regulation-proposals.pdf

15. Fraud Advisory: Social Engineering Scams Target Social Security Beneficiaries. Social Security Administration. November 21, 2012. Accessed February 2, 2019. https://oig.ssa.gov/newsroom/news-releases/advisory21

16. Fight Back Against Tax Identity Theft. Federal Trade Commission. Gressin, Seena. January 30, 2019. Accessed February 2, 2019. https://www.consumer.ftc.gov/blog/2019/01/fight-back-against-tax-identity-theft

2

THE CONTINUUM OF SOCIAL ENGINEERING APPROACHES

During the last few years, many social engineering approaches to deceive unsuspecting users have grown in popularity. These include the offer to fill out a survey for an online banking site with a monetary reward if the user includes account information, and email messages claiming to be from hotel reward clubs, asking users to verify credit card information that a customer may store on the legitimate site for reservation purposes. Included in the message is a uniform resource locater (URL) for the victim to use, which then directs the user to a site to enter their personal information. This site is crafted to closely mimic the look and feel of the legitimate site. The information is then collected and used by **criminal enterprises**. Over time, these fake emails and websites have evolved to become more technically deceiving to casual investigation.

The definition of phishing has grown to encompass a wider variety of electronic financial crimes. In addition to the widespread use of these fake email messages and websites to lure users into divulging their personal information, there has also been an increase in the amount of malicious code that specifically targets user account information and spies on communications with websites in order to collect account information.[1] This chapter examines a continuum of social engineering strategies, tactics, and motivations

2.1 What Social Engineering Attackers Want

There is a variety of outcomes that social engineering attackers pursue. Often in the past, they were just vandals and delinquents. In 1999, the Melissa computer virus, which was widely considered a denial of service attack that was akin to juvenile vandalism in its intent. In 2000, The Love Bug virus, however, was much more sinister in its intent and was socially engineered to get people to click on an attachment to the email. Like Melissa, it targeted Microsoft Outlook users. But unlike Melissa, it spread to a victim's entire address book instead of just the first 50 names. It deleted picture and sound files from the hard drive and apparently attempted to steal the computer's password. Perhaps of greatest concern is the fact that experts were united in saying that the virus was such a simple program that even a sixth grader with Visual Basic scripting knowledge could have created it in a few hours. Indeed, the alleged perpetrators were students at a computer school without much training who simply copied source codes from previous viruses, purportedly with the intention of stealing computer passwords. The Love Bug underscored the need to recognize and effectively combat the risks that can potentially create severe business disruption, economic calamity, and national security breaches.

Although many will argue the semantics of I LOVE YOU: Was it a virus, a worm, or a Trojan Horse? All agreed that it qualified as malicious code, that is, code that does something other than what the user wants it to do. The modus operandi was very similar to Melissa, in that the malicious code arrived via email, probably from someone you knew, with an attachment called LOVE-LETTER-FOR-YOU.TXT.VBS. The suffix VBS meant that the attachment was executable code, not just text. Once the reader clicked on this file, I LOVE YOU attacked Microsoft Outlook and mailed a copy of itself to everyone on the victim's mailing list, while Melissa just used the first 50 names. It infected the software that supports chat rooms so that anytime a chat room was set up, I LOVE YOU was sent out to all the chatters. It looked for picture, video, and music files to overwrite them with itself, since those files tend to get executed more often. It then infected Internet Explorer with its password stealing program, which was activated when the system restarted.

The I LOVE YOU virus spread more effectively than Melissa for two main reasons: First, it sent itself out to everyone on the mailing list; and second, it came during the week, not on a weekend, and spread it did. By 6:00 p.m. on May 4, 2000, the Computer

Emergency Readiness Team (CERT) at Carnegie Mellon estimated that approximately 420,000 hosts were infected. The next day, variants entitled Mother's Day, Very Funny, and the like were sent out. The Department of Defense's Joint Task Force Computer Network Defense Group had identified at least 14 variants of I LOVE YOU, one of which, entitled Virus Alert, was more dangerous than the others since it corrupted and overwrote critical system files. The Love Bug hit large corporations like AT&T, TWA, Ford, the Washington Post, ABC News, the British Parliament, the International Monetary Fund (IMF), at least 14 US government agencies, as well as myriad schools, credit unions, and individual citizens.[2]

The I Love You bug was certainly malicious and resulted in billions of dollars of damage. Since then there have been numerous social engineering traps on the Internet designed to get computer users to follow links to websites laden with malicious code. Anna Kournikova and other celebrities have been used as click bait to draw in naive Internet users. However, Internet vandals and petty thieves have now been overshadowed by **criminal group** elements who have little interest in vandalism or delinquency and are focused on making money through their criminal exploits.

Some social engineers are focused on short-term, hit-and-run attacks while others are playing a long-term game. The short-term approach is like a hit-and-run exercise with the goal of quick money through ransoms or the theft and sale of user credentials, passwords, credit card numbers, and various types of personal or corporate information that can be used to set the stage for more severe attacks. Regardless of their goals, the US Council of Economic Advisers estimated that cybercriminals' malicious activity cost the US economy between $57 billion and $109 billion in 2016.[3] According to government and industry sources, malicious cyber activity is a growing concern for both the public and private sectors. Between 2013 and 2015, according to the Office of the Director of National Intelligence (DNI), cyber threats were the most important strategic threat the United States was facing. Cyber threat actors fall into six broad groups (see Box 2.1), each driven by distinct objectives and motivations.

BOX 2.1   CYBER THREAT ACTORS

Nation-states
Corporate competitors
Hacktivists
Organized criminal groups
Opportunists
Company insiders

Nation-states: The main actors are Russia, China, Iran, and North Korea, according to the DNI in 2017. These groups are well funded and often engage in sophisticated, targeted attacks. Nation-states are typically motivated by political, economic, technical, or military agendas, and they have a range of goals that vary at different times. Nation-states frequently engage in industrial espionage. If they have funding needs, they may conduct ransom attacks and electronic thefts of funds. Nation-states frequently target **Personally Identifiable Information (PII)** in order to spy on certain individuals. Furthermore, through interviews of cybersecurity experts, nation-states may engage in business destruction involving one or more firms, potentially as retaliation against sanctions or other actions taken by the international community.

Corporate competitors: These are firms that seek illicit access to proprietary intellectual property including financial, strategic, and workforce-related information on their competitors; and many such corporate actors are backed by nation-states.

Hacktivists: These are generally private individuals or groups around the globe who have a political agenda and seek to carry out high-profile attacks. These attacks help hacktivists to distribute propaganda or to cause damage to opposition organizations for ideological reasons.

Organized criminal groups: These are criminal collectives that engage in targeted attacks motivated by profit-seeking. They collect profits by selling stolen PII on the dark web and by collecting ransom payments from both public and private entities by means of disruptive attacks.

Opportunists: These are usually amateur hackers driven by a desire for notoriety. Opportunists typically attack organizations using widely available codes and techniques, and thus usually represent the least advanced form of adversaries.

Company insiders: These are typically disgruntled employees or ex-employees looking for revenge or financial gain. Insiders can be especially dangerous when working in tandem with external actors, allowing these external actors to easily bypass even the most robust defenses.

Ultimately, any organization is fair game for cyber threat actors, though at different times a different set of firms may face higher risks. For example, corporate competitors typically target firms in their industry. So-called hacktivists, motivated by ideological consider-ations, may pile on to attack a different set of organizations at different times, typically because these organizations have somehow offended the hacktivists. When a nation-state faces sanctions targeting a cer-tain industry, the nation-state may use cyber-enabled means to target firms in that same industry in the country or countries that imposed the sanctions. That said, every firm is a potential target, independent of its age, size, sector, location, or employee composition.[3]

2.2 Common Types of Fraud

Social engineering is an age-old art and that is reflected in the type of fraudulent schemes that keep reoccurring over a long period of time. Organized criminal groups or criminal collectives that engage in targeted attacks motivated by profit-seeking are often involved in some type of fraudulent scheme. The pitch for these schemes, or how criminals convince people to get trapped in the schemes, is truly the art of social engineering. One approach to better understand social engineering is to understand the fraudulent schemes that are powered by social engineering. This section provides an overview of commonly occurring fraudulent schemes. The Federal Bureau of Investigation (FBI) warns against several types of fraud.

An advance fee scheme or **advance fee fraud** is when the victim pays money to someone in anticipation of receiving something of greater value, such as a loan, contract, investment, or gift and then receives little or nothing in return. The variety of advance fee schemes is limited only by the imagination of the con artists who offer them and they are all presented to the potential victim in as appealing a manner that a social engineer can craft. They may involve the sale of products or services, the offering of investments, lottery winnings, found money, or many other opportunities. For example, clever con artists will offer to find financing arrangements for their clients who pay a finder's fee in advance. They require their clients to sign contracts in which the clients agree to pay the fee when they are introduced to the financing source. Victims often learn that they are ineligible for financing only after they have paid the finder according to the contract. Such agreements may be legal unless it can be shown that the finder never had the intention or the ability to provide financing for the victims.

Business fraud consists of dishonest and illegal activities perpetrated by individuals or companies in order to provide an advantageous financial outcome to those persons or establishments. Also known as corporate fraud, these schemes often appear under the guise of legitimate business practices. A wide array of crimes falls under business fraud, including the following:

- Charity fraud: Using deception to get money from individuals believing they are making donations to legitimate charity organizations, especially charities representing victims of natural disasters shortly after the incident occurs (**disaster fraud**).
- Internet auction fraud: A fraudulent transaction or exchange that occurs in the context of an online auction site.
- Non-delivery of merchandise: Fraud occurring when a payment is sent but the goods and services ordered are never received.
- Non-payment of funds: Fraud occurring when goods and services are shipped or rendered but payment for them is never received.
- Overpayment scheme: An individual is sent a payment significantly higher than an owed amount and is instructed to deposit the money in their bank account and wire transfer the excess funds back to the bank of the individual or company that sent it. The sender's bank is usually located overseas, in Eastern Europe, for example, and the initial payment is found to be fraudulent, often after the wire transfer has occurred.

- Reshipping scheme: An individual is recruited to receive merchandise at their place of residence and subsequently repackage the items for shipment, usually abroad. Unbeknownst to them, the merchandise was purchased with fraudulent credit cards, often opened in their name.
- Credit card fraud is the unauthorized use of a credit or debit card, or similar payment tool (automated clearinghouse (ACH), electronic funds transfer (EFT), recurring charges, etc.), to fraudulently obtain money or property. Credit and debit card numbers can be stolen from unsecured websites or can be obtained in an identity theft scheme.
- Investment fraud involves the illegal sale or purported sale of financial instruments. The typical investment fraud schemes are characterized by offers of low- or no-risk investments, guaranteed returns, overly consistent returns, complex strategies, or unregistered securities. Examples of investment fraud include advance fee fraud, Ponzi schemes, pyramid schemes, and market manipulation fraud. More complex approaches to investment fraud are discussed in the next section.
- Legitimate letters of credit are never sold or offered as investments. They are issued by banks to ensure payment for goods shipped in connection with international trade. Payment on a letter of credit generally requires that the paying bank receive documentation certifying that the goods ordered have been shipped and are en route to their intended destination. Letters of credit frauds are often attempted against banks by providing false documentation to show that goods were shipped when, in fact, no goods or inferior goods were shipped. Other letters of credit frauds occur when con artists offer a letter of credit or bank guarantee as an investment wherein the investor is promised huge interest rates, of the order of 100–300% annually. Such investment opportunities simply do not exist.
- Market manipulation fraud, commonly referred to as a pump and dump, creates artificial buying pressure for a targeted security, generally a low-trading volume issuer in the over-the-counter securities market largely controlled by the fraud perpetrators. This artificially increased trading volume has the effect of artificially increasing the price of the

targeted security (i.e., the pump), which is rapidly sold off into the inflated market for the security by the fraud perpetrators (i.e., the dump). This results in illicit gains for the perpetrators and losses for innocent third-party investors. Typically, the increased trading volume is generated by inducing unwitting investors to purchase shares of the targeted security through false or deceptive sales practices and/or public information releases. A modern variation on this scheme involves largely foreign-based computer criminals gaining unauthorized access to the online brokerage accounts of unsuspecting victims in the United States. These victim accounts are then utilized to engage in coordinated online purchases of the targeted security to affect the pump portion of a manipulation, while the fraud perpetrators sell their pre-existing holdings in the targeted security into the inflated market to complete the dump.

• Criminals post fraudulent online classified advertisements offering vehicles for sale that are not, nor have ever been, in their possession. The fake advertisements usually include photos matching the description of the vehicle and a phone number or email address to contact the supposed seller. Once contact is established, the criminal sends the intended buyer additional photos along with an explanation for the discounted price and the urgency of the transaction. Common reasons provided include: The seller is moving or being deployed by the military, the seller received the vehicle as part of a divorce settlement, or the vehicle belonged to a relative who has died.

The criminal makes the fraud appear legitimate by deceptively claiming partnership with a reputable company, such as eBay, and assuring that the transaction will occur through a third party's buyer protection program. They may go so far as to send a fraudulent toll-free number that impersonates the third party. The buyer is told to purchase pre-paid gift cards in the sale amount and to share the card codes with the criminal, who then notifies the buyer they will be receiving the vehicle in a number of days. After the transaction is complete, the criminal typically ignores all follow-up calls, text messages, or emails from the buyer or may demand additional payments. In the end, the vehicle is not delivered and the buyer is most often unable to recuperate their losses.

Other frauds include counterfeit prescription drugs that are illegal and may be hazardous to your health. They are fake medicines not produced to the pharmacological specifications of the drugs they claim to be. These counterfeit prescription drugs may be contaminated or contain the wrong ingredients or no active ingredient. They also could have the right active ingredient but with the wrong dosage. Many people are fooled by fake prescription drugs masquerading as legitimate medicines, and using them may worsen their health conditions.

Fraudulent cosmetics and anti-aging product scams have increased the volume of counterfeit cosmetics arriving in the United States. The Internet has given consumers widespread access to health and beauty products (some labeled with anti-aging properties) that are fakes. Counterfeiters of personal care products increasingly view dealing in these fake items as a low-risk crime since many of them are located outside the United States. Government and industry studies and testing have discovered dangerous ingredients within counterfeit anti-aging products. Fraudulent cosmetics may contain arsenic, beryllium, and cadmium (all known carcinogens) along with high levels of aluminum and dangerous levels of bacteria from sources such as urine. Some of these products have caused conditions like acne, psoriasis, rashes, and eye infections.

Funeral and cemetery fraud have grown in popularity. Millions of Americans enter into contracts to prearrange their funerals and pre-pay some or all of the expenses involved, to ease the financial and emotional burdens on their families. Laws in individual states regulate the industry, and various states have laws to help ensure that these advance payments are available when they are needed. However, protections vary widely from state to state, sometimes providing a window of opportunity for unscrupulous operators to overcharge expenses and list themselves as financial beneficiaries.

Healthcare-related schemes attempt to defraud private or government healthcare programs, which usually involve healthcare providers, companies, or individuals. These schemes may include offers for (fake) insurance cards; health insurance marketplace assistance; stolen health information; medications, supplements, weight loss products; or pill mill practices. Medical equipment fraud occurs when insurers are charged for products that were not needed and/or may not have been delivered. Rolling lab schemes involve unnecessary and some-times fake tests, which are given to individuals at health clubs, retire-ment homes, or shopping malls, and billed to insurance companies or Medicare.

Medicare fraud can take the form of any of the health insur-ance frauds described above. Senior citizens are frequent targets of Medicare schemes, especially by medical equipment manufacturers who offer seniors free medical products in exchange for their Medicare numbers. Because a physician has to sign a form certifying that equip-ment or testing is needed before Medicare pays for it, con artists fake signatures or bribe corrupt doctors to sign the forms. Once a signature is in place, the manufacturers bill Medicare for merchandise or ser-vice that was not needed or was not ordered.

Nigerian letter frauds combine the threat of impersonation fraud with a variation of an advance fee scheme in which a letter mailed, or emailed, from Nigeria offers the recipient the opportunity to share in a percentage of millions of dollars that the author, often a self-proclaimed government official, is trying to transfer illegally out of Nigeria. The recipient is encouraged to send information to the author, such as blank letterhead stationery, bank name and account numbers, and other identifying information using a fax number given in the letter or return email address provided in the message. The scheme relies on convincing a willing victim, who has demonstrated a propensity for larceny by responding to the invitation, to send money to the author of the letter in Nigeria in several installments of increas-ing amounts for a variety of reasons.

Payment of taxes, bribes to government officials, and legal fees are often described in great detail with the promise that all expenses will be reimbursed as soon as the funds are spirited out of Nigeria. In actu-ality, the millions of dollars do not exist, and the victim eventually ends up with nothing but loss. Once the victim stops sending money, the perpetrators have been known to use the personal information and checks that they received to impersonate the victim, draining bank accounts and credit card balances. While such an invitation impresses most law-abiding citizens as a laughable hoax, millions of dollars in losses are caused by these schemes annually. Some victims have been lured to Nigeria, where they have been imprisoned against their will along with losing large sums of money. The Nigerian government is not sympathetic to victims of these schemes, since the victim actually conspires to remove funds from Nigeria in a manner that is contrary to Nigerian law. The schemes themselves violate Section 419 of the Nigerian criminal code, hence the label 419 fraud.

Redemption/Strawman/Bond fraud is common, with proponents of this scheme claiming that the US government or the Treasury Department control bank accounts, often referred to as US Treasury Direct Accounts, for all US citizens that can be accessed by submitting paperwork with state and federal authorities. Individuals promoting this scam frequently cite various discredited legal theories and may refer to the scheme as Redemption, Strawman, or Acceptance for Value. Trainers and websites will often charge large fees for kits that teach individuals how to perpetrate this scheme. They will often imply that others have had great success in discharging debt and purchasing merchandise such as cars and homes. Failures to implement the scheme successfully are attributed to individuals not following instructions in a specific order or not filing paperwork at correct times.

This scheme predominately uses fraudulent financial documents that appear to be legitimate. These documents are frequently referred to as bills of exchange, promissory bonds, indemnity bonds, offset bonds, sight drafts, or comptrollers' warrants. In addition, other official documents are used outside of their intended purpose, like IRS forms 1099, 1099-OID, and 8300. This scheme frequently intermingles legal and pseudo-legal terminology in order to appear lawful. Notaries may be used in an attempt to make the fraud appear legitimate.

The FBI and the US Department of Housing and Urban Development Office of Inspector General (HUD-OIG) urge consumers, especially senior citizens, to be vigilant when seeking reverse mortgage products. Reverse mortgages, also known as home equity conversion mortgages (HECM), have increased more than 1,300% between 1999 and 2008, creating significant opportunities for fraud perpetrators.

Reverse mortgage scams are engineered by unscrupulous professionals in a multitude of real estate, financial services, and related companies to steal the equity from the property of unsuspecting senior citizens or to use these seniors to unwittingly aid the fraudsters in stealing equity from a flipped property. In many of the reported scams, senior victims are offered free homes, investment opportunities, and foreclosure or refinance assistance. They are also used as straw buyers in property flipping scams. Seniors are frequently targeted through local churches and investment seminars, as well as television, radio, billboard, and mailer advertisements. However, a legitimate HECM loan product is insured by the Federal Housing Authority. It enables eligible homeowners to access the equity in their homes by providing funds without incurring a monthly payment. Eligible borrowers must be 62 years or older, occupy their property as their primary residence, and own their property or have a small mortgage balance.

Telemarketers call constantly, and during times of the year when taxes are due or health insurance paperwork must be processed, they call more often. They have also started using emails, some of which draw victims further into a trap while others just infect computers with spyware or ransomware. When individuals send money to people they do not know personally or give personal or financial information to unknown callers, they increase the chances of becoming a victim of telemarketing fraud. Here are some warning signs of telemarketing fraud—what a caller may say:

- You must act now or the offer won't be good.
- You've won a free gift, vacation, or prize. But you have to pay for postage and handling or other charges.
- You must send money, give a credit card or bank account number, or have a check picked up by courier. You may hear this before you have had a chance to consider the offer carefully.
- You don't need to check out the company with anyone. (The callers say you do not need to speak to anyone at all, including your family, lawyer, accountant, local Better Business Bureau, or consumer protection agency).
- You don't need any written information about the company or their references.
- You can't afford to miss this high-profit, no-risk offer.[4]

2.3 Socially Engineered Larger-Scale Investment Scams

Investment fraud comes in many forms. Whether you are a first-time investor or have been investing for many years, there are some basic facts you should know about different types of fraud.[5] The Securities and Exchange Commission (SEC) focuses on fraud where social engineers specifically target investors. Box 2.2 shows the types of fraud that the SEC warns investors about. The Commodity Futures Trading Commission (CFTC) works to protect market users and their funds, consumers, and the public from fraud, manipulation, and abusive practices related to derivatives and other products that are subject to the Commodity Exchange Act (CEA).

Many types of investment fraud are discussed above but many warrant additional explanation and are covered in the following paragraphs. In this section, more information is provided on how to identify the socially engineered information that fraudsters are providing the potential victim. This provides greater insight into the social engineering process employed when the social engineering attacker is playing a long game and plans to keep the victim on the hook as long as possible in order to increase the possibility of successful fraud.

BOX 2.2   TYPES OF INVESTMENT FRAUD

Affinity fraud
Advance fee fraud
Binary options fraud
High yield investment programs
Internet and social media fraud
Microcap fraud
Ponzi scheme
Pre-IPO investment scams
Pyramid schemes
Prime bank investments
Promissory notes
Pump and dump schemes

Affinity fraud almost always involves either a fake investment or an investment where the fraudster lies about important details (such as the risk of loss, the track record of the investment, or the background of the promoter of the scheme). Many affinity frauds are Ponzi or pyramid schemes, where money given to the promoter by new investors is paid to earlier investors to create the illusion that the so-called investment is successful. This tricks new investors into investing in the scheme, and lulls existing investors into believing their investments are safe. In reality, even if there really is an actual investment, the investment typically makes little or no profit. The fraudster simply takes new investors' money for their own personal use, often using some of it to pay off existing investors who may be growing suspicious. Eventually, when the supply of investor money dries up and current investors demand to be paid, the scheme collapses and investors discover that most or all of their money is gone.

Fraudsters who carry out affinity scams frequently are (or pretend to be) members of the group they are trying to defraud. The group could be a religious group, such as a particular denomination or church. It could be an ethnic group or an immigrant community. It could be a racial minority. It could be members of a particular workforce—even members of the military have been targets of these frauds. Fraudsters target any group they think they can convince to trust them with the group members' hard-earned savings. That is the key to this type of social engineering.

At its core, affinity fraud exploits the trust and friendship that exist in groups of people who have something in common. Fraudsters use a number of methods to get access to the group. A common way is by enlisting respected leaders from within the group to spread the word about the scheme. Those **civil society leaders** may not realize the investment is actually a scam, and they may become unwitting victims of the fraud themselves.

Because of the tight-knit structure of many groups, it can be difficult for regulators or law enforcement officials to detect an affinity scam. Victims often fail to notify authorities or pursue legal remedies. Instead, they try to work things out within the group. This is particularly true where the fraudsters have used respected community or religious leaders to convince others to join the investment.[6]

The SEC's Office of Investor Education and Advocacy issued an Investor Alert to warn investors that fraudsters may socially engineer investment schemes through purported online binary options trading platforms. While some binary options are listed on registered exchanges or traded on a designated contract market that is subject to oversight by US regulators such as the SEC or the Commodity Futures Trading Commission, respectively, this is only a portion of the binary options market. Much of the binary options market operates through Internet-based trading platforms that are not necessarily complying with applicable US regulatory requirements.

A binary option is a type of options contract in which the payout will depend entirely on the outcome of a yes/no (binary) proposition. When the binary option expires, the option holder will receive either a predetermined amount of cash or nothing at all. Given the all-or-nothing payout structure, binary options are sometimes referred to as all-or-nothing options or fixed-return options.

Typically, a representative of a binary options website will ask a customer to deposit money into an account where the customer can purchase binary options contracts. A customer may be asked to, for example, pay $50 for a binary option contract that promises a 50% return if the stock price of XYZ company is above $5 per share when the binary option expires.

Representatives of binary options websites may use fictitious names and tout socially engineered credentials, qualifications, and experience. They may misrepresent where they are calling from (e.g., pretending that they are in the United States). Supposedly unbiased sources reviewing or ranking binary options websites may have been paid to promote or criticize particular websites. Fraudsters may warn you that the binary options website you are using is a scam in order to gain your trust and get you to deposit even more money in another website that they also run. People considering investing money with a binary options website should look out for these red flags:

- Unsolicited offers: Unsolicited offers (you didn't ask for it and don't know the sender) to earn investment returns that seem too good to be true may be part of a fraudulent investment scheme.

- High-pressure sales tactics or threats: Representatives of binary options websites may use high-pressure sales tactics or even threats (e.g., threatening to file a lien against your property) to swindle you.
- Identity theft: Representatives of binary options websites may falsely claim that the government requires photocopies of your credit card, passport, driver's license, utility bills, or other personal data. Protect yourself and safeguard your personal information.
- Constant turnover of representatives: Be skeptical if the names of the persons you are dealing with at a binary options website seem to change frequently or if you are told your former broker has been fired.
- Issues with withdrawals: Representatives of binary options websites may use delay tactics to hold up your withdrawal request until it is too late for you to dispute the charge(s) with your credit card company. The Fair Credit Billing Act (FCBA) provides consumer protection if you are charged for goods and services you did not accept or that were not delivered as agreed, but you must send a letter disputing the charges that reaches the creditor within 60 days after the first bill with the error was mailed to you. Also, be skeptical if someone tries to convince you to pay more money for a premium account with fewer restrictions on withdrawals.
- Credit card abuse: If you used a credit card to fund your account, keep an eye out for unauthorized charges on your credit card statements. Even if you signed a form purportedly waiving your right to dispute any credit card charges, report all unauthorized charges to your credit card company immediately.
- Government impersonators: If someone claiming to be affiliated with the SEC contacts you and asks you to pay money to help you recover binary options investment-related losses, submit a complaint at www.sec.gov/oig to the SEC's Office of Inspector General (OIG) or call the OIG's toll-free hotline at (833) SEC-OIG1 (732-6441). It is important for all investors to know that the SEC never makes people pay to get their money back.[7]

In addition to perpetrating socially engineered fraudulent investment schemes, the operators of binary options websites may be violating the federal securities laws through other illegal conduct, including:

- Offering or selling securities that have not been registered with the SEC (and no exemption to registration is available);
- Operating as unregistered broker-dealers;
- Operating as unregistered securities exchanges; and
- Making material misrepresentations to investors (e.g., overstating the average return on investment, overstating the long-term profitability of investing in binary options over the course of multiple trades, or understating the risk of binary options trading).

Furthermore, if any of the products offered by binary options trading websites are security-based swaps, additional requirements will apply.

The term microcap stock (sometimes referred to as penny stock) applies to companies with low or micro-market capitalizations. Companies with a market capitalization of less than $250 or $300 million are often called microcap stocks, although many have market capitalizations of far less than those amounts. The smallest public companies, with market capitalizations of less than $50 million, are sometimes referred to as nanocap stocks.

Many microcap stocks trade in the over-the-counter (OTC) market. Quotes for microcap stocks may be available directly from a broker-dealer or on OTC systems such as the OTC Bulletin Board (OTCBB), OTC Link LLC (OTC Link), or Global OTC.

Microcap stocks differ from other stocks in several ways. Often, the biggest difference between a microcap stock and other stocks is the amount of reliable publicly available information about the company. Most large public companies file reports with the SEC that any investor can get for free from the SEC's website. Professional stock analysts regularly research and write about larger public companies, and it is easy to find their stock prices on the Internet or in newspapers and other publications. In contrast, the same information about microcap companies can be extremely difficult to find, making them more vulnerable to socially engineered investment fraud schemes and making it less likely that quoted prices will be based on full and accurate information about the company.

Companies that list their stocks on exchanges must meet minimum listing standards. For example, they must have minimum amounts of net assets and minimum numbers of shareholders. In contrast, companies quoted on the OTCBB, OTC Link, or Global OTC generally do not have to meet any minimum listing standards, but are typically subject to some initial and ongoing requirements. Investors can find the OTCBB's eligibility requirements for stocks at http://www.finra.org/industry/faq-otcbb-frequently-asked-questions, and additional information about OTC Link and Global OTC can be found at www.otcmarkets.com and www.globalotc.com, respectively.

While all investments involve risk, microcap stocks are among the riskiest. Many microcap companies are new and have no proven track record. Some of these companies have no assets, operations, or revenues. Others have products and services that are still in development or have yet to be tested in the market. Another risk that pertains to microcap stocks involves the low volumes of trade, which may make it difficult for investors to sell shares when they want to do so. Because many microcap stocks trade in low volumes, any size trade can have a large percentage impact on the price of the stock. Microcap stocks may also be susceptible to fraud and manipulation.[8]

People considering investing in this grade of stock need to be cautious of misinformation about the company. Potential buyers can ask their investment professional if the company files reports with the SEC and to provide written information about the company and its business, finances, and management. Potential investors should also remember that they should never use unsolicited emails, message board postings, and company news releases as the sole basis for investment decisions. Unfortunately, some of the information people receive may be false or misleading, or may be distributed by persons with an undisclosed interest in causing investors to buy stock for more than it is worth. Just because a company appears to have readily available company information or files reports with a regulator, does not mean it is safe to invest in that company.[9]

Often, the biggest difference between a microcap stock and other stocks is the amount of reliable publicly available information about the company. Most large public companies file reports with the SEC that any investor can get for free from the SEC's website. Professional stock analysts regularly research and write about larger public companies, and it is easy to find their stock prices on the Internet or in newspapers and other publications. In contrast, the same information about microcap companies can be extremely difficult to find, making them more vulnerable to investment fraud schemes and making it less likely that quoted prices will be based on full and accurate information about the company.

Companies quoted on the OTCBB, OTC Link, or Global OTC do not have to meet any minimum listing standards, but are typically subject to some initial and ongoing requirements. Historically, microcap stocks have been less liquid than the stocks of larger companies. Before investing in a microcap company, buyers should carefully consider that they may have difficulty selling the stock later or that the sale will have a noticeable impact on the stock's selling price.

While all stocks experience volatility to some degree, microcap stocks have historically been more volatile than stocks of larger companies. Before investing in microcap stocks, people should carefully consider the possibility that these stocks may be susceptible to sudden large price changes; particularly in light of the potential difficulty investors may have in selling these stocks.

Reliable, publicly available information about microcap stocks is often limited. Also, the stocks of microcap companies are historically less liquid and more thinly traded (lower volume) than the stocks of larger companies. These factors make it easier for fraudsters to manipulate the stock price or trading volume of microcap stocks.

When weighing the legitimacy of a potential investment in a microcap company several things should be examined. These include any SEC trading suspensions if there is a lack of current and accurate information concerning the company and its stock; whether a company's stock seems to be more heavily promoted than its products or services; unexplained increases or decreases in stock price or trading volume; history of operational success; insiders owning large amounts of stock; few or no assets, minimal revenues, or implausible press releases may suggest no real business operations.

Potential investors should look beyond **publicly available social media** and press releases to obtain independent information about the company's management and its directors and never deal with brokers who refuse to provide you with written information about the investments they are promoting. All materials given to potential investors

should be carefully reviewed and verified especially financial statements, particularly if they are not audited by a certified public accountant (CPA). If a broker has solicited you to purchase this stock and
cannot provide you with basic information regarding the company
(e.g., the company's financial statistics), carefully consider whether
this is an appropriate investment.[10]

The SEC's Office of Investor Education and Advocacy issued an
updated Investor Alert to warn investors about investment scams that
purport to offer investors the opportunity to buy pre-initial public
offering (pre-IPO) shares of companies, including social media and
technology companies such as Facebook and Twitter. SEC staff are
aware of a number of complaints and inquiries about these types of
frauds, which may be promoted on social media and Internet sites, by
telephone, email, in person, or by other means. In September 2010, a
judgment order was entered in favor of the SEC based on allegations
that a scam artist had misappropriated more than $3.7 million from
45 investors in four states by offering fake pre-IPO shares of companies, including AOL/Time Warner, Inc., Google, Inc., and Rosetta
Stone, Inc., before the companies went public. Investors should be
mindful of the risks involved with an offer to purchase pre-IPO
shares in a company. Remember that the people and companies that
promote fraudulent pre-IPO offerings often use socially engineered,
impressive-looking websites, bulletin board postings, and email spam
to exploit investors who scour the Internet looking for e-businesses in
which to invest. To lure investors in, they make unfounded compari-
sons between their company and other established, successful Internet
companies. But these and other claims that sound so believable at first
often turn out to be false or misleading. Always be skeptical when
considering any pre-IPO offerings promoted through the Internet.[11]

Commodity pool fraud is a type of fraud that involves individuals and firms, often unregistered, offering investments in commodity
pools. In these fraudulent schemes, investor money is misused (often
spent on improper expenses). The pool operators advertise based on
socially engineered false claims of high profits and low risk. Signs of
a possible fraudulent sales pitch include:

- Leading people to believe they can profit from current news
  already known to the public. For example, "As a result of that
  hurricane, the price of oil futures will increase substantially."

- Making contact through word of mouth referrals or emails from friends, relatives, members of churches, or social groups—one fraudulent pool operator even solicited his cancer support group.
- Claiming to know unique market trends or to have a record of highly profitable trading.
- Making promises of quick, large, and guaranteed returns.
- Asking for personal information such as a person's full name, phone number, and email or home address.
- Requesting cash immediately.

Frequently, socially engineered persuasion tactics include:

- Dangling the prospect of wealth and enticing people with something they want, but can't have. For example, "This gold purchase is guaranteed to double in three months!"
- Trying to build credibility by claiming to be with a reputable firm or to have special credentials or experience. For example, "Believe me, as a senior vice president of EZY Money Inc., I would never sell an investment that doesn't produce."
- Leading people to believe that other savvy investors have already invested. For example, "This is how Bob got his start. I know it's a lot of money, but I'm in and so are my mom and half her club and it's worth every dime."
- Offering to do a small favor for people in return for a big favor. For example, "I'll give you a break on my commission if you buy now, half off."
- Creating a false sense of urgency by claiming limited supply. For example, "There are only two units left, so I'd sign up today if I were you."[12]

The foreign exchange (Forex) market is volatile and carries substantial risks. It is not the place to put any money that you cannot afford to lose, such as retirement funds, as you can lose most or all of it very quickly. The CFTC has witnessed a sharp rise in Forex trading scams in recent years and advises investors on how to identify potential fraud. Signs of a possible fraudulent sales pitch include most of the same socially engineered pitches and persuasion tactics employed in commodity pool fraud.[13]

A Fraud Advisory from the CFTC concerning profits from the War on Terrorism urges investors to beware of promises of profits from commodity futures and options trading based on the events of September 11, 2001, and other terrorist attacks as well as public information relating to the war on terrorism. Companies often use telephone call solicitations, email messages, Internet advertisements, websites, Internet chat room discussions, or radio and television advertisements and infomercials to promote commodity futures and options trading. Solicitations may promise quick riches, such as turning $5,000 into $20,000 in just a few months with predetermined risk. We are aware of pitches that a purchase of futures or options in crude oil will be profitable because unrest in oil-producing countries will drive up the price of this commodity.

These sales pitches are socially engineered and false, increases in the demand for commodities due to world events do not necessarily result in the increase in value of an option or futures contracts. The market has already factored such demand into the price of futures and options. Markets respond immediately to new information, within a few minutes or hours. The prices of commodity options and futures contracts already take into account all known or predictable market conditions. Claims that the risk of purchasing commodity futures and options can be predetermined or fixed are misleading. Purchasers of commodity options contracts can lose every penny and because futures contracts are leveraged or margined, customers may be liable for losses in excess of their initial deposits.[14]

Precious metals fraud is often initiated with some very well socially engineered promises of easy profits from rising prices in precious metals such as gold, silver, palladium, and platinum. The socially engineered pitches and persuasion tactics employed in commodity pool fraud and Forex market fraud are routinely employed in precious metal fraud schemes. There are a few different twists like: "Since that mine disaster, you are certain to earn big returns on your deposit," or the claim that precious metals transactions are not regulated by the CFTC or the National Futures Association.[15]

2.4 Ways Social Engineering Attackers Work

In a social engineering attack, an attacker uses basic human interaction (social skills) to get a recipient of a message, posting, or advertisement to perform a desired action. This can be as simple as opening a file or clicking on a link, as with the I Love You attack. It can also involve obtaining compromising information about an organization, its operations, or computer systems that is helpful in penetrating and attacking networks and systems. In a more complex attack, content can be socially engineered to draw the reader into a more complex situation that results in fraud or theft. Regardless of the attacker's desired results, social engineering the message has proven to be an effective method to support the criminal enterprise or further a social or political agenda.

A good attacker will seem unassuming and respectable, possibly claiming to be a new employee, repair person, or researcher, or supporter, and even offering credentials to support that identity. However, by asking questions, they often piece together enough information to further infiltrate organization operations, networks, systems, or data. If an attacker does not harvest enough information from one source, they usually contact other sources within the same organization utilizing the information from the first source to add to the credibility and the appearance of legitimacy. Attackers work on building whatever level of relationship necessary to achieve their goals.

Phishing is a form of social engineering that most often uses email, social media, or malicious websites to solicit personal information by posing as a legitimate, trustworthy organization. One tactic frequently employed is where an attacker may send an email, seemingly from a reputable credit card company or financial institution, that requests account information, often suggesting that there is a problem. When users respond with the requested information, attackers can use it to gain further access to accounts or systems.

Phishing attacks may also appear to come from other types of organizations such as charities or government agencies. Attackers often take advantage of current events or certain times of the year, such as natural disasters like Hurricane Katrina, or human suffering like epidemics and health scares, economic concerns, major political elections, or even holidays. However, phishing attacks can also be executed by employees from inside an organization or relatives of employees who gain access to organization resources that can be used to collect additional information or increase their access.[16]

In a telephone social engineering attack, the hacker contacts the victim pretending to be someone else, such as a service technician or fellow employee, and attempts to gather information that may seem innocuous to the victim. Social engineers may try to collect information about their victims at trade shows or conferences related to the victims' line of work, personal interest, or hobby. Social engineers leverage a variety of emotions and human characteristics ranging from the desire to be helpful to wanting friendship, or, most often in the case of financial fraud, plain old greed on the part of a potential victim.

In situations where the social engineer can physically interact with potential victims, such as at trade shows or fairs, they will wander around the venue striking up conversations with potential victims. The event gives them a common interest with which to break the ice. They may also go as far as setting up a display or booth to collect information under the pretense of offering a solution or a product related to the event.[17]

2.5 Conclusion

The technologies that social engineers exploit will be covered in later chapters along with additional real-world social engineering attacks. It is, however, important to note that the technology used by social engineering attackers will constantly change and can often be difficult for the non-technical person to understand and identify. The material covered in this chapter shows a wide array of social engineering attacker goals that should turn on alarm bells for computer users if they suspect any of the potential click bait approaches or ploys discussed are at play.

2.6 Key Points

Key points covered in this chapter include:

- Fake emails and websites have evolved to become more technically deceiving to casual investigation and this makes it difficult for many non-technical users to identify malicious content.
- The definition of phishing has grown to encompass a wider variety of electronic financial crimes, beyond fake email messages and websites, taking into account the increase in the amount of malicious code that specifically targets user account

information and spies on communications with websites to collect account information.

- The Love Bug underscored the need to recognize and effectively combat the risks that can potentially create severe business disruption, economic calamity, and national security breaches.
- Some social engineers are focused on short-term hit-and-run attacks while others are playing a long-term game.
- Nation-states' social engineers are well funded and often engage in sophisticated, targeted attacks. Nation-states are typically motivated by political, economic, technical, or military agendas, and they have a range of goals that vary at different times.
- Corporate competitors seek illicit access to proprietary intellectual property including financial, strategic, and workforce-related information on their competitors; and many such corporate actors are backed by nation-states.
- Hacktivists are generally private individuals or groups around the globe who have a political agenda and seek to carry out high-profile attacks.
- Organized criminal groups often engage in targeted attacks motivated by profit-seeking. They collect profits by selling stolen PII on the dark web and by collecting ransom payments from both public and private entities by means of disruptive attacks.
- Opportunists are usually amateur hackers driven by a desire for notoriety and typically attack organizations using widely available codes and techniques, and thus usually represent the least advanced form of adversaries.
- Company insiders often employ social engineering attacks looking for revenge or financial gain.
- One approach to better understanding social engineering is to understand the fraudulent schemes that are powered by social engineering.
- Investment fraud comes in many forms. Whether you are a first-time investor or have been investing for many years, there are some basic facts you should know about different types of fraud.
- Frequently socially engineered persuasion tactics include dangling the prospect of wealth and enticing people with something they want, but can't have.

- In a social engineering attack, an attacker uses basic human interaction (social skills) to get a recipient of a message, posting, or advertisement to perform a desired action.
- A good attacker will seem unassuming and respectable, possibly claiming to be a new employee, repair person, researcher, or supporter, and even offering credentials to support that identity.
- In a telephone social engineering attack, the hacker contacts the victim pretending to be someone else, such as a service technician or fellow employee, and attempts to gather information that may seem innocuous to the victim.

2.7 Seminar Discussion Topics

Discussion topics for graduate- or professional-level seminars are:

- What experience have seminar participants had in situations where they or people they know have been victims of an Internet fraud scheme?
- How did the victims of the fraud schemes resolve their situation and recover any lost funds?
- What are the perceptions of participants regarding the ability of individual Internet users to readily identify a socially engineered attack or fraud scheme?

2.8 Seminar Group Project

Seminar participants will interview three to five people who have encountered Internet fraud or other forms of social engineering attacks and write a one-page summary of the interviews. Participants should be prepared to discuss their findings in the discussion group setting.

Key Terms

Advance fee fraud: are fee schemes that require victims to advance relatively small sums of money in the hope of realizing much larger gains. Not all advance fee schemes are investment frauds. In those that are, however, victims are told that in order to have the opportunity to be an investor (in an initial offering of a promising security, investment, or commodity, etc.), the victim must first send funds to cover taxes or processing fees, etc.

Affinity fraud: perpetrators of affinity fraud take advantage of the tendency of people to trust others with whom they share similarities, such as religion or ethnic identity, to gain their trust and money.

Civil society leaders: are individuals who hold government, business, or religious positions that enable them to influence their societies, communities, and individuals.

Criminal groups: are comprised of people who are organized for the purpose of committing criminal activity for economic gain, political clout, or dominance in a specific geographical area.

Criminal enterprises: the FBI defines a criminal enterprise as a group of individuals with an identified hierarchy, or comparable structure, engaged in significant criminal activity.

Disaster fraud: is often committed by individuals who seek to profit via false claims of damages; there are also non-insurance-related disaster frauds as many organizations and individuals solicit contributions for the victims of the disaster. Fraud victims may be approached through unsolicited emails asking for donations to a legitimate-sounding organization. The schemer will instruct the victim to send a donation via a money transfer.

Personally Identifiable Information (PII): is information that can be used to distinguish or trace an individual's identity, either alone or when combined with other personal or identifying information that is linked or linkable to a specific individual.

Publicly available social media: covers social media applications and content that can be accessed and viewed by a general public without restrictions.

References

1. Technical Trends in Phishing Attacks. US-CERT. Milletary, Jason. Accessed February 2, 2019. www.us-cert.gov/sites/default/files/publications/phishing_trends0511.pdf

2. The Love Bug Virus: Protecting Lovesick Computers from Malicious Attack. Wednesday, May 10, 2000. House of Representatives, Committee on Science, Subcommittee on Technology, Washington, DC. Accessed February 4, 2019. http://commdocs.house.gov/committees/science/hsy131170.000/hsy131170_1.HTM

3. The Cost of Malicious Cyber Activity to the US Economy. The Council of Economic Advisers. February 2018. Accessed February 4, 2019. https://www.whitehouse.gov/wp-content/uploads/2018/03/The-Cost-of-Malicious-Cyber-Activity-to-the-U.S.-Economy.pdf

4. Scams and Safety Common Fraud Schemes. Federal Bureau of Investigation. Accessed February 4, 2019. https://www.fbi.gov/scams-and-safety/common-fraud-schemes

5. Types of Fraud. US Securities and Exchange Commission. Accessed February 5, 2019. https://www.investor.gov/protect-your-investments/fraud/types-fraud

6. Investor Bulletin: Affinity Fraud. US Securities and Exchange Commission. Accessed February 5, 2019. https://www.investor.gov/additional-resources/news-alerts/alerts-bulletins/investor-bulletin-affinity-fraud

7. Investor Alert: Binary Options Websites May be Used for Fraudulent Schemes. US Securities and Exchange Commission. Accessed February 5, 2019. https://www.investor.gov/investing-basics/avoiding-fraud/types-fraud/binary-options-fraud

8. Investor Bulletin: Microcap Stock Basics (Part 1 of 3: General Information). US Securities and Exchange Commission. Accessed February 5, 2019. https://www.investor.gov/additional-resources/news-alerts/alerts-bulletins/investor-bulletin-microcap-stock-basics-part-1-3

9. Investor Bulletin: Microcap Stock Basics (Part 2 of 3: Research). US Securities and Exchange Commission. Accessed February 5, 2019. https://www.investor.gov/additional-resources/news-alerts/alerts-bulletins/investor-bulletin-microcap-stock-basics-part-2-3

10. Investor Bulletin: Microcap Stock Basics (Part 3 of 3: Risk). US Securities and Exchange Commission. Accessed February 5, 2019. https://www.investor.gov/additional-resources/news-alerts/alerts-bulletins/investor-bulletin-microcap-stock-basics-part-3-3

11. Investor Alert: Pre-IPO Investment Scams (updated). US Securities and Exchange Commission. Accessed February 5, 2019. https://www.investor.gov/additional-resources/news-alerts/alerts-bulletins/investor-alert-pre-ipo-investment-scams-updated

12. Commodity Pool Fraud. US Commodity Futures Trading Commission (CFTC). Accessed February 5, 2019. https://www.cftc.gov/About/MissionResponsibilities/index.htm

13. Foreign Currency Trading (Forex) Fraud. US Commodity Futures Trading Commission (CFTC). Accessed February 5, 2019. https://www.cftc.gov/ConsumerProtection/FraudAwarenessPrevention/CFTCFraudAdvisories/fraudadv_forex.html

14. Fraud Advisory from the CFTC: Profits from the War on Terrorism. US Commodity Futures Trading Commission (CFTC). Accessed February 5, 2019. https://www.cftc.gov/ConsumerProtection/FraudAwarenessPrevention/CFTCFraudAdvisories/fraudadv_wtcattack.html

15. Precious Metals Fraud. U.S. Commodity Futures Trading Commission (CFTC). Accessed February 5, 2019. https://www.cftc.gov/Consumer Protection/FraudAwarenessPrevention/CFTCFraudAdvisories/frau-dadv_preciousmetals.html
16. Security Tip (ST04-014), Avoiding Social Engineering and Phishing Attacks. The National Cybersecurity and Communications Integration Center (NCCIC). Original release date: October 22, 2009. Last revised: November 21, 2018. Accessed February 1, 2019. https://www.us-cert. gov/ncas/tips/ST04-014
17. Types of Social Engineering. Federal Emergency Management Agency (FEMA). Accessed February 1, 2019. https://emilms.fema.gov/is906/ WSA0101610text.htm

3

CRIMINAL SOCIAL ENGINEERING ACTIVITIES

Phishing scams have flourished in recent years due to favorable economic and technological conditions. The technical resources needed to execute phishing attacks can be readily acquired through public and private sources. Some technical resources have been streamlined and automated, allowing use by non-technical criminals. This makes phishing both economically and technically viable for a larger population of less sophisticated criminals.[1]

The mission of the Internet Crime Complaint Center (IC3) is to provide the public with a reliable and convenient reporting mechanism to submit information to the Federal Bureau of Investigation (FBI) concerning suspected Internet-facilitated criminal activity and to develop effective alliances with law enforcement and industry partners. Since 2000, the IC3 has received complaints crossing the spectrum of cybercrime matters to include online fraud in its many forms. It has become increasingly evident that, regardless of the label placed on a cybercrime matter, the potential for it to overlap with another referred matter is substantial. In addition, many of these crimes are perpetrated through social engineering.[2]

The Federal Trade Commission (FTC) works to prevent fraudulent, deceptive, and unfair business practices in the marketplace and to provide information to help consumers to spot, stop, and avoid them. Many of the complaints received by the FTC are regarding business practices that are perpetrated through social engineering.[3] The Securities and Exchange Commission (SEC) oversees the key participants in the securities world, including securities exchanges, securities brokers and dealers, investment advisors, and mutual funds. The SEC is concerned primarily with promoting the disclosure of important market-related information, maintaining fair dealing, and protecting against fraud. Many of the complaints handled by the SEC are regarding crimes perpetrated through the use of social engineering.[4] This chapter reviews several instances of social engineering being employed to commit criminal acts, which violate laws that the above agencies are responsible for enforcing.

3.1 The Tech Support Scam

This social engineering attack is still going on and in 2017 the IC3 received approximately 11,000 complaints related to tech support fraud. The claimed losses amounted to nearly $15 million, which represented an 86% increase in losses from 2016. While a majority of tech support fraud involves victims in the United States, IC3 has received complaints of this scenario of **computer fraud** from victims in 85 different countries.

Criminals may pose as a security, customer, or technical support representative offering to resolve such issues as a compromised email or bank account, a virus on a computer, or to assist with a software license renewal. Some recent complaints involve criminals posing as technical support representatives for GPS, printer, or cable companies, or support for virtual currency exchangers. As this type of fraud has become more commonplace, criminals have started to pose as government agents, even offering to recover supposed losses related to tech support fraud schemes or to request financial assistance with apprehending criminals. Initial contact with the victim typically occurs through the methods shown in Box 3.1.

BOX 3.1   TECH SUPPORT FRAUD INITIAL VICTIM CONTACT METHODS

Telephone: A victim receives an unsolicited telephone call from an individual claiming the victim's device or computer is infected with a virus or is sending error messages to the caller. Callers are generally reported to have strong, foreign accents.

Search Engine Advertising: Individuals in need of tech support may use online search engines to find technical support companies. Criminals pay to have their fraudulent tech support company's link show higher in search results, hoping victims will choose one of the top links in search results.

Pop-Up Message: The victim receives an on-screen pop-up message claiming a virus has been found on their computer. In order to receive assistance, the message requests the victim call a phone number associated with the fraudulent tech support company.

Locked Screen on a Device: The victim's device displays a frozen, locked screen with a phone number and instructions to contact a fraudulent tech support company. Some victims have reported being redirected to alternative web sites before the locked screen occurs.

Pop-ups and locked screens are often accompanied by a recorded, verbal message to contact a phone number for assistance. In other instances, a uniform resource locater (URL) is programmed into links for advertisements or popular topics on social media, which are disguised because web addresses of popular websites (such as social media or financial websites) are **typosquatted** to result in a pop-up or locked screen if the victim incorrectly types the intended website address.

Another approach is that a victim receives a phishing email warning of a possible intrusion to their computer or an email warning of a fraudulent account charge to their bank accounts or credit cards. The email provides a phone number for the recipient to contact the fraudulent tech support. Once the fraudulent tech support company representative makes verbal contact with the victim, the criminal tries to convince the victim to provide remote access to the victim's device. If the device is a tablet or smartphone, the criminal often instructs the victim to connect the device to a computer. Once remotely connected the criminal claims to find expired licenses, viruses, malware, or **scareware**. The criminal will inform the victim the issue can be removed for a fee. Criminals usually request payment through personal/electronic check, bank/wire transfer, debit/credit card, pre-paid card, or virtual currency.

Another widespread issue is the **fake refund**. In this scheme, the criminal contacts the victim offering a refund for tech support services previously rendered. The criminal requests access to the victim's device and instructs the victim to login to their online bank account to process a refund. As a result, the criminal gains control of the victim's device and bank account. With this access, the criminal makes it appear as if too much money was refunded to the victim's account and requests the victim return the difference back to the criminal's company via a wire transfer or pre-paid cards. In reality, there was no refund at all. Instead, the criminal transferred funds among the victims own accounts (checking, savings, retirement, etc.) to make it appear as though funds were deposited. The victim returns their own money to the criminal. The refund and return process can occur multiple times, resulting in the victim potentially losing thousands of dollars.

Tech support fraud was originally an attempt by criminals to gain access to devices to extort payment for fraudulent services. However, criminals are creating new techniques and versions of the scheme to advance and perpetuate the fraud. These include **re-targeting** previous victims and contacts by criminals posing as government officials or law enforcement officers. The criminal offers assistance in recovering losses from a previous tech support fraud incident. The criminal either requests funds from the victim to assist with the investigation or to cover fees associated with returning the lost funds. Criminals also pose as collection services claiming the victim did not pay for prior tech support services. The victim is often threatened with legal action if the victim does not pay a settlement fee.

Virtual currency is increasingly targeted by tech support criminals, with individual victim losses often in thousands of dollars. Criminals pose as virtual currency support personnel. Victims contact fraudulent virtual currency support numbers usually located via open source searches. The fraudulent support asks for access to the victim's virtual currency wallet and transfers the victim's virtual currency to another wallet for temporary holding during maintenance. The virtual currency is never returned to the victim, and the criminal ceases all communication. Criminals who have access to a victim's electronic device use the victim's personal information and credit card to purchase and transfer virtual currency to an account controlled by the criminal.

There has also been increasing use of victim's personal information and accounts to conduct additional fraud. Criminals use the victim's personal information to request bank transfers or open new accounts to accept and process unauthorized payments. They also send phishing emails to the victim's personal contacts from the victim's computer and download personal files containing financial accounts, passwords, and personal data (health records, social security numbers, tax information, etc.). Additionally, IC3 complaints report:

- Criminals who took control of victims' devices and/or accounts and did not release control unless a ransom was paid.
- Viruses, **key-logging software,** and malware were installed on victims' devices.
- Criminals have become more belligerent, hostile, and abusive if challenged by victims.

Computer users should always remember that legitimate customer, security, or tech support companies will not initiate unsolicited contact with individuals and that they should be cautious of customer support numbers obtained via open source searching. Phone numbers listed in a sponsored results section are likely boosted as a result of search engine advertising. It is wise to learn to recognize fraudulent attempts and cease all communication with the criminal.[5]

3.2 Business Email Compromise

Business Email Compromise (BEC)/Email Account Compromise (EAC) is a sophisticated scam targeting both businesses and individuals performing wire transfer payments. The scam is frequently carried out when a perpetrator compromises legitimate business email accounts through social engineering or computer intrusion techniques to conduct unauthorized transfers of funds. The scam may not always be associated with a request for transfer of funds. A variation of the scam involves compromising legitimate business email accounts and requesting Personally Identifiable Information (PII) or Wage and Tax Statement (W-2) forms for employees.

The BEC/EAC scam continues to grow and evolve, targeting small, medium, and large businesses and personal transactions. Between December 2016 and May 2018, there was a 136% increase in identified global exposed losses. The scam has been reported in all 50 states in the United States and in 150 countries. Victim complaints filed with the IC3 and financial sources indicate fraudulent transfers have been sent to 115 countries.

Table 3.1   BEC/EAC Scam Statistics
(October 2013 and May 2018)

Worldwide incidents	78,617
Worldwide losses	$12,536,948,299
US victims	41,058
US losses	$2,935,161,457
Non-US victims	2,565
Non-US losses	$671,915,009

Based on the financial data, Asian banks located in China and Hong Kong remain the primary destinations of fraudulent funds; however, financial institutions in the United Kingdom, Mexico, and Turkey have also been identified recently as prominent destinations. Between October 2013 and May 2018, there were 78,617 incidents reported by domestic and international sources and the dollar loss was staggering. Statistics are shown in Table 3.1.

In recent years, BEC/EAC actors heavily targeted the real estate sector. Victims participating at all levels of a real estate transaction have reported such activity to IC3. This includes title companies, law firms, real estate agents, buyers, and sellers. Victims most often report a fabricated email being sent or received on behalf of one of these real estate transaction participants with instructions directing the recipient to change the payment type and/or payment location to a fraudulent account. The funds are usually directed to a fraudulent domestic account and are then quickly dispersed through cash or check withdrawals. The funds may also be transferred to a secondary fraudulent domestic or international account. Funds sent to domestic accounts are often depleted rapidly making recovery difficult.

Domestic **money mules** are frequently identified in connection with the BEC/EAC real estate trend. BEC/EAC actors often recruit money mules through confidence/romance scams. The BEC/EAC actor may groom a victim and then direct them to open accounts under the guise of sending or receiving funds as directed by the BEC/EAC actor. The accounts opened to facilitate this activity are typically used for a short period of time. Once the account is flagged by the financial institutions, it may be closed and the BEC/EAC actor will either direct the scam victim to open a new account or move on to grooming a new victim. It is noteworthy that some victims reported they were unable to distinguish fraudulent phone conversations from legitimate conversations. One way to counteract this fraudulent activity is to establish code phrases that would only be known to the two legitimate parties.

Based on victim complaint data, BEC/EAC scams targeting the real estate sector are on the rise. From calendar years 2015 to 2017, there was an over 1,100% rise in the number of BEC/EAC victims reporting the real estate transaction angle and an almost 2,200% rise in the reported monetary loss or over $18 billion.[6]

3.3 Social Engineering of Education Scams

The FTC has charged three individuals and nine businesses with bilking more than $125 million from thousands of consumers with a fraudulent business education program called MOBE (My Online Business Education). A federal court halted the scheme and froze the defendants' assets at the FTC's request. According to the FTC, the defendants behind this international operation target US consumers, including service members, veterans, and older adults, through online ads, social media, direct mailers, and live events held throughout the country. This action follows the agency's recent action against Digital Altitude, LLC, which was a competing business opportunity scheme that was also halted by court order.

The FTC alleged that the defendants falsely claimed that their business education program would enable people to start their own online businesses and earn substantial incomes. The defendants claimed to have a proven 21-step system for making substantial sums of money quickly and easily from Internet marketing, which they promise to provide to those who join their program. According to the complaint, consumers who paid the initial $49 entry fee for the 21-step program were then bombarded with sales pitches for membership packages that cost thousands of dollars, which the defendants pressured them to buy in order to continue through the 21 steps. The defendants eventually revealed that their proven system for making money is for consumers to sell the same memberships to others in the hopes of earning commissions on those sales. Most people who buy into the program and pay for the expensive memberships are unable to recoup their costs, and many experience crippling losses or mounting debts, including some who have lost more than $20,000, the FTC alleged.

The FTC also alleged that the defendants offer refunds and money-back guarantees to further mislead people to believe the program is risk-free, but they often refuse to honor a refund request, or they provide refunds only after buyers make persistent demands or threaten to complain to the Better Business Bureau or law enforcement agencies.[7]

In a similar situation, online ads and in person workshops for Sellers Playbook claim to offer secrets to making big money on Amazon. But, like a lot of name-droppers, the truth doesn't live up to the hype. That is what the FTC and the Minnesota Attorney General (AG) alleged in a lawsuit they filed. According to the complaint, Sellers Playbook lures consumers in with promises like "Potential Net Profit: $1,287,463.38" and "Starting with $1000 … 1 year later over $210,000," but the FTC and AG say few people, if anybody, makes that kind of money, despite shelling out thousands to learn the company's so-called secrets. What is even more deceptive is that Sellers Playbook had no affiliation with Amazon other than dropping the online giant's name in its ads. If the tactics sound familiar, that is because some of the defendants behind Sellers Playbook were affiliated with Amazing Wealth Systems, a venture whose bogus big money claims were the subject of an earlier FTC lawsuit.

The FTC and the Minnesota AG have charged Sellers Playbook with making misleading earnings claims. The FTC also says the defendants have violated the Business Opportunity Rule, a consumer protection provision that requires sellers of money-making ventures to disclose certain facts up front to people thinking about signing up. In addition, the lawsuit alleged that the defendants violated the Consumer Review Fairness Act, which is a new law that bans contract provisions that try to silence consumers from posting their honest opinions about a company's products or customer service.[8]

3.4 The Avalanche Takedown

In December 2016, the Department of Justice (DOJ) announced a multinational operation involving arrests and searches in four countries to dismantle a complex and sophisticated network of computer servers known as Avalanche. The Avalanche network allegedly hosted more than two dozen of the world's most pernicious types of malicious software and several money laundering campaigns. However,

Avalanche is considered to be just one example of a criminal infrastructure dedicated to facilitating privacy invasions and financial crimes on a global scale.

The Avalanche network offered cybercriminals a secure infrastructure, designed to thwart detection by law enforcement and cybersecurity experts, over which the criminals conducted malware campaigns as well as money laundering schemes known as money mule schemes. Online banking passwords and other sensitive information stolen from victims' malware-infected computers were redirected through the intricate network of Avalanche servers and ultimately to back-end servers controlled by the cybercriminals. Access to the Avalanche network was offered to the cybercriminals through postings on exclusive, underground online criminal forums.

The operation also involved an unprecedented effort to seize, block, and sinkhole—meaning redirect traffic from infected victim computers to servers controlled by law enforcement instead of the servers controlled by cybercriminals—more than 800,000 malicious domains associated with the Avalanche network. Such domains are needed to funnel information, such as sensitive banking credentials, from the victims' malware-infected computers, through the layers of Avalanche servers, and ultimately back to the cybercriminals. This was accomplished, in part, through a temporary restraining order obtained by the US in the Western District of Pennsylvania.

The types of malware and money mule schemes operating over the Avalanche network varied. Ransomware such as Nymain, for example, encrypted victims' computer files until the victim paid a ransom (typically in a form of electronic currency) to the cybercriminal. Other malware, such as GozNym, was designed to steal victims' sensitive banking credentials and use those credentials to initiate fraudulent wire transfers. The money mule schemes operating over Avalanche involved highly organized networks of mules that purchased goods with stolen funds, enabling cybercriminals to launder the money they acquired through the malware attacks or other illegal means.

The Avalanche network, which had been operating since at least 2010, was estimated to serve clients operating as many as 500,000 infected computers worldwide on a daily basis. The monetary losses associated with malware attacks conducted over the Avalanche network are estimated to be in the hundreds of millions of dollars worldwide, although exact calculations are difficult due to the high number of malware families present on the network.

The US Attorney's Office of the Western District of Pennsylvania, the FBI, and the Criminal Division's Computer Crime and Intellectual Property Section (CCIPS) conducted the operation in close cooperation with the Public Prosecutor's Office, Verden, Germany; the Luneburg Police, Germany; Europol; Eurojust, located in the Hague, the Netherlands; and investigators and prosecutors from more than 40 jurisdictions, including India, Singapore, Taiwan, and Ukraine. Other agencies and organizations partnering in this effort included the Department of Homeland Security's US-Computer Emergency Readiness Team (US-CERT), the Shadowserver Foundation, Fraunhofer Institute for Communication, Registry of Last Resort, ICANN, and domain registries from around the world. The Criminal Division's Office of International Affairs also provided significant assistance.[9] The goal was to dismantle the operation but also to accomplish **effective prosecution**.

3.5 Takedown of the Gameover Zeus and Cryptolocker Operations

Evgeniy Bogachev and the members of his criminal network devised and implemented the kind of cybercrimes that you might not believe if you saw them in a science fiction movie. By secretly implanting viruses on computers around the world, they built a network of infected machines, or bots, that they could infiltrate, spy on, and even control, from anywhere they wished. Sitting quietly at their own computer screens, the cybercriminals could watch as the Gameover Zeus malware intercepted the bank account numbers and passwords that unwitting victims typed into computers and networks in the United States. Then the criminals turned that information into cash by emptying the victims' bank accounts and diverting the money to themselves. Typically, by the time victims learned they had been infected with Gameover Zeus, it was too late.

The Cryptolocker scheme, by contrast, was brutally direct about obtaining victims' money. Rather than watch and wait, the cybercriminals simply took the victim's computer hostage until the computer owner agreed to pay a ransom directly to them. They used sophisticated encryption tools, originally designed to protect data from theft, to make it impossible for victims to access any data stored on their computers. The criminals effectively held for ransom every private email, business plan, child's science project, or family photograph—every single important and personal file stored on the victim's computer. In order to get their data back, computer owners had to hand over their cash. As with Gameover Zeus, once a computer user learned they were infected with the Cryptolocker malware, it was too late.

On May 7, 2014, in coordination with the FBI, the Ukrainian authorities and the DOJ seized and copied key Gameover Zeus command servers in Kiev and Donetsk. Then, on Monday, May 19, they obtained sealed criminal charges against Bogachev in Pittsburgh charging him with illegal hacking, fraud, and money laundering. On Wednesday, May 28, they obtained civil court orders against Bogachev and his co-conspirators based on federal laws that prohibit ongoing fraud and the illegal interception of communications. These orders allowed the DOJ to cause the computers infected with Gameover Zeus to cease communicating with computer servers controlled by the criminals and instead contact a server established by the court order. The court also authorized the collection of information necessary to identify the victim computers so that the DOJ could provide that information to public- and private-sector entities that could help the victims rid their computers of the infection. At the same time, foreign law enforcement partners seized critical computer servers used to operate Cryptolocker, which resulted in Cryptolocker being unable to encrypt victim files.

Beginning in the early morning hours on Friday, May 30, and continuing through the weekend, the FBI and law enforcement around the world began the coordinated seizure of computer servers that had been the backbone of Gameover Zeus and Cryptolocker. These seizures took place in Canada, France, Germany, Luxembourg, the Netherlands, Ukraine, and the United Kingdom. Recognizing that seizures alone would not be enough because cybercriminals can quickly establish new servers in other locations, the team began a carefully timed sequence of technical measures to wrest from the criminals the ability to send commands to hundreds of thousands of infected computers, and to direct those computers to contact the server that the court had authorized the DOJ to establish. Working from command posts in the United States and at the European Cybercrime Centre in the Hague, the Netherlands, the FBI and their foreign counterparts, assisted by numerous private-sector partners, worked feverishly around the clock to accomplish this redirection and to defeat various defenses built into the malware, as well as countermeasures attempted in real time over the weekend by the cybercriminals who were trying to retain control over their network.

Those actions caused a major disruption of the Gameover Zeus botnet. Over the weekend, more than 300,000 victim computers had been freed from the botnet. By Saturday, Cryptolocker was no longer functioning and its infrastructure had been effectively dismantled. Over the next few days and weeks, investigators and prosecutors worked with private-sector partners to notify infected victims and provide links to safe and trusted tools that can help them rid themselves of Gameover Zeus and Cryptolocker and then close the vulnerabilities through which their computers were infected.[10]

3.6 Social Engineers are Striking on Numerous Fronts

Criminal social engineers are striking everywhere they think they can succeed. The following social engineer attacks do not seem to be as widespread as the tech support attack, or do as much damage to a single entity as the business email attacks, but they are directed at very vulnerable segments of the population. These attacks include:

- Cybercriminals utilize social engineering techniques to obtain employee credentials to conduct payroll diversion attacks. The IC3 has received complaints reporting that cybercriminals are targeting the online payroll accounts of employees in a variety of industries. Institutions most affected are education, healthcare, and commercial airway transportation.
- Cybercriminals target employees through phishing emails designed to capture an employee's login credentials. Once the cybercriminal has obtained an employee's credentials, the credentials are used to access the employee's payroll account in order to change their bank account information. Rules are added by the cybercriminal to the employee's account preventing the employee from receiving alerts regarding direct

deposit changes. Direct deposits are then changed and redirected to an account controlled by the cybercriminal, which is often a pre-paid card.[11]

The FTC has been hearing about a social engineering attack targeting people who are selling their cars online. Sellers get calls or texts from people who claim to be interested in buying the car but first want to see a car history report. They ask the seller to get the report from a specific website, where the seller needs to enter some information and pay about $20 by credit card for the report. The seller then sends it to the supposed buyer but never hears back. When the car sellers go to one of these websites, they're automatically redirected to sites ending in .vin, which seems like it might be related to a car's vehicle identification number (VIN). Scammers hope they will think that, but no. In this case, .vin is a relatively new website domain like .com or .org that groups can apply to use. This domain was intended to be used for sites that relate to wine, since vin is the French word for wine, but others are not prevented from using it. So yes, that's a clever take on .vin for cars. However, sellers still might want to think twice if anyone asks them to do car-related business on a site ending in .vin. Sellers may have no way of knowing who operates the site, especially if it's one they have never heard of. It might be a ruse to get personal information, including credit card account numbers. It also could be a way for companies called lead generators to get information, which they sell to third parties for advertising and marketing purposes.[12]

In February 2019, the US Secret Service announced the indictment of 20 people, including 16 foreign nationals, for their involvement in an online auction fraud scheme designed to defraud users looking to purchase merchandise via the Internet. It is alleged that this transnational organized fraud ring stole millions of dollars from unsuspecting victims across the United States in a sophisticated fraud scheme that relied on the increasing popularity of e-commerce marketplaces such as Craigslist™ and eBay™. Using these sites, fraudsters post false advertisements for merchandise that does not exist. Then, using a multitude of social engineered and convincing methods, these cybercriminals persuade victims to send money for the non-existent goods.

The indictment alleged that the defendants participated in a criminal conspiracy primarily located in Alexandria, Romania, that engaged in a large-scale scheme of online auction fraud. Specifically, Romania-based members of the conspiracy and their associates posted false advertisements to popular online auction and sales websites such as Craigslist™ and eBay™ for high-cost goods (typically vehicles) that did not actually exist. According to the indictment, these members would convince American victims to send money for the advertised goods by crafting persuasive narratives, for example, by impersonating a military member who needed to sell the advertised item before deployment. The members of the conspiracy are alleged to have created fictitious online accounts to post these advertisements and communicate with victims, often using the stolen identities of Americans to do so.[13]

The United States Patent and Trademark Office (USPTO) and the FTC have made public announcements that there are companies pretending to be the USPTO or a partner of the USPTO. These companies are tricking patent and trademark holders into paying them fees for services, but they are not the USPTO. They often send official-looking solicitations that offer to do things like renew a trademark registration, sign people up for trademark monitoring services, record trademarks with government agencies, or list them on a private registry. Nearly always, the services offered are overpriced, unnecessary, or outright deceptive.

The names and emblems these imposters use on their forms help them seem like they are connected with the USPTO, copying the look of official government forms, according to information from the USPTO. Some patent or trademark holders have paid imposters hundreds or even thousands of dollars mistakenly thinking they were paying fees to the USPTO, or paying fees the USPTO requires, to maintain and protect their patents and trademarks. Thus potential buyers must read any notice about patents or trademarks very carefully. Official mail from the USPTO will come from the US Patent and Trademark Office in Alexandria, Virginia. If it comes via email, the domain will be @uspto.gov.[14]

The SEC issued a Report of Investigation regarding certain cyber-related frauds and public company issuer internal accounting controls requirements. The Report discusses a type of cyber fraud called business email compromise where perpetrators pretended in emails to be high-level company executives or vendors, and then

BOX 3.2 OTHER RECENT SOCIAL ENGINEERING ATTACKS

Timeshare resale scheme preyed on older adults

Google business listing will be removed

Publishers Clearing House imposters

FTC asking for access to your computer

Student loan forgiveness

The Secretary of State is emailing you

Love interest asking for money

US Marshals calling you about jury duty

Equifax calling you

Phantom debt collectors impersonate law firms[16]

convinced company personnel to transmit large wire transfers to accounts controlled by the perpetrators.[15] Other recent social engineered attacks resulting in fraud are shown in Box 3.2.

3.7 The North Korean Connection

In September 2018, a criminal complaint was unsealed charging Park Jin Hyok (박진혁; aka Jin Hyok Park and Pak Jin Hek), a North Korean citizen, for his involvement in a conspiracy to conduct multiple destructive cyber attacks around the world, resulting in damage to massive amounts of computer hardware, and the extensive loss of data, money, and other resources.

The complaint alleged that Park was a member of a government-sponsored hacking team known to the private sector as the Lazarus Group and worked for a North Korean government front company, Chosun Expo Joint Venture (aka Korea Expo Joint Venture or KEJV), to support the Democratic People's Republic of Korea (DPRK) government's malicious cyber actions. The conspiracy's malicious activities included the creation of the malware used in the 2017 WannaCry 2.0 global ransomware attack; the 2016 theft of $81 million from Bangladesh Bank; the 2014 attack on Sony Pictures Entertainment (SPE); and numerous other attacks or intrusions on the entertainment, financial services, defense, technology, virtual currency industries, academia, and electric utilities.

The complaint alleged that the North Korean government, through a state-sponsored group, robbed a central bank and citizens of other nations, retaliated against free speech in order to chill it half-a-world away, and created disruptive malware that indiscriminately affected victims in more than 150 other countries, causing hundreds of millions, if not billions, of dollars' worth of damage. The complaint charged members of this North Korean-based conspiracy with being responsible for cyber attacks that caused unprecedented economic damage and disruption to businesses in the United States and around the globe. The FBI traced the attacks back to the source and mapped their commonalities, including similarities among the various programs used to infect networks across the globe. Park was charged with one count of conspiracy to commit computer fraud and abuse, which carried a maximum sentence of five years in prison, and one count of conspiracy to commit wire fraud, which carried a maximum sentence of 20 years in prison.

Security researchers that independently investigated these activities referred to this hacking team as the Lazarus Group. The conspiracy's methods included spear phishing campaigns, destructive malware attacks, exfiltration of data, theft of funds from bank accounts, ransomware extortion, and propagating worm viruses to create botnets. The complaint described a broad array of the conspiracy's alleged malicious cyber activities, both successful and unsuccessful, in the United States and elsewhere, with a particular focus on four specific examples:

- In November 2014, the conspirators launched a destructive attack on Sony Pictures Entertainment (SPE) in retaliation for the movie *The Interview*, a farcical comedy that depicted the assassination of the DPRK's leader. The conspirators gained access to SPE's network by sending malware to SPE employees, and then stole confidential data, threatened SPE executives and employees, and damaged thousands of computers. Around the same time, the group sent spear phishing messages to other members in the entertainment industry, including a movie theater chain and a UK-based company that was producing a fictional series involving a British nuclear scientist taken prisoner in DPRK.

- In February 2016, the conspiracy stole $81 million from Bangladesh Bank. As part of the cyber heist, the conspiracy accessed the bank's computer terminals that interfaced with the Society for Worldwide Interbank Financial Telecommunication (SWIFT) communication system after compromising the bank's computer network with spear phishing emails. It then sent fraudulently authenticated SWIFT messages directing the Federal Reserve Bank of New York to transfer funds from Bangladesh to accounts in other Asian countries. The conspiracy attempted to and gained access to several other banks in various countries from 2015 through 2018 using similar methods and **watering hole attacks,** attempting the theft of at least $1 billion through such operations.
- In 2016 and 2017, the conspiracy targeted a number of US defense contractors, including Lockheed Martin, with spear phishing emails. These malicious emails used some of the same aliases and accounts seen in the SPE attack, at times accessed from North Korean IP addresses, and contained malware with the same distinct data table found in the malware used against SPE and certain banks, the complaint alleged. The spear phishing emails sent to the defense contractors were often sent from email accounts that purported to be from recruiters at competing defense contractors, and some of the malicious messages made reference to the Terminal High Altitude Area Defense (THAAD) missile defense system deployed in South Korea. The attempts to infiltrate the computer systems of Lockheed Martin, the prime contractor for the THAAD missile system, were not successful.
- In May 2017, a ransomware attack known as WannaCry 2.0 infected hundreds of thousands of computers around the world, causing extensive damage, including a significant impact on the United Kingdom's National Health Service. The conspiracy is connected to the development of WannaCry 2.0, as well as two prior versions of the ransomware, through similarities in form and function to other malware developed by the hackers, and by spreading versions of the ransomware through the same infrastructure used in other cyber attacks.

Park and his co-conspirators were linked to these attacks, intrusions, and other malicious cyber-enabled activities through a thorough investigation that identified and traced: Email and social media accounts that connected to each other and were used to send spear phishing messages; aliases; malware collector accounts used to store stolen credentials; common malware code libraries; proxy services used to mask locations; and North Korean, Chinese, and other IP addresses. Some of this malicious infrastructure was used across multiple instances of the malicious activities described herein. Taken together, these connections and signatures, which were revealed in charts attached to the criminal complaint, showed that the attacks and intrusions were perpetrated by the same actors.

In connection with the unsealing of the criminal complaint, the FBI and prosecutors provided cybersecurity providers and other private-sector partners with detailed information on accounts used by the conspiracy in order to assist these partners in their own independent investigative activities and disruption efforts.[17]

3.8 Conclusion

There have been countless social engineering attacks, some of which merely amounted to delinquency while others have had a global financial and business impact. Activities like the Tech Support Scam and Business Email Compromise have impacted thousands of businesses and private computer users. Some social engineering efforts like those of North Korea and Avalanche have been subparts of larger criminal conspiracies. This chapter has reviewed real-world exploits and crimes involving social engineering.

3.9 Key Points

Key points presented in this chapter are as follows:

- The technical resources needed to execute phishing attacks can be readily acquired through public and private sources.
- Tech support fraud was originally an attempt by criminals to gain access to devices to extort payment for fraudulent

services. However, criminals are creating new techniques and versions of the scheme to advance and perpetuate the fraud.

- While a majority of tech support fraud involves victims in the United States, IC3 has received complaints from victims in 85 different countries.
- Business Email Compromise (BEC)/Email Account Compromise (EAC) is a sophisticated scam targeting both businesses and individuals performing wire transfer payments and is frequently carried out when a perpetrator compromises legitimate business email accounts through social engineering or computer intrusion.
- The Avalanche network allegedly hosted more than two dozen of the world's most pernicious types of malicious software and several money laundering campaigns. However, Avalanche is considered to be just one example of a criminal infrastructure dedicated to facilitating privacy invasions and financial crimes on a global scale.
- A criminal network devised and implemented the kind of cybercrimes that you might not believe if you saw them in a science fiction movie. By secretly implanting viruses on computers around the world, they built a network of infected machines or bots that they could infiltrate, spy on, and even control, from anywhere they wished.
- Criminal social engineers are striking everywhere they think they can succeed and many attacks are directed at already very vulnerable segments of the population.
- Online auction fraud is a sophisticated fraud scheme that relies on the increasing popularity of e-commerce market-places such as Craigslist™ and eBay™.
- North Korea's alleged malicious activities include the creation of the malware used in the 2017 WannaCry 2.0 global ransomware attack; the 2016 theft of $81 million from Bangladesh Bank; the 2014 attack on Sony Pictures Entertainment (SPE); and numerous other attacks or intrusions on the entertainment, financial services, defense, technology, and virtual currency industries, academia, and electric utilities.

3.10 Seminar Discussion Topics

Discussion topics for graduate- or professional-level seminars are:

- What experience have seminar participants had with any of the social engineering attacks covered in this chapter?
- Discuss the perspective of the participants regarding the accusations against North Korea. Do participants think North Korea is the perpetrator of all things they have been accused of doing?
- Why do participants think that people keep falling into the same type of socially engineered traps year after year?

3.11 Seminar Group Project

Divide participants into multiple groups with each group taking 10 to 15 minutes to develop a list of ways that computer users could be trained or educated not to respond to socially engineered click bait. Meet as a group and discuss the ways that groups have listed to train or educate computer users to not respond to socially engineered click bait.

Key Terms

Computer fraud: is crime involving deliberate misrepresentation, alteration, or disclosure of data in order to obtain something of value (usually for monetary gain).

Effective prosecution: is the successful prosecution of intellectual crime perpetrators while simultaneously protecting trade secrets and other intellectual property of the victim organization.

Fake refund: is a socially engineered scheme where criminals contact a victim, offering a refund for tech support services allegedly provided previously. The criminal requests access to the victim's device and instructs the victim to login to their online bank account to process a refund. This action provides the criminal control of the victim's device and access to their bank account.

Key-logging software: captures and records the keys struck on a keyboard, typically covertly, so that the person using the keyboard is unaware that their actions are being monitored. The information can be retrieved by the person who is operating or who installed the logging program.

Money mules: are defined as persons who transfer money illegally on behalf of others.

Re-targeting: is when a scammer who has attempted to or who has successfully exploited a user in the past makes a second attempt at exploiting that user for financial gain or access to additional information or systems.

Scareware: is socially engineered malware designed to cause shock or the perception of a threat in order to manipulate users into buying malicious software. It is a type of malicious attack that can include rogue security software, ransomware, and other scams that get computer users to be concerned that their computer is infected with malicious code and often suggests that they pay a fee to fix their computer.

Typosquatting (typosquatted): also called URL hijacking, is cybersquatting (sitting on sites under someone else's brand or copyright) that targets Internet users who incorrectly type a website address into their web browser. When users make typical typographical errors they can be sent to a website owned by a hacker, which is often designed for criminal purposes.

Watering hole attacks: are malware attacks in which the attacker determines the websites frequently visited by a victim or a particular victim group, and infects those websites with malware, which in turn infects the computer of the visiting website users, and thus can infect members of the targeted victim group.

References

1. Technical Trends in Phishing Attacks. US-CERT. Milletary, Jason. Accessed February 2, 2019. www.us-cert.gov/sites/default/files/publications/phishing_trends0511.pdf
2. IC3 Mission Statement/About Us. Federal Bureau of Investigation Internet Crime Complaint Center (IC3). Accessed February 7, 2019. https://www.ic3.gov/about/default.aspx

3. About Us. Federal Trade Commission Consumer Information. Accessed February 7, 2019. https://www.consumer.ftc.gov/about-us

4. What We Do. Securities and Exchange Commission. Accessed February 7, 2019. https://www.sec.gov/Article/whatwedo.html

5. Tech Support Fraud. Federal Bureau of Investigation. March 28, 2018. Accessed February 7, 2019. https://www.ic3.gov/media/2018/180328.aspx

6. Business Email Compromise The 12 Billion Dollar Scam. Federal Bureau of Investigation. March 28, 2018. Accessed February 7, 2019. https://www.ic3.gov/media/2018/180712.aspx

7. FTC Action Halts MOBE, A Massive Internet Business Coaching Scheme. Federal Trade Commission. Puig, Alvaro. June 11, 2018. Accessed February 8, 2019. https://www.ftc.gov/news-events/press-releases/2018/06/ftc-action-halts-mobe-massive-internet-business-coaching-scheme

8. Promoter Pitches Secrets to Big Bucks on Amazon. Federal Trade Commission. Fair, Lesley. August 6, 2018. Accessed February 8, 2019. https://www.consumer.ftc.gov/blog/2018/08/promoter-pitches-secrets-big-bucks-amazon

9. Avalanche Network Dismantled in International Cyber Operation. Department of Justice US Attorney's Office Western District of Pennsylvania. December 5, 2016. Accessed February 8, 2019. https://www.justice.gov/usao-wdpa/pr/avalanche-network-dismantled-international-cyber-operation

10. Assistant Attorney General Leslie R. Caldwell Delivers Remarks for the Gameover Zeus and Cryptolocker Operations and Related Criminal Charges. Washington, DC. June 2, 2014. Accessed February 8, 2019. https://www.justice.gov/opa/speech/assistant-attorney-general-leslie-r-caldwell-delivers-remarks-gameover-zeus-and

11. Cybercriminals Utilize Social Engineering Techniques to Obtain Employee Credentials to Conduct Payroll Diversion. Federal Bureau of Investigation. September 18, 2018. Accessed February 7, 2019. https://www.ic3.gov/media/2018/180918.aspx

12. Steering Clear of Vehicle History Report Scams. Federal Trade Commission. Tressler, Colleen. October 19, 2018. Accessed February 7, 2019. https://www.consumer.ftc.gov/blog/2018/10/steering-clear-vehicle-history-report-scams

13. Secret Service Investigation Leads to Indictment of Organized Transnational Cyber-Crime Ring Targeting US Consumers. United States Secret Service. February 7, 2019. Accessed February 8, 2019. https://www.secretservice.gov/data/press/releases/2019/19-FEB/Secret_Service_Press_Release-Transnational_Online_Auction_Fraud_Ring.pdf

14. Scammers Can Be Inventive. Federal Trade Commission. Lake, Lisa. July 10, 2017. Accessed February 8, 2019. https://www.consumer.ftc.gov/blog/2017/07/scammers-can-be-inventive

15. Report of Investigation Pursuant to Section 21(a) of the Securities Exchange Act of 1934: Certain Cyber-Related Frauds Perpetrated Against Public Companies and Related Internal Accounting Controls

Requirements. US Securities and Exchange Commission. October 16, 2018. Accessed February 8, 2019. https://www.sec.gov/spotlight/cybersecurity-enforcement-actions

16. Most Recent Scam Alerts. Federal Trade Commission. Accessed February 8, 2019. https://www.consumer.ftc.gov/features/scam-alerts

17. North Korean Regime-Backed Programmer Charged with Conspiracy to Conduct Multiple Cyber Attacks and Intrusions. Department of Justice Office of Public Affairs. September 6, 2018. Accessed February 8, 2019. https://www.justice.gov/opa/pr/north-korean-regime-backed-programmer-charged-conspiracy-conduct-multiple-cyber-attacks-and

4
SECURING ORGANIZATIONS AGAINST SOCIAL ENGINEERING ATTACKS

An organization's security culture contributes to the effectiveness of its information security program. The information security program is more effective when security processes are deeply embedded in the institution's culture and there is a high level of **security awareness**. The management team should understand and support information security and provide appropriate resources for developing, implementing, and maintaining the information security program. The result of this understanding and support is a program in which both management and employees are committed to integrating the program into lines of business, support functions, and third-party management programs.[1]

4.1 The Basics of Security for Social Engineering Attacks

Protection against social engineering attacks and other **security threats** is essential for all organizations. Attackers use malware to obtain access to an organization's network and computer environment and to execute an attack within the environment. Malware may enter through public or private networks and from devices attached to the network. Although protective mechanisms may block most malware before they do any damage, even a single malicious executable file may create a significant potential for loss.

The implementation of an in-depth defensive program to protect, detect, and respond to malware is an important basic step. Businesses can use many tools to block malware before it enters the network and to detect it and respond if it is not blocked. Methods or systems that management should consider include the following:

- Hardware-based roots of trust, which use cryptographic means to verify the integrity of software.
- Servers that run active content at the gateway and disallow content based on policy.
- Blacklists that disallow code execution based on code fragments, Internet locations, and other factors that correlate with malicious code.
- White lists of allowed programs.
- Port monitoring to identify unauthorized network connections.
- Network segregation.
- Computer configuration to permit the least amount of privileges necessary to perform the user's job.
- Application **sandboxing**.
- Monitoring for unauthorized software and disallowing the ability to install unauthorized software.
- Monitoring for anomalous activity for malware and polymorphic code.
- Monitoring of network traffic.
- User education in awareness, **security vigilance**, safe computing practices, indicators of malicious code, and response actions.[2]

Training is absolutely essential for security against social engineering and malicious code attacks, but it is neglected by far too many organizations. Training ensures personnel have the necessary knowledge and skills to perform their job functions. Training should support security awareness and strengthen compliance with security and acceptable use policies. Ultimately, management's behavior and priorities heavily influence employee awareness and policy compliance, so training and the commitment to security should start with management. Organizations should educate users about their security roles and responsibilities and communicate them through acceptable use policies. Management should hold all employees, officers, and contractors accountable for complying with security and acceptable use policies and should ensure that the institution's information and other assets are protected. Management should also have the ability to impose sanctions for noncompliance.

Training materials for most users focus on issues such as endpoint security, login requirements, and password administration guidelines. Training programs should include scenarios capturing areas of significant and growing concern, such as phishing and social engineering attempts, loss of data through email or removable media, or unintentional posting of confidential or proprietary information on social media. As the risk environment changes, so should the training. Management should collect signed acknowledgments of the employee **acceptable use policy** as part of the annual training program.[3]

Acceptable use policies should emphasize that an organization's computer and networks will not be used for personal activities. This is a very important principle. Employee's **personal use** expands the profile of a network and domain and can open the environment to a larger number of social engineering attacks and malware infestations. Employees may feel this is harsh but the goal of a security plan and security policy is to protect the networks and electronic assets so that operations are not disrupted.

4.2 Applying the Cybersecurity Framework is an Ongoing Process

Recognizing that national and economic security of the United States depends on the reliable functioning of critical infrastructure, the president issued Executive Order (EO) 13636, Improving Critical Infrastructure Cybersecurity, in February 2013. The Order directed the National Institute of Standards and Technology (NIST) to work with stakeholders to develop a voluntary framework for reducing cyber risks to critical infrastructure. The Cybersecurity Enhancement Act of 2014 reinforced NIST's EO 13636 role.

Created through collaboration between industry and government, the voluntary Framework consists of standards, guidelines, and practices to promote the protection of critical infrastructure. The prioritized, flexible, repeatable, and cost-effective approach of the Framework helps owners and operators of critical infrastructure to manage cybersecurity-related risk. The Cybersecurity Framework consists of three main components: the Core, Implementation Tiers, and Profiles.

The Framework Core provides a set of desired cybersecurity activities and outcomes using common language that is easy to understand. The Core guides organizations in managing and reducing their cybersecurity risks in a way that complements an organization's existing cybersecurity and risk management processes.

The Framework Implementation Tiers assist organizations by providing context for an organization to view cybersecurity risk management. The Tiers guide organizations to consider the appropriate level of rigor for their cybersecurity program and are often used as a communication tool to discuss risk appetite, mission priority, and budget.

Framework Profiles are an organization's unique alignment of their organizational requirements and objectives, risk appetite, and resources against the desired outcomes of the Framework Core. Profiles are primarily used to identify and prioritize opportunities for improving cybersecurity at an organization.[4]

The Framework will help an organization better understand, manage, and reduce its cybersecurity risks. It will assist in determining which activities are most important to assure critical operations and service delivery. In turn, that will help prioritize investments and maximize the impact of each dollar spent on cybersecurity. By providing a common language to address cybersecurity risk management, it is especially helpful in communicating inside and outside the organization. That includes improving communication, awareness, and understanding between and among information technology (IT), planning, and operating units, as well as senior executives of organizations. Organizations can also readily use the Framework to communicate current or desired cybersecurity posture between a buyer and supplier.

The Framework is guidance. It should be customized by different sectors and individual organizations to best suit their risks, situations, and needs. Organizations will continue to have unique risks as they face different threats and have different vulnerabilities and risk tolerances, and how they implement the practices in the Framework to achieve positive outcomes will vary. The Framework should not be implemented using a one-size-fits-all approach for critical infrastructure organizations or as an un-customized checklist.

Organizations are using the Framework in a variety of ways. Many have found it helpful in raising awareness and communicating with stakeholders within their organizations, including the executive

BOX 4.1   HIGH PRIORITY AREAS FOR DEVELOPMENT IN THE CYBERSECURITY FRAMEWORK

Authentication
Automated indicator sharing
Conformity assessment
Cybersecurity workforce
Data analytics
Federal agency cybersecurity alignment
International aspects, impacts, and alignment
Supply chain risk management
Technical privacy standards

leadership. The Framework is also improving communication across organizations, allowing cybersecurity expectations to be shared with business partners, suppliers, and among sectors. By mapping the Framework to current cybersecurity management approaches, organizations are learning and showing how they match up with the Framework's standards, guidelines, and best practices. Some parties are using the Framework to reconcile and de-conflict internal policy with legislation, regulation, and industry best practice. The Framework is also being used as a strategic planning tool to assess risks and current practices.

The Framework can be used by organizations that already have extensive cybersecurity programs, as well as by those just beginning to think about putting cybersecurity management programs in place. The same general approach works for any organization, although the way in which they make use of the Framework will differ depending on their current state and priorities. The high-priority areas for the development of practices, standards, and technologies necessary to support the Framework are shown in Box 4.1.[5]

4.3 The Framework Components

The Framework Core is a set of cybersecurity activities, desired outcomes, and applicable references that are common across critical infrastructure sectors. An example of Framework outcome language is physical devices and systems within the organization are inventoried.

The Core presents industry standards, guidelines, and practices in a manner that allows for communication of cybersecurity activities and outcomes across the organization from the executive level to the implementation/operations level. The Framework Core consists of five concurrent and continuous Functions, which are shown in Box 4.2. When considered together, these Functions provide a high-level, strategic view of the lifecycle of an organization's management of cybersecurity risk. The Framework Core then identifies underlying key Categories and Subcategories for each Function and matches them with example Informative References, such as existing standards, guidelines, and practices for each Subcategory.

A Framework Profile represents the cybersecurity outcomes based on business needs that an organization has selected from the Framework Categories and Subcategories. The Profile can be characterized as the alignment of standards, guidelines, and practices to the Framework Core in a particular implementation scenario. Profiles can be used to identify opportunities for improving cybersecurity posture by comparing an as is security condition to a desired security condition. To develop a Profile, an organization can review all the Categories and Subcategories and, based on business drivers and a risk assessment, determine which ones are most important for them. They can also add Categories and Subcategories as needed to address the organization's risks. The Current Profile can then be used to support prioritization and measurement of progress toward the Target Profile, while factoring in other business needs including cost-effectiveness and innovation. Profiles can be used to

---

BOX 4.2   THE FRAMEWORK CORE: CONCURRENT AND CONTINUOUS FUNCTIONS

Identify
Protect
Detect
Respond
Recover

conduct self-assessments and communicate within an organization or between organizations.

Framework Implementation Tiers provide the context for how an organization views cybersecurity risk and the processes in place to manage that risk. Tiers describe the degree to which an organization's cybersecurity risk management practices exhibit the characteristics defined in the Framework (e.g., risk and threat aware, repeatable, and adaptive). The Tiers characterize an organization's practices over a range, from Partial (Tier 1) to Adaptive (Tier 4). These Tiers reflect a progression from informal, reactive responses to approaches that are agile and risk-informed. During the Tier selection process, an organization should consider its current risk management practices, threat environment, legal and regulatory requirements, business/mission objectives, and organizational constraints.

The Framework Implementation Tiers are not intended to be maturity levels. The Tiers are intended to provide guidance to organizations on the interactions and coordination between cybersecurity risk management and operational risk management. The key tenet of the Tiers is to allow organizations to take stock of their current activities from an organization-wide point of view and determine if the current integration of cybersecurity risk management practices is sufficient, given their mission, regulatory requirements, and risk appetite. Progression to higher Tiers is encouraged when such a change would reduce cybersecurity risk and would be cost-effective.

The companion Roadmap was initially released in February 2014 in unison with the publication of the Framework version 1.0. The Roadmap discusses NIST's next steps with the Framework and identifies key areas of development, alignment, and collaboration. These plans are based on input and feedback received from stakeholders through the Framework development process. This list of high-priority areas is not intended to be exhaustive, but these are important areas identified by NIST and stakeholders that should inform future versions of the Framework. For that reason, the Roadmap will be updated over time in alignment with the most impactful stakeholder cybersecurity activities and the Framework itself.

Each organization's cybersecurity resources, capabilities, and needs are different. So the time to implement the Framework will vary among organizations, ranging from as short as a few weeks to several years. The Framework Core's hierarchical design enables organizations to apportion steps between current state and desired state in a way that is appropriate to their resources, capabilities, and needs. This allows organizations to develop a realistic action plan to achieve Framework outcomes in a reasonable time frame, and then build upon that success in subsequent activities.

The Framework provides guidance relevant to the entire organization. The full benefits of the Framework will not be realized if only the IT department uses it. The Framework balances comprehensive risk management, with a language that is adaptable to the audience at hand. More specifically, the Function, Category, and Subcategory levels of the Framework correspond well to organizational, mission/business, and IT and operational technology (OT)/industrial control system (ICS) professionals at the systems level. This enables accurate and meaningful communication from the C-suite to individual operating units and with supply chain partners. It can be especially helpful in improving communications and understanding between IT specialists, OT/ICS operators, and senior managers of the organization.[6] The complete Cybersecurity Framework can be found at www.nist.gov/cyberframework.

4.4 Developing Security Policies

While policies themselves do not solve problems, and in fact can actually complicate things unless they are clearly written and observed, they do define the ideal toward which all organizational efforts should point. By definition, security policy refers to clear, comprehensive, and well-defined plans, rules, and practices that regulate access to an organization's system and the information included in it. A good policy protects not only information and systems, but also individual employees and the organization as a whole. It also serves as a prominent statement to the outside world about the organization's commitment to security.

Tenable security policy must be based on the results of a risk assessment. Findings from a risk assessment provide policymakers with an accurate picture of the security needs specific to their organization. Risk assessments also help expose **gaps in security**, which is imperative for proper policy development, something that requires several steps on the part of decision-makers as are shown in Box 4.3.

> ## BOX 4.3   STEPS DECISION-MAKERS MUST TAKE TO DEVELOP SECURITY POLICIES
>
> Identify sensitive information and critical systems
> Incorporate local, state, and federal laws, as well as relevant ethical standards
> Define institutional security goals and objectives
> Set a course for accomplishing those goals and objectives
> Ensure that necessary mechanisms for accomplishing the goals and objectives are in place

Although finalizing organizational policy is usually a task reserved for top-level decision-makers, contributing to the development of policy should be an organization-wide activity. While every employee doesn't necessarily need to attend each security policy planning session, top-level managers should include representatives from all job levels and types in the information gathering phase (just as in the case of brainstorming during risk assessment). Non-administrative employees have an especially unique perspective to share with policymakers that simply cannot be acquired by any other means. Meeting with staff on a frequent basis to learn about significant issues that affect their work is a big step toward ensuring that there is buy-in at all levels of the organization.

It was pointed out in previous chapters that all organizations are vulnerable to social engineering attacks and indeed organizations from all sectors have been impacted by such attacks. Although an organization's risk assessment informs managers of their system's specific security needs, in the case of social engineering attacks all types and sizes of organizations need to take steps to mitigate such attacks. Regardless of any findings from a risk assessment, the following general questions should be addressed clearly and concisely in any security policy:

- What is the reason for the policy?
- Who developed the policy?
- Who approved the policy?
- Whose authority sustains the policy?
- Which laws or regulations, if any, are the policies based on?

- Who will enforce the policy?
- How will the policy be enforced?
- Whom does the policy affect?
- What assets must be protected?
- What are users actually required to do?
- How should security breaches and violations be reported?
- What are the effective date and expiration date of the policy?

Policies should be written in plain language and understandable to their intended audience. They should be concise and focus on expectations and consequences, but it is helpful to explain why the policies are being put into place. In addition, any term that could potentially confuse a reader needs to be defined. By keeping things as simple as possible, employee participation becomes a realistic aspiration. But bear in mind that unless the organization educates its users, there is little reason to expect security procedures to be implemented properly.

Employee training that is specifically tailored to meet the requirements of the security policy should be implemented. Policy makers should recognize that many computer users may not be trained to use technology properly and what little training they have had was probably aimed at overcoming their fears and teaching them how to turn on their machines. At most, they may have learned how to use a particular piece of software for a specific application. Thus, the majority of an organization's employees would have little understanding of security issues, and there would be no reason to expect that to change unless the organization does its part to correct the situation and provide appropriate training. Reluctance on the part of the organization to adequately prepare employees for making security policy a part of the work environment makes the rest of the effort an exercise in the theoretical—and theory will not protect a system from threats that are all too real.

Expecting every employee to become a security expert is wholly unrealistic. Instead, recommended security practices should be broken down into manageable pieces that are tailored to meet individual job duties. A single, short, and well-focused message each week will be better received than a monthly volume of information that is overly ambitious.

Without proof that an employee agreed to abide by security regulations, the sometimes necessary tasks of reprimanding, dismissing, or even prosecuting security violators can be difficult to pursue. One aim of a successful security policy is that it should limit the need for trust in the system. While this may seem like a terribly cynical philosophy, it actually serves to protect both the organization's employees and the organization itself. But before the benefits of security can be realized, staff must be properly informed of their roles, responsibilities, and organizational expectations. Employees must be told in writing including what is and is not acceptable use of equipment and that security will be a part of performance reviews.

Whenever security is threatened, whether it is a disk crash, an external intruder attack, or a natural disaster, it is important to have planned for the potential adverse events in advance. The only way to be sure that you have planned in advance for such troubles is to plan now, because you can never predict exactly when a security breach will happen. It could happen in a year, a month, or this afternoon. Planning for emergencies beforehand goes beyond good policy. There is no substitute for security breach response planning and other overarching contingency planning.[7]

4.5 Protecting Small Businesses from Social Engineering Attacks

There are numerous opportunities for small businesses to fill needed niches in industry or business services. Broadband and information technology are powerful factors in small businesses reaching new markets and increasing productivity and efficiency. However, many small businesses may not have all the resources they need to have a strong cybersecurity posture but they still need a cybersecurity strategy to protect their own business, their customers, and their data from growing cybersecurity threats. The Federal Communications Commission (FCC), the Department of Homeland Security (DHS), and the Small Business Administration have all provided advice for small businesses.

The 30 million small businesses in the United States create about two out of every three new jobs in the US each year, and more than half of Americans either own or work for a small business. Small businesses play a key role in the economy and in the nation's supply chain, and they are increasingly reliant on information technology to store, process, and communicate information. Protecting this information against increasing cyber threats is critical.

Small employers often do not consider themselves targets for cyber attacks due to their size or the perception that they don't have anything worth stealing. However, small businesses have valuable information cybercriminals seek, including employee and customer data, bank account information and access to the business's finances, and intellectual property. Small employers also provide access to larger networks such as supply chains.

While some small employers already have robust cybersecurity practices in place, many small firms lack sufficient resources or personnel to dedicate to cybersecurity. Given their role in the nation's supply chain and economy, combined with fewer resources than their larger counterparts to secure their information, systems, and networks, small employers are an attractive target for cybercriminals.[8]

The National Cybersecurity and Communications Integration Center (NCCIC) received multiple reports of WannaCry ransomware infections worldwide. Ransomware is a type of malicious software that infects and restricts access to a computer until a ransom is paid. Although there are other methods of delivery, ransomware is frequently delivered through social engineering attacks and phishing emails, and it exploits unpatched vulnerabilities in software. Phishing emails are crafted to appear as though they have been sent from a legitimate organization or known individual. These emails often entice users to click on a link or open an attachment containing malicious code. After the code is run, a computer may become infected with malware.

A commitment to cyber hygiene and **best practices** is critical to protecting organizations and users from cyber threats, including malware. In advice specific to the recent social engineering attacks and WannaCry ransomware threat, users should:

- Be careful when clicking directly on links in emails, even if the sender appears to be known; attempt to verify web addresses independently (e.g., contact the organization's help desk or search the Internet for the main website of the organization or topic mentioned in the email).
- Exercise caution when opening email attachments. Be particularly wary of compressed or ZIP file attachments.
- Be suspicious of unsolicited phone calls, visits, or email messages from individuals asking about employees or other

internal information. If an unknown individual claims to be from a legitimate organization, try to verify his or her identity directly with the company.

- Avoid providing personal information or information about the organization, including its structure or networks, unless you are certain of a person's authority to have the information.
- Avoid revealing personal or financial information in emails, and do not respond to email solicitations for this information. This includes following links sent in emails.
- Be cautious about sending sensitive information over the Internet before checking a website's security.[9]

If you are unsure whether an email request is legitimate, try to verify it by contacting the company directly. Do not use the contact information provided on a website connected to the request; instead, check previous statements for contact information. Small businesses should also do the following:

- Train employees in security principles and establish basic security practices and policies for employees, such as requiring strong passwords, and establish appropriate Internet use guidelines that detail penalties for violating company cybersecurity policies.
- Protect information, computers, and networks from cyber attacks by keeping clean machines: Having the latest security software, web browser, and operating systems are the best defenses against viruses, malware, and other online threats. Set anti-virus software to run a scan after each update. Install other key software updates as soon as they are available.
- Provide firewall security for the Internet connection and make sure the operating system's firewall is enabled or install free firewall software available online. If employees work from home, ensure that their home system(s) are protected by a firewall.
- Mobile devices can create significant security and management challenges, especially if they hold confidential information or can access the corporate network. Require users to password-protect their devices, encrypt their data, and install security apps to prevent criminals from stealing information

while the phone is on public networks. Be sure to set reporting procedures for lost or stolen equipment.

- Regularly back up the data on all computers. Critical data
includes word processing documents, electronic spreadsheets,
databases, financial files, human resources files, and accounts
receivable/payable files. Back up data automatically if possible, or at least weekly and store the copies either off-site or
in the cloud.

- Prevent access to or use of business computers by unauthorized individuals. Laptops can be particularly easy targets for
theft or can be lost, so lock them up when unattended. Make
sure a separate user account is created for each employee and
require strong passwords. Administrative privileges should
only be given to trusted IT staff and key personnel.

- Ensure that the Wi-Fi network for the workplace is secure,
encrypted, and hidden. To hide the Wi-Fi network, the wireless access point or router should be set up such that it does
not broadcast the network name, known as the Service Set
Identifier (SSID). Also, access to the router should be password protected.

- Work with banks or processors to ensure the most trusted
and validated tools and anti-fraud services are being used.
Companies may also have additional security obligations
pursuant to agreements with their bank or processor. They
should ensure that payment systems are isolated from other,
less secure programs and that the same computer is not used
to process payments and surf the Internet.

- Ensure that no one employee is provided with access to all
data systems. Employees should only be given access to the
specific data systems that they need for their jobs, and should
not be able to install any software without permission.

- Require employees to use unique passwords and change passwords every three months. Consider implementing multifactor authentication that requires additional information
beyond a password to gain entry. Check with vendors that
handle sensitive data, especially financial institutions, to see if
they offer multifactor authentication for your account.[10]

- Make sure each of your business's computers is equipped with anti-virus software and anti-spyware, and updated regularly. Such software is readily available online from a variety of vendors. All software vendors regularly provide patches and updates to their products to correct security problems and improve functionality. Configure all software to install updates automatically.
- Educate employees about online threats and how to protect the business's data, including the safe use of social networking sites. Depending on the nature of the business, employees might be introducing competitors to sensitive details about the firm's internal business via social networking sites. Employees should be informed about how to post online in a way that does not reveal any trade secrets to the public or competing businesses.
- Protect all pages on public-facing websites, not just the checkout and sign-up pages.[11]

4.6 Establishing a Culture of Security

When managing a network, developing an app, or even organizing paper files, sound security is no accident. Companies that consider security from the start assess their options and make reasonable choices based on the nature of their business and the sensitivity of the information involved. Threats to data may transform over time, but the fundamentals of sound security remain constant.

From personal data on employment applications to network files with customers' credit card numbers, sensitive information pervades every part of many companies. Business executives often ask how to manage confidential information. The key first step is to start with security. Factor it into the decision-making in every department of the organization including personnel, sales, accounting, information technology. Collecting and maintaining information just because it can be collected is no longer a sound business strategy. Savvy companies think through the implications of their data decisions. Making conscious choices about the kind of information to collect, how long to keep it, and who can access it, can reduce the risk of a data compromise down the road. Of course, all of those decisions will depend on the nature of the business.

Sometimes it's necessary to collect personal data as part of a transaction. But once the deal is done, it may be unwise to keep it. In the Federal Trade Commission's (FTC's) BJ's Wholesale Club case, the company collected customers' credit and debit card information to process transactions in its retail stores. But according to the complaint, it continued to store that data for up to 30 days, long after the sale was complete. Not only did that violate bank rules but, by holding on to the information without a legitimate business need, the FTC said BJ's Wholesale Club created an unreasonable risk. By exploiting other weaknesses in the company's security practices, hackers stole the account data and used it to make counterfeit credit and debit cards. The business could have limited its risk by securely disposing of the financial information once it no longer had a legitimate need for it.

If employees do not have to use personal information as part of their job, there is no need for them to have access to it. For example, in the Goal Financial case, the FTC alleged that the company failed to restrict employee access to personal information stored in paper files and on its network. As a result, a group of employees transferred more than 7,000 consumer files containing sensitive information to third parties without authorization. The company could have prevented that misstep by implementing proper controls and ensuring that only authorized employees with a business need had access to people's personal information.

Passwords like 121212 or qwerty are not much better than no password at all. That's why it's wise to give some thought to the password standards you implement. In the Twitter case, for example, the company let employees use common dictionary words as administrative passwords, as well as passwords they were already using for other accounts. According to the FTC, those lax practices left Twitter's system vulnerable to hackers who used password-guessing tools or tried passwords stolen from other services in the hope that Twitter employees used the same password to access the company's system. Twitter could have limited those risks by implementing a more secure password system, for example, by requiring employees to choose complex passwords and training them not to use the same or similar passwords for both business and personal accounts.

In the Guidance Software case, the FTC alleged that the company stored network user credentials in clear, readable text that helped a hacker gain access to customer credit card information on the network. Similarly, in the Reed Elsevier case, the FTC charged that the business allowed customers to store user credentials in a vulnerable format in cookies on their computers. In Twitter, too, the FTC said the company failed to establish policies that prohibited employees from storing administrative passwords in plain text in personal email accounts. In each of those cases, the risks could have been reduced if the companies had policies and procedures in place to store credentials securely.

In the Lookout Services case, the FTC charged that the company failed to adequately test its web application for widely known security flaws, including one called predictable resource location. As a result, a hacker could easily predict patterns and manipulate URLs to bypass the web app's authentication screen and gain unauthorized access to the company's databases. The company could have improved the security of its authentication mechanism by testing for common vulnerabilities.

Data does not stay in one place. That's why it's important to consider security at all stages if transmitting information is a necessity for your business. In the Superior Mortgage Corporation case, for example, the FTC alleged that the company used Secure Sockets Layer (SSL) encryption to secure the transmission of sensitive personal information between the customer's web browser and the business's website server. But once the information reached the server, the company's service provider decrypted it and emailed it in clear, readable text to the company's headquarters and branch offices. That risk could have been prevented by ensuring the data was secure throughout its lifecycle and not just during the initial transmission.

The FTC's actions against Fandango and Credit Karma alleged that the companies used SSL encryption in their mobile apps, but turned off a critical process known as SSL certificate validation without implementing other compensating security measures. That made the apps vulnerable to man-in-the-middle attacks, which could allow hackers to decrypt sensitive information the apps transmitted. Those risks could have been prevented if the companies' implementations of SSL had been properly configured.

In the Dave & Buster's case, the FTC alleged that the company did not use an intrusion detection system and did not monitor system logs for suspicious activity. The FTC said something similar happened in the Cardsystem Solutions case. The business did not use sufficient measures to detect unauthorized access to its network. Hackers exploited weaknesses, installing programs on the company's network, which collected stored sensitive data and sent it outside the network every four days. In each of these cases, the businesses could have reduced the risk of a data compromise, or the breadth of that compromise, by using tools to monitor activity on their networks.

In cases like MTS, HTC America, and TRENDnet, the FTC alleged that the companies failed to train their employees in secure coding practices. The upshot: Questionable design decisions, including the introduction of vulnerabilities into the software. For example, according to the complaint in HTC America, the company failed to implement readily available secure communication mechanisms in the logging applications it pre-installed on its mobile devices. As a result, malicious third-party apps could communicate with the logging applications, placing consumers' text messages, location data, and other sensitive information at risk. The company could have reduced the risk of vulnerabilities like that by adequately training its engineers in secure coding practices.

Security cannot be a take-our-word-for-it thing. Including security expectations in contracts with service providers is an important first step, but it is also important to build oversight into the process. The FTC Upromise case illustrates that point. There, the company hired a service provider to develop a browser toolbar. Upromise claimed that the toolbar, which collected consumers' browsing information to provide personalized offers, would use a filter to remove any personally identifiable information before transmission. But, according to the FTC, Upromise failed to verify that the service provider had implemented the information collection program in a manner consistent with Upromise's privacy and security policies and with the terms in the contract designed to protect consumer information. As a result, the toolbar collected sensitive personal information—including financial account numbers and security codes from secure web pages—and transmitted it in clear text. How could the company have reduced that risk? By asking questions and following up with the service provider during the development process.[12]

Responding to the dramatic changes in computing power, use of the Internet, and development of networked systems, the Organization of Economic Cooperation and Development (OECD) guidelines provide a set of principles to help ensure the security of contemporary interconnected communication systems and networks. They are applicable to all, from those who manufacture, own, and operate information systems to those individual users who connect through home PCs. Importantly, the guidelines call for new ways of thinking and behaving when using information systems. They encourage the development of a **culture of security** as a mindset to respond to the threats and vulnerabilities of communication networks. The nine principles address: Awareness, Responsibility, Response, Ethics, Democracy, Risk Assessment, Security Design and Implementation, Security Management, and Reassessment. The guidelines were developed with the full cooperation of the OECD's Business Industry Advisory Council (BIAC) and representatives of civil society.

In October 2001, the OECD Committee on Information, Computer, and Communication Policy (ICCP) responded positively to a US proposal for an expedited review of the security guidelines. The OECD member countries, businesses, civil society, and the OECD Secretariat shared a sense of urgency and responded with full cooperation and support. The text of the guidelines is available at www.oecd.org.

Completion of the guidelines is only the first step. US government agencies used the guidelines in their outreach activities to the private sector, the public, and other governments and encouraged business, industry, and consumer groups to join in using the guidelines as they developed their own approaches to the security of information systems and networks, and in the development of a culture of security for information systems and networks.[13]

4.7 Conclusion

Defending against social engineering attacks is a necessity for all types and sizes of organizations. The information security program is more effective when security processes are deeply embedded in the institution's culture. Effective security must be a substantive part of organization culture and training must occur on an ongoing basis.

4.8 Key Points

Important points presented in this chapter are as follows:

- Training is absolutely essential to security against social engineering and malicious code attacks but it is neglected by far too many organizations.
- The Cybersecurity Framework consists of three main components: The Core, Implementation Tiers, and Profiles. Profiles are primarily used to identify and prioritize opportunities for improving cybersecurity in an organization.
- The Framework is guidance. It should be customized by different sectors and individual organizations to best suit their risks, situations, and needs. Organizations will continue to have unique risks, face different threats, and have different vulnerabilities and risk tolerances. How they implement the practices in the Framework to achieve positive outcomes will vary.
- The term security policy refers to clear, comprehensive, and well-defined plans, rules, and practices that regulate access to an organization's system and the information included in it.
- Policies should be concise and focus on expectations and consequences, but it is helpful to explain why the policies are being put into place.
- Many small businesses may not have all the resources they need to have a strong cybersecurity posture. However, businesses need a cybersecurity strategy to protect their own organization, customers, and data from growing cybersecurity threats.
- Companies that consider security from the start assess their options and make reasonable choices based on the nature of their business and the sensitivity of the information involved.
- Making conscious choices about the kind of information to collect, how long to keep it, and who can access it, can reduce the risk of a data compromise down the road.
- The Organization of Economic Cooperation and Development (OECD) guidelines encourage the development of a culture of security as a mindset to respond to the threats and vulnerabilities of communication networks.

4.9 Seminar Discussion Topics

Discussion topics for graduate- or professional-level seminars are:

- What experience have seminar participants had in assessing the state of security in an organization? What were the results of those assessments?
- What experience have seminar participants had in developing security policies for an organization? What type of policies did they develop?
- What experience have seminar participants had in reassessing security practices and policies after a security breach occurred in an organization? What were the results of the reassessment?

4.10 Seminar Group Project

Participants should interview people from five different organizations to determine what the interviewees understand about cybersecurity in their organizations. They should then write up a one-page summary of each interview and share them in a discussion group in the seminar.

Key Terms

Acceptable use policy: is a document that establishes an agreement between users and the enterprise and defines for all parties the ranges of use that are approved before users can gain access to a network or the Internet.

Best practices: are techniques or methodologies that, through experience and research, have reliably led to a desired or optimum result.

Culture of security: is an organization culture in which security pervades every aspect of daily life as well as all in all operational situations.

Gaps in security: are security measures or mitigation methods that are inadequate to protect an asset or do not thoroughly protect the asset that they were deployed to protect.

Personal use: means using a service or an item for personal reasons and goals that do not have any relationship to the organization employing the individual using the item or service.

Sandboxing: is the use of a restricted, controlled execution environment that prevents potentially malicious software, such as mobile code, from accessing any system resources except those for which the software is authorized to limit the access and functionality of the executed code.

Security awareness: is the basic level of understanding of security and recognition of the importance of security.

Security threats: are conditions, people, or events that can jeopardize the security of a nation, organization, a facility, or any asset belonging to the threatened entity.

Security vigilance: is a constant attention given to security during day-to-day operations; it contributes to security by encouraging the reporting of security violations, and it makes suggestions on how to improve security when weaknesses are observed.

References

1. Security Culture. Federal Financial Institutions Examination Council. Accessed February 10, 2019. https://ithandbook.ffiec.gov/it-booklets/information-security/i-governance-of-the-information-security-program/ia-security-culture.aspx
2. Malware Mitigation. Federal Financial Institutions Examination Council. Accessed February 10, 2019. https://ithandbook.ffiec.gov/it-booklets/information-security/ii-information-security-program-management/iic-risk-mitigation/iic12-malware-mitigation.aspx
3. Training. Federal Financial Institutions Examination Council. Accessed February 10, 2019. https://ithandbook.ffiec.gov/it-booklets/information-security/ii-information-security-program-management/iic-risk-mitigation/iic7-user-security-controls/iic7(e)-training.aspx
4. New to Framework. NIST. December 11, 2018. Accessed February 10, 2019. https://www.nist.gov/cyberframework/new-framework#background
5. Framework Basics. NIST. December 11, 2018. Accessed February 10, 2019. https://www.nist.gov/cyberframework/questions-and-answers#framework
6. Framework Components. NIST. December 11, 2018. Accessed February 10, 2019. https://www.nist.gov/cyberframework/questions-and-answers#framework
7. Security Policy: Development and Implementation. US Department of Education, the Institute of Education Sciences (IES). Accessed February 10, 2019. https://nces.ed.gov/pubs98/safetech/chapter3.asp

8. Introduction to Cybersecurity. US Small Business Administration. Accessed February 10, 2019. https://www.sba.gov/managing-business/cybersecurity/introduction-cybersecurity

9. Protect Against Ransomware. US Small Business Administration. Accessed February 10, 2019. https://www.sba.gov/managing-business/cybersecurity/protect-against-ransomware

10. Cybersecurity for Small Business. US Federal Communications Commission. Accessed February 10, 2019. https://www.fcc.gov/general/cybersecurity-small-business

11. Top Ten Cybersecurity Tips. US Small Business Administration. Accessed February 10, 2019. https://www.sba.gov/managing-business/cybersecurity/top-ten-cybersecurity-tips

12. Start with Security: A Guide for Business. FTC. June 2005. Accessed February 11, 2019. https://www.ftc.gov/tips-advice/business-center/guidance/start-security-guide-business#start

13. OECD Calls for Culture of Security for Information Systems. Organization of Economic Cooperation and Development (OECD). August 2002. Accessed February 11, 2019. https://2001-2009.state.gov/r/pa/prs/ps/2002/12518.htm

5

SOCIAL ENGINEERING ATTACKS LEVERAGING PII

Social engineering attacks are more effective when the bait or the ploy fits into a context that the recipient of a message relates to as routine or normal. That message could be about football or baseball, making it of interest to sports fans. Bait messages promising nude photos of celebrities have also worked well in the past. The vast amount of Personally Identifiable Information (PII) available on the Internet makes it easy for social engineering attackers to find subject matter that is relatable to individuals in their private lives and to corporate employees in the pursuit of their business activities. Thus, the information that is publicly available about individuals or organizations has become a security issue, because it can be used in socially engineered attacks on systems or in attempts to defraud or steal identities. This chapter reviews the security issues surrounding PII.

5.1 Defining Personally Identifiable Information (PII)

One perspective on Personally Identifiable Information (PII) refers to information that can be used to distinguish or trace an individual's identity, either alone or when combined with other personal or identifying information that is linked or linkable to a specific individual. The definition of PII is not necessarily anchored to any single category of information or technology. Rather, it requires a case-by-case assessment of the specific risk that an individual can be identified from the information. In performing this assessment, it is important for an agency to recognize that non-PII can become PII whenever additional information is made publicly available in any medium and from any source that, when combined with other available information, could be used to identify an individual.[1]

Another perspective on PII contends that it is any representation of information that permits the identity of an individual to whom the information applies to be reasonably inferred by either direct or indirect means. Further, PII is defined as information that directly identifies an individual (name, address, social security number (SSN) or other identifying number or code, telephone number, email address, etc.) or by which an agency intends to identify specific individuals in conjunction with other data elements, that is, indirect identification. (These data elements may include a combination of gender, race, birth date, geographic indicator, and other descriptors.) Additionally, information permitting the physical or online contacting of a specific individual is the same as personally identifiable information. This information can be maintained in either paper or electronic or other media.[2]

According to the General Accountability Office (GAO), PII is any information about an individual maintained by an agency, including any information that can be used to distinguish or trace an individual's identity, such as name, social security number, date and place of birth, mother's maiden name, or biometric records; and any other information that is linked or linkable to an individual, such as medical, educational, financial, and employment information. Examples of PII include, but are not limited to:

- Name, such as full name, maiden name, mother's maiden name, or alias.
- Personal identification number, such as social security number, passport number, driver's license number, taxpayer identification number, or financial account or credit card number.
- Address information, such as street address or email address.
- Personal characteristics, including photographic image (especially of the face or other identifying characteristics), fingerprints, handwriting, or other biometric data (e.g., retina scan, voice signature, facial geometry).
- Information about an individual that is linked or linkable to one of the above (e.g., date of birth, place of birth, race, religion, weight, activities, geographical indicators, employment information, medical information, education information, financial information).

- Asset information, such as Internet Protocol (IP) or Media Access Control (MAC) address, or other host-specific, persistent, static identifiers that consistently link to a particular person or small, well-defined group of people.
- Information identifying personally owned property, such as vehicle registration number or title number and related information.

Linked information is information about or related to an individual that is logically associated with other information about the individual. In contrast, linkable information is information about or related to an individual for which there is a possibility of logical association with other information about the individual. For example, if two databases contain different PII elements, then someone with access to both databases may be able to link the information from the two databases and identify individuals, as well as access additional information about or relating to the individuals. If the secondary information source is present on the same system or a closely related system and does not have security controls that effectively segregate the information sources, then the data are considered linked. If the secondary information source is maintained more remotely, such as in an unrelated system within the organization, available in public records, or otherwise readily obtainable (e.g., Internet search engine), then the data is considered linkable.[3]

5.2 Why PII is a Problem

Unauthorized access, use, or disclosure of PII can seriously harm individuals, by contributing to **cyber-stalking**, identity theft, blackmail, or embarrassment, as well as harming the organization holding the PII, by reducing public trust in the organization or creating legal liability. Harm means any adverse effects that would be experienced by an individual whose PII was the subject of a loss of confidentiality, as well as any adverse effects experienced by the organization that maintains the PII. Harm to an individual includes any negative or unwanted effects (i.e., that may be socially, physically, or financially damaging). Examples of types of harm to individuals include, but are not limited to, the potential for blackmail, identity theft, physical harm, discrimination, or emotional distress. As a result, more and more people are using **identity monitoring** services or having **identity theft insurance**.

PII can also be used in phishing attacks, as was allegedly the case in the February 2019 revelation that Iranian intelligence staff used the PII of US intelligence staff to socially engineer an attack that compromised the US staff and resulted in Iran gaining access to US intelligence information.

Organizations may also experience harm as a result of a loss of confidentiality of PII maintained by the organization, including but not limited to administrative burden, financial losses, loss of public reputation and public confidence, and legal liability. The following describe the three impact levels, low, moderate, and high, which are based on the potential impact of a security breach involving a particular system. The impact levels are summarized in Box 5.1.

The potential impact is *low* if the loss of confidentiality, integrity, or availability could be expected to have a limited adverse effect on organizational operations, organizational assets, or individuals. A limited adverse effect means that the loss of confidentiality, integrity, or availability might, for example, cause a degradation in mission capability to an extent and duration that the organization is able to perform its primary functions, but the effectiveness of the functions is noticeably reduced; result in minor damage to organizational assets; result in minor financial loss; or result in minor harm to individuals.

The potential impact is *moderate* if the loss of confidentiality, integrity, or availability could be expected to have a serious adverse effect

---

BOX 5.1   IMPACT LEVELS OF PII COMPROMISES

LOW if the loss of confidentiality, integrity, or availability could be expected to have a limited adverse effect.

MODERATE if the loss of confidentiality, integrity, or availability could be expected to have a serious adverse effect.

HIGH if the loss of confidentiality, integrity, or availability could be expected to have a severe or catastrophic adverse effect.

on organizational operations, organizational assets, or individuals. A serious adverse effect means that the loss of confidentiality, integrity, or availability might, for example, cause a significant degradation in mission capability to an extent and duration that the organization is able to perform its primary functions, but the effectiveness of the functions is significantly reduced; result in significant damage to organizational assets; result in significant financial loss; or result in significant harm to individuals that does not involve loss of life or serious life-threatening injuries.

The potential impact is *high* if the loss of confidentiality, integrity, or availability could be expected to have a severe or catastrophic adverse effect on organizational operations, organizational assets, or individuals. A severe or catastrophic adverse effect means that the loss of confidentiality, integrity, or availability might, for example, cause a severe degradation in or loss of mission capability to an extent and duration that the organization is not able to perform one or more of its primary functions; result in major damage to organizational assets; result in major financial loss; or result in severe or catastrophic harm to individuals involving loss of life or serious life-threatening injuries.

Harm to individuals as described in these impact levels is easier to understand with examples. A breach of the confidentiality of PII at the low-impact level would not cause harm greater than inconvenience, such as changing a telephone number. The types of harm that could be caused by a breach involving PII at the moderate-impact level include financial loss due to identity theft or denial of benefits, public humiliation, discrimination, and the potential for blackmail. Harm at the high-impact level involves serious physical, social, or financial harm, resulting in potential loss of life, loss of livelihood, or inappropriate physical detention.

An organization that is subject to any obligations to protect PII should consider such obligations when determining the PII confidentiality impact level. Many organizations are subject to laws, regulations, or other mandates governing the obligation to protect personal information, such as the Privacy Act of 1974, OMB memoranda, and the Health Insurance Portability and Accountability Act of 1996 (HIPAA). Additionally, some federal agencies, such as the Census Bureau and the Internal Revenue Service (IRS), are subject to additional specific legal obligations to protect certain types of PII. Some organizations are also subject to specific legal requirements based on their role. For example, organizations acting as financial institutions by engaging in financial activities are subject to the Gramm-Leach-Bliley Act (GLBA). Also, some agencies that collect PII for statistical purposes are subject to the strict confidentiality requirements of the Confidential Information Protection and Statistical Efficiency Act (CIPSEA). Violations of these laws can result in civil or criminal penalties. Organizations may also be obliged to protect PII by their own policies, standards, or management directives.

Decisions regarding the applicability of a particular law, regulation, or mandate should be made in consultation with an organization's legal counsel and privacy officer because relevant laws, regulations, and mandates are often complex and change over time.[3]

5.3 Identity Theft is Made Easy with PII

Identity theft and identity fraud are terms used to refer to all types of crime in which someone wrongfully obtains and uses another person's personal data in some way that involves fraud or deception, typically for economic gain. Several common types of identity theft that can affect individuals are shown in Box 5.2.

BOX 5.2   COMMON TYPES OF IDENTITY THEFTS

Tax ID theft—Someone uses your social security number to falsely file tax returns with the IRS or your state.

Medical ID theft—Someone steals your Medicare ID or health insurance member number. Thieves use this information to get medical services or send fake bills to your health insurer.

Social ID theft—Someone uses your name and photos to create a fake account on social media.[4]

Some of the most common ways that identity theft or fraud can happen include:

- In public places, for example, criminals may engage in shoulder surfing watching from a nearby location as people punch in their telephone calling card number or credit card number, or listening to their conversation if they give a credit card number over the telephone.
- If people receive applications for pre-approved credit cards in the mail but discard them without tearing up the enclosed materials, criminals may retrieve them and try to activate the cards for their use without your knowledge. Also, if mail is delivered to a place where others have ready access to it, criminals may simply intercept and redirect mail to another location.
- Many people respond to spam (social engineering attack) that promises them some benefit but requests identifying data, without realizing that in many cases, the requester has no intention of keeping that promise. In some cases, criminals reportedly have used computer technology to steal large amounts of personal data.

The Department of Justice (DOJ) prosecutes cases of identity theft and fraud under a variety of federal statutes. In the fall of 1998, for example, Congress passed the Identity Theft and Assumption Deterrence Act. This legislation created a new offense of identity theft, which prohibits knowingly transfer[ring] or us[ing], without lawful authority, a means of identification of another person with the intent to commit, or to aid or abet, any unlawful activity that constitutes a violation of federal law, or that constitutes a felony under any applicable state or local law. This offense, in most circumstances, carries a maximum term of 15 years' imprisonment, a fine, and criminal forfeiture of any personal property used or intended to be used to commit the offense.

Schemes to commit identity theft or fraud may also involve violations of other statutes as shown in Box 5.3. Each of these federal offenses is a felony that carries substantial penalties, in some cases, as high as 30 years' imprisonment, fines, and criminal forfeiture.[5]

BOX 5.3   FEDERAL LAWS IDENTITY THEFT VIOLATE

Identification fraud (18 USC § 1028)
Credit card fraud (18 USC § 1029)
Computer fraud (18 USC § 1030)
Mail fraud (18 USC § 1341)
Wire fraud (18 USC § 1343)
Financial institution fraud (18 USC § 1344)

Federal prosecutors work with federal investigative agencies such as the Federal Bureau of Investigation (FBI), the US Secret Service, and the US Postal Inspection Service to prosecute identity theft and fraud cases. In addition, several private companies are providing **identity theft protection** and **identity recovery services**.

In March 2015, the Internal Revenue Service convened a public-private partnership to respond to the growing threat of tax identity theft and stolen identity refund fraud. This group, called the IRS Security Summit, is made up of IRS officials, CEOs of leading tax preparation firms, software developers, payroll and tax financial product processors, financial institutions, tax professionals, and state tax administrators.

The summit has improved safeguards in the tax return submission pipeline, keeping false returns out of the system, improving internal fraud filters, and preventing fraudulent refunds from being paid out. Between 2015 and 2017, the number of reported tax identity theft victims fell by nearly 65%, and tax returns with confirmed identity theft decreased by about 30% between 2016 and 2017.

The Identity Theft Tax Refund Fraud Information Sharing and Analysis Center (IDTTRF-ISAC, also known as ISAC), a partnership between the IRS, the states, and the private sector, was established to form a new line of defense to protect the tax ecosystem and taxpayers by merging ideas, addressing legal barriers, and opening channels of communication. The IDTTRF-ISAC is serving as the Trusted Third Party (TTP) between all of the entities cooperating to reduce fraudulent tax returns.

As of 2018, all states and virtually all major stakeholders in private industry are participating in the ISAC. Members agree that seeing what others are doing will help them get a bigger picture and identify more instances of fraud. The ability to connect in the ISAC portal is unprecedented because it enables members to build a network and learn new strategies and tactics by leveraging others' knowledge and expertise. Partners note the usefulness of the ISAC portal, an open but secure (NIST 800-53 and IRS Publication 4812 compliant with two-factor authentication) environment that allows states, the IRS, and industry to quickly, easily, and confidentially share best practices and techniques. Especially for some partners from smaller entities with limited resources, the ISAC enables them to connect with and learn from more mature and experienced partners.[6]

5.4 Self Disclosure of PII is also a Problem

The Internet has been available for widespread public use since the early 1990s. Many people cannot recall how society functioned without it. Compared with the lifespan of the Internet, social media, which began to evolve in 2003, remains in its adolescent stage. Users add their own content to any social media site that allows it. Websites such as Facebook and Wikipedia are not static; individuals continually modify them by adding commentary, photos, and videos. The web is no longer a fixed object for passive observation. It has become a dynamic venue for proactive and often passionate interaction. The growth, power, and influence of social media have proven phenomenal, as evidenced by the decline of traditional newspapers and the outcome of recent elections.

Information obtained from public records (e.g., birth, death, and real estate) has been available online for years. By increasing exposure of personal information, social media has raised the threat level on identity theft and other forms of criminal activity. This new entity has a unique nature that makes it powerful and unpredictable. Several characteristics combine to make it especially threatening to some types of people including military personnel and law enforcement officers:

- The structure of social media encourages **self-promotion**.
- It offers easy access to an unlimited pool of potential friends.
- Individuals who crave validation can achieve a feeling of connection not available in their offline lives.

- People who have a desire for attention, notoriety, or fame are attracted to it. To get noticed, they often post entertaining or provocative information.

Constraints do not exist for social media. Anyone can post anything online with little fear of repercussion. The anonymous online environment can encourage inflammatory and shocking behavior. Individuals sometimes create screen names or new identities that allow them to act outside their normal inhibitions and sometimes participate in caustic and less ethical activities that they would otherwise avoid. Anonymity hampers efforts to control these actions. In the past, simple things, such as post office boxes and license plate confidentiality, provided some identity protection.[7]

Social media and professional networking websites, as well as those websites that are the home of online communities for hobbyists and enthusiasts, generally ask for or offer the participants to post a personal profile. These profiles are filled with PII including name, email addresses, locations, educational background, marital status, parental status, and a long list of information items that can assist the social engineering criminal to steal identities and commit other intrusive acts toward individuals. Privacy settings and security on many of these websites have left a lot to be desired. Many warnings have surfaced over the last decade about what people need to be cautious about when voluntarily posting on the Internet, but people keep posting and keep exposing themselves to potential criminal actions or social harassment by groups that have some issue about what a person has done or does in their life.

5.5 The Harassment of Doxxing

Doxxing refers to gathering an individual's PII and disclosing or posting it publicly, usually for malicious purposes such as public humiliation, stalking, identity theft, or to target an individual for harassment. Doxxers may target government employees for such purposes as identifying law enforcement or security personnel, demonstrating their hacking capabilities, or attempting to embarrass the government.

Doxxers may use hacking, social engineering, or other malicious cyber activities to access personal information. One common practice is getting access to a victim's email account. A doxxer could use social engineering to get a password by posing as a representative from the IT help desk or an Internet Service Provider. Once a doxxer has access to an email account, he or she will attempt to obtain more personal information from the account or break into other web-based accounts (e.g., social media, online storage, and financial records) by using email-based password resets or harvesting information in order to answer website security questions. The doxxer may also attempt to use the same email address and password combination on other sites to gain access to additional accounts.

Doxxers may collect information about individuals from Internet sources, such as property records, social media postings, obituaries, wedding announcements, newsletters, public conferences, and web forums. Most, if not all, of this information is publicly available. The doxxer compiles information from multiple public-facing sources to reveal sensitive information about the victim, such as the victim's home address, family members, photos, workplace, and information about the individual's habits, hobbies, or interests. In this mosaic effect, the seemingly innocuous information posted or shared online can be put together to develop a detailed dossier.

Doxxers may also use data brokers or people-search sites that compile information from public and commercial sources and then sell this information to companies or the public. These brokers may obtain commercial data from retailers, catalog companies, magazines, and websites (e.g., news, travel).

In some cases, the Doxxer can be a person an individual is acquainted with in some way or who works within the same organization. When co-workers or employees commit identity theft or misappropriation of proprietary information it is considered **insider misconduct** and is often dealt with by the employer.

To mitigate the threat of doxxing the Department of Homeland Security recommends that people limit what they share online. Some of the publicly available information (e.g., public records) may be out of an individual's control, but people should remember that anything they post on the Internet might be misused, including photos. Once it's online, they probably cannot take it back.

It is also recommended to avoid posting information that may increase the chances of being targeted for doxxing. Not all information has the same sensitivity level. For example, do not post information about employment on social media, especially sensitive details about job duties or physical location. Also avoid posting information that might be used to answer website security questions, such as a pet's name or place of birth. People should also:

- Turn on privacy settings on social media, mobile applications, and other websites and be careful about the connections or friends they may have on these sites.
- Limit their use of third-party applications on social media and the use of social media accounts to login to other websites. These third-party applications receive PII from user profiles when they use the application.
- Consider removing themselves from data brokers. Unfortunately, this can be a time-consuming process, and their information may reappear when data brokers receive new or updated data sources, so everyone must weigh the potential benefit against the effort required.
- Practice good cyber hygiene. Set up two-step verification, use complex passwords, and avoid using the same password for multiple accounts to help prevent the hacking or hijacking of accounts.
- If doxxers publish PII on social media, report it immediately and ask that it be taken down.
- Document any threats they received, and if they think they are in danger, they should call the police. If they believe they are the victim of identity theft, they should file a report with the local police office. Even if the police do nothing, it's better to get a report on file. Ask to speak with an officer who specializes in online crimes.[8]

Law enforcement personnel, members of the military, and public officials may be at an increased risk of cyber attack. These attacks can be precipitated by someone scanning networks or opening infected emails containing malicious attachments or links. Hacking collectives are effective at leveraging open source, publicly available information that identifies officers, their employers, and their families. With this in mind, officers and public officials should be aware of their online presence and exposure. For example, posting images wearing uniforms displaying name tags or listing their police department or military unit on social media sites can increase the risk of being targeted or attacked.

Many legitimate online posts are linked directly to personal social media accounts. Law enforcement personnel and public officials need to maintain an enhanced awareness of the content they post and how it may reflect on themselves, their families, and their employers, or how it could be used against them in court or during online attacks. Recent activity suggests family members of law enforcement and military personnel and public officials are also at risk of cyber attack and doxxing activity. Targeted information may include PII, public information, and pictures from social media websites.

Another dangerous attack often used by criminals is known as **swatting**. This involves calling law enforcement authorities to report a hostage situation or other critical incident at the victim's residence when there is no emergency situation. While eliminating exposure in the current digital age is nearly impossible, law enforcement and public officials can take steps to minimize their risk in the event they are targeted. The FBI recommends that social media users:

- Turn on all privacy settings on social media sites and refrain from posting pictures showing any affiliation to law enforcement.
- Be aware of security settings on home computers and wireless networks.
- Limit personal postings on media sites and carefully consider comments.
- Restrict driver license and vehicle registration information with the Department of Motor Vehicles.
- Request real estate and personal property records be restricted from online searches with the person's county of residence.
- Routinely update hardware and software applications, including anti-virus.
- Pay close attention to all work and personal emails, especially those containing attachments or links to other websites. These suspicious or phishing emails may contain infected attachments or links.
- Routinely conduct online searches of their own name to identify what public information is already available.

- Enable additional email security measures to include two-factor authentication on personal email accounts. This is a security feature offered by many email providers. The feature will cause a text message to be sent to your mobile device prior to accessing your email account.
- Closely monitor credit and banking activity for fraudulent activity.
- Passwords should be changed regularly. It is recommended to use a password phrase of 15 characters or more. Example of a password phrase: Thi$$isthirdmonthof7eptem$er,2014.
- Be aware of suspicious phone calls or emails from people phishing for information or pretending to know them. Social engineering is a skill often used to trick people into divulging confidential information and continues to be an extremely effective method for criminals.
- Advise family members to turn on security settings on *all* social media accounts. Family member associations are public information and family members can become online targets of opportunity.[9]

5.6 Pending Congressional Legislation Addressing Doxxing

House of Representatives Bill 3067 of the 115th Congress, 1st Session to amend title 18, US Code, to establish certain criminal violations for various aspects of harassment using the interstate telecommunications system, and for other purposes June 27, 2017, introduced by Ms. Clark of Massachusetts (for herself, Mrs. Brooks of Indiana, and Mr. Meehan) was referred to the Committee on the Judiciary. Title III—Interstate Doxxing Prevention addressed doxxing in amending Section 301: Disclosure of personal information with the intent to cause harm, intends to amend Chapter 41 of title 18, U.S. Code, by adding at the end the following:

§ 881. Publication of personally identifiable information with the intent to cause harm
(a) Criminal violation.—
     Whoever uses the mail or any facility or means of interstate or foreign commerce, to knowingly publish a person's personally identifiable information—
     (1) with the intent to threaten, intimidate, or harass any person, incite or facilitate the commission of a crime

of violence against any person, or place any person in reasonable fear of death or serious bodily injury; or

(2) with the intent that the information will be used to threaten, intimidate, or harass any person, incite or facilitate the commission of a crime of violence against any person, or place any person in reasonable fear of death or serious bodily injury, shall be fined under this title or imprisoned not more than 5 years, or both.

(b) Civil action.—

(1) IN GENERAL.—An individual who is a victim of an offense under this section may bring a civil action against the perpetrator in an appropriate district court of the United States and may recover damages and any other appropriate relief, including reasonable attorney's fees.

(2) JOINT AND SEVERAL LIABILITY.—An individual who is found liable under this subsection shall be jointly and severally liable with each other person, if any, who is found liable under this subsection for damages arising from the same violation of this section.

(3) Stay Pending Criminal Action—(A) Any civil action filed under this subsection shall be stayed during the pendency of any criminal action arising out of the same occurrence in which the claimant is the victim.

(c) Definitions.—In this section:

(1) PUBLISH.—The term publish means to circulate, deliver, distribute, disseminate, transmit, or otherwise make available to another person.

(2) CRIME OF VIOLENCE.—The term crime of violence has the meaning given the term in section 16.

(3) PERSONALLY IDENTIFIABLE INFORMATION.—The term "personally identifiable information" means—

(A) any information that can be used to distinguish or trace an individual's identity, such as name, prior legal name, alias, mother's maiden name, social security number, date or place of birth, address, phone number, or biometric data;

(B) any information that is linked or linkable to an individual, such as medical, financial, education, consumer, or employment information, data, or records; or

(C) any other sensitive private information that is linked or linkable to a specific identifiable individual, such as gender identity, sexual orientation, or any sexually intimate visual depiction.[10]

5.7 Real Examples of Doxxing and Cyberbullying

Doxxing, which has resulted in online and real-life harassment, has done harm to many people over the last several years. Without identifying individuals by name or other PII, there are several major examples when doxxing resulted in harassment:

* The harassment of those people that have publicly advocated stricter gun control.
* The harassment of individuals who have opposed recommended appointees to political or judicial positions as happened with Brett Kavanaugh and Donald Trump accusers.
* The harassment of those people from non-white Christian backgrounds that have pursued political office.
* The harassment of individuals that worked in abortion clinics, performed abortions, or supported reproductive freedom of choice.

Gun control advocates usually become more active after a mass shooting has occurred, participating in protest and posting and commenting on social media. The pro-gun factions also become more active and the Internet trolling of the anti-gun factions has become common on the part of the pro-gun factions. In many cases, this has resulted in threats of violence online but has also resulted in physical harassment, intimidation, and physical assault.

In the case of accusers being harassed, there have been very organized and constant attacks in social media as well as physical intimidation and threats of more intense physical violence. In some cases, accusers and their families have had to move from their homes and literally hide out for their own personal safety. Much of this harassment is the result of a tribal response to perceived threats, but there have also been indications that some of the harassment was well-organized trolls targeting and attacking individuals.

With the reawakening of racism and xenophobia in the United States, many non-white people and non-Christians that became involved in local or national politics have faced threats of violence and cyberbullying with increasing frequency. There has also been increased physical violence and attempted physical violence against ethnic, racial, and religious minorities.

Those people that work in abortion clinics have long been the target of physical violence and intimidation as well as online harassment. Some have even been killed. There have been numerous cases of doxxing of these individuals and that continues to occur and go unchecked by law enforcement.

Doxxing has often resulted in cyberbullying, which is bullying that takes place over digital devices like cell phones, computers, and tablets. Cyberbullying can occur through SMS, text, and apps, or online in social media, forums, or gaming, where people can view, participate in, or share content. Cyberbullying includes sending, posting, or sharing negative, harmful, false, or mean content about someone else. It can include sharing personal or private information about someone else causing embarrassment or humiliation. Some cyberbullying crosses the line into unlawful or criminal behavior. The most common places where cyberbullying occurs are:

- Social media, such as Facebook™, Instagram™, Snapchat™, and Twitter™.
- SMS, also known as text messaging, sent through devices.
- Instant message (via devices, email provider services, apps, and social media messaging features).
- Email.

With the prevalence of social media and digital forums, comments, photos, posts, and content shared by individuals can often be viewed by strangers as well as acquaintances. The content an individual shares online, both their personal content as well as any negative, mean, or hurtful content, creates a kind of permanent public record of their views, activities, and behavior. This public record can be thought of as an online reputation, which may be accessible to schools, employers, colleges, clubs, and others who may be researching an individual now or in the future. Cyberbullying can harm the online reputations of everyone involved, not just the person being bullied, but also those doing the bullying or participating in the activities.[11] Cyberbullying raises many unique concerns, which are shown in Box 5.4.

In 2014, the US Centers for Disease Control and the US Department of Education released the first federal, uniform definition of bullying for research and surveillance. The core elements of the definition include unwanted aggressive behavior, observed or perceived power imbalance, and repetition of behaviors or high likelihood of repetition. However, there are many different modes and types of bullying.

Most research on bullying focuses on minors and does not address the impact on adults. The current definition acknowledges two modes and four types by which youth can be bullied or can bully others. The two modes of bullying include direct (e.g., bullying that occurs in the presence of a targeted youth) and indirect (e.g., bullying not directly communicated to a targeted youth, such as spreading rumors). In addition to these two modes, the four types of bullying include broad categories of physical, verbal, relational (e.g., efforts to harm the reputation or relationships of the targeted youth), and damage to property.

Electronic bullying or cyberbullying involves primarily verbal aggression (e.g., threatening or harassing electronic communications)

BOX 5.4   UNIQUE CONCERNS REGARDING CYBERBULLYING

Persistence: Digital devices offer an ability to immediately and continuously communicate 24 hours a day, so it can be difficult for children experiencing cyberbullying to find relief.

Permanence: Most information communicated electronically is permanent and public, if not reported and removed. A negative online reputation, including for those who bully, can impact college admissions, employment, and other areas of life.

Hard to notice: It is harder to recognize because teachers and parents may not overhear or see cyberbullying taking place.

and relational aggression (e.g., spreading rumors electronically). Electronic bullying or cyberbullying can also involve property damage resulting from electronic attacks that lead to the modification, dissemination, damage, or destruction of a youth's privately stored electronic information. However, some bullying actions can fall into criminal categories, such as harassment, hazing, or assault.

Journalists and other content creators can use this definition to determine whether an incident they are covering is actually bullying. Media pieces often mistakenly use the word bullying to describe events such as one-time physical fights, online arguments, or incidents between adults.

Bullying prevention is a growing research field that has made great strides in answering important questions. We now know much more about how complex bullying is, and how it affects youth not only at the time they experience it but also as adults. Yet many questions remain. Journalists and other content creators can serve the public by representing the state of the science as transparently as possible.[12]

5.8 Conclusion

Social engineering is most effective when the message matches what will prompt a recipient to take the bait and perform the action that the perpetrator desires. The vast amount of PII on the Internet make it easy for a social engineering attacker to design a phish to fit the individual who posted that information on social media or other websites.

5.9 Key Points

The points covered in this chapter include:

- The definition of PII is not necessarily anchored to any single category of information or technology. Rather, it requires a case-by-case assessment of the specific risk that an individual can be identified.
- Improper use of PII can contribute to identity theft, blackmail, or embarrassment, as well as harm the organization holding the PII by reducing public trust in the organization or creating legal liability.

- Many organizations are subject to laws, regulations, or other mandates governing the obligation to protect personal information.
- Doxxing refers to gathering an individual's PII and disclosing or posting it publicly, usually for malicious purposes, such as public humiliation, stalking, identity theft, or targeting an individual for harassment.
- People should avoid posting information that may increase the chances of being targeted for doxxing.
- Doxxing has often resulted in cyberbullying, which is bullying that takes place over digital devices like cell phones, computers, and tablets.

5.10 Seminar Discussion Topics

Discussion topics for graduate- or professional-level seminars are:

- What experience have seminar participants or people they know had with their PII being improperly obtained?
- How do participants handle posting or not posting PII on social media or networking websites?
- How do participants attempt to protect their PII that they find on the Internet?

5.11 Seminar Group Project

Participants should interview five people about their perspective on and experience with PII, then write brief summaries of the interview results and share them in a group discussion.

Key Terms

Cyber-stalking: is the use of the Internet, email, social media, or other electronic communication devices to stalk another person.

Doxxing: is the process of gathering an individual's PII and disclosing or posting it publicly, usually for malicious purposes, such as public humiliation, stalking, identity theft, or targeting an individual for harassment.

Identity monitoring: provides alerts when personal information, such as bank account information or social security number, driver's license, passport, or medical ID number, is being used in ways that generally will not show up on a credit report.

Identity recovery services: are designed to help regain control of a name and finances after identity theft occurs.

Identity theft insurance: is offered by most of the major identity theft protection services, and it generally covers out-of-pocket expenses directly associated with reclaiming an identity.

Identity theft protection: offers monitoring and recovery services that watch for signs that an identity thief may be using personal information and helps to deal with the effects of identity theft after it happens.

Insider misconduct: conduct by an employee that is against organization policies or procedures or that can otherwise harm the employing organization.

Self-promotion: in the case of social media, this means providing information or making claims that are designed to result in personal or financial gain for the individual using social media accounts.

Swatting: is when people call law enforcement authorities to report a hostage situation or other critical incident at a victim's residence, when there is no emergency situation. When the police arrive, it may result in a potentially dangerous situation.

References

1. Rules and Policies—Protecting PII—Privacy Act. General Services Administration. Accessed February 12, 2019. https://www.gsa.gov/reference/gsa-privacy-program/rules-and-policies-protecting-pii-privacy-act
2. Guidance on the Protection of Personal Identifiable Information. Department of Labor. Accessed February 12, 2019. https://www.dol.gov/general/ppii
3. Guide to Protecting the Confidentiality of Personally Identifiable Information (PII). Special Publication 800-122.NIST. Accessed February 12, 2019. https://csrc.nist.gov/publications/detail/sp/800-122/final
4. Identity Theft. Accessed February 12, 2019. https://www.usa.gov/identity-theft#item-206115

5. What Are Identity Theft and Identity Fraud? US Department of Justice. February 2017. Accessed February 12, 2019. https://www.justice.gov/criminal-fraud/identity-theft/identity-theft-and-identity-fraud

6. Identity Theft Tax Refund Fraud. Information Sharing and Analysis Center (ISAC) Annual Report. April 2018. Accessed February 12, 2019. https://www.irs.gov/pub/newsroom/IDTTRF%20ISAC%20April%202018%20Annual%20Report.pdf

7. Social Media and Law Enforcement Potential Risks. FBI. November 2012. Accessed February 12, 2019. https://leb.fbi.gov/articles/featured-articles/social-media-and-law-enforcement

8. How to Prevent Online Harassment from Doxxing. Department of Homeland Security Privacy Office. Accessed February 13, 2019. https://www.dhs.gov/sites/default/files/publications/How%20to%20Prevent%20Online%20Harrassment%20From%20Doxxing.pdf

9. Hacktivists Threaten to Target Law Enforcement Personnel and Public Officials. IC3. April 21, 2015. Accessed February 13, 2019. https://www.ic3.gov/media/2015/150421.aspx

10. Text: HR3067—115th Congress (2017–2018). Accessed February 13, 2019. https://www.congress.gov/bill/115th-congress/house-bill/3067/text?r=1#toc-H0D33F5FDEA39493AACF3128A8222CD38

11. What Is Cyberbullying. stopbullying.gov. Accessed February 13, 2019. https://www.stopbullying.gov/cyberbullying/what-is-it/index.html

12. Other Types of Aggressive Behavior. stopbullying.gov. Accessed February 13, 2019. https://www.stopbullying.gov/what-is-bullying/other-types-of-aggressive-behavior/index.html

6

HACKING THE DEMOCRATIC
ELECTORAL PROCESS

There has been considerable debate and speculation regarding the exploitation of social media for foreign organizations to influence the outcome of the 2016 and 2018 elections in the US and 2019 in Europe. There is little doubt that Russian organizations and perhaps those of other nations have indeed used social media to attempt to influence elections. Chapter 1 provides a brief overview of the testimony of social media executives before the US Congress. This chapter examines the activities of foreign players as well as domestic organizations and individuals' using social engineering to influence election outcomes.

6.1 How Active Measures Have Progressed Over Time

A considerable amount of the discussion about outside interference in elections has focused on the activities of Russia. Indeed the Russians have had a history of using **active measures** to influence events around the world according to Roy Godson, Ph.D., Emeritus Professor of Government at Georgetown University, in his testimony of March 2017 in a US Senate hearing entitled Disinformation: A Primer in Russian Active Measures and Influence Campaigns.

Professor Godson reviewed Russian active measures operations since the 1920s and 1930s when Russia created an enormous apparatus of whole organizations, overt and covert, throughout the world; organizations that were able to challenge all the major powers of Europe and the United States. After the Second World War, Russia used this apparatus to be able to influence the politics of Europe. They had also used it during the war to help them, and sometimes the United States, in fighting the Nazis and the Italian fascists. But in a major way, they were also preparing for being able to influence the outcome of the struggle for the balance of power in Europe following the Second World War.

So, while they were a US ally at the time, they were also planning to undermine democratic and liberal parties in both Europe and the United States,. In fact, they were able to take advantage of the fact that the United States was friendly and that they and Russia were working together. The Russians used their apparatus, which has been up since the 1920s, to achieve political goals in the late 1970s and 1980s. Since then, they have modernized this apparatus and are spending billions of dollars a year extending it, with a possible 10,000 to 15,000 people involved worldwide, in addition to the trolls and other kinds of cyber capabilities they have.

Professor Godson pointed out that there were some people both inside and outside the US government who had warned the government about the Soviet use of active measures, starting in 2016, and had asked them to be more mindful of Soviet active measures. Unfortunately, many felt that the government did not take the warnings seriously.[1]

Eugene B. Rumer, Ph.D., Senior Fellow and Director, Russia and Eurasia Program, with the Carnegie Endowment for International Peace, followed Professor Godson's presentation with a similar analysis, asserting that the Russian use of active measures and their interference in the US presidential campaign were the most contentious issues in our national conversation. He believed that Russian **intelligence operations** and their proxies intervened in the election in 2016, and it was the totality of Russian efforts in plain sight to mislead, misinform, and exaggerate that was more convincing than any cyber evidence. Russia Today (RT) broadcasts, Internet trolls, and fake news are an integral part of modern Russian foreign policy. Their content is designed to appeal to **domestic anti-social groups** and **domestic fanatics**.

He further pointed out that the 1990s was a terrible decade for Russia, but a great decade for the West. For Russian leaders and many regular Russians, the dominance of the West came at the expense of Russia's loss in the Cold War. But Russia would not remain weak and its economic recovery led to a return to a much more assertive and aggressive posture on the world stage, as was seen in the crushing of Georgia in 2008, in the annexation of Crimea in 2014, and currently in the ongoing war in Eastern Ukraine. For the West, Russia's return to the world stage has been nothing more than pure **revanchism**. For Russia, it is restoring some balance in their relationship with the West. The narrative of restoring the balance, correcting the injustice and the distortions of the 1990s, has been absolutely essential to Russian propaganda since the beginning of the Putin era.

Dr. Rumer contended that Russian meddling in the US presidential election was most likely viewed by the Kremlin as an unqualified success. The payoffs included, but were not limited to: (1) a major distraction to the US by spreading **hate messages** among other content; (2) damage to US leadership in the world; and, perhaps most importantly, (3) the demonstration effect—The Kremlin could do this to the world's sole remaining global superpower without consequence.

Later, during the hearing, Mr. Clint Watts of the Foreign Policy Research Institute discussed a petition that appeared on the WhiteHouse.gov website in April of 2014 entitled Alaska Back to Russia. It appeared as a public campaign to give America's largest state back to the nation from which it was purchased. Even though satirical or nonsensical petitions appearing on the White House website are not out of the norm, this petition was different, having gained more than 39,000 online signatures in a short period. An examination of those signing and posting on this petition showed that it appeared to be the work of bots. A closer look at those bots tied in closely with other social media campaigns pushing Russian propaganda months before. Hackers proliferated on the networks and could be spotted among recent data breaches and website defacements. Closely circling those hackers were honeypot accounts, attractive-looking women and political partisans that were trying to social engineer other users.

During the same period of time, **synchronized trolling accounts** using an **online alias** and **spoofing** tactics would attack political targets using similar talking patterns and points. Those accounts, some of which overtly support the Kremlin, promoted Russian foreign policy positions targeting key English-speaking audiences throughout Europe and North America. Thus the conclusion was that Soviet active measures strategy and tactics had been reborn and updated for the modern Russian regime and the digital age. Mr. Watts contended that Russia hoped to win the second Cold War through the force of politics, as opposed to the politics of force. While Russia certainly sought to promote Western candidates sympathetic to their worldview and foreign policy objectives, winning a single election is not their end goal. Russian active measures hope to topple democracies through the pursuit of five complementary objectives, which are shown in Box 6.1.

From these objectives, the Kremlin can crumble democracies from the inside out, achieving two key milestones: (1) The dissolution of the European Union; and (2) the breakup of the North Atlantic Treaty Organization (NATO). Achieving these two victories against the West will allow Russia to reassert its power globally and pursue its foreign policy objectives bilaterally through military, diplomatic, and economic aggression.

In late 2014 and throughout 2015, Foreign Policy Research Institute observers watched active measures being used on nearly every disaffected US audience. Whether it was claims about the US military declaring martial law during the Jade Helm exercise, chaos during Black Lives Matter protests, or a standoff at the Bundy Ranch, Russia's state-sponsored RT and Sputnik News, characterized as white outlets, churned out manipulated truths, false news stories, and conspiracies. The activities generally lined up under four themes, which are shown in Box 6.2.

BOX 6.1   RUSSIAN SOCIAL ENGINEERING OBJECTIVES

1. Undermine citizen confidence in democratic governance
2. Foment and exacerbate divisive political fissures
3. Erode trust between citizens and elected officials and their institutions
4. Popularize Russian policy agendas within foreign populations
5. Create general distrust or confusion over information sources by blurring the lines between fact and fiction, a very pertinent issue today in the United States

BOX 6.2   MAJOR THEMES IN RUSSIAN SOCIAL ENGINEERING

Political messages—designed to tarnish democratic leaders and institutions

Financial propaganda—created to weaken confidence in financial markets and capitalist economies

Social unrest—crafted to amplify divisions amongst democratic populaces

Global calamity—pushed to incite fear of global demise, such as nuclear war or catastrophic climate change

From these overt Russian **propaganda outlets**, a wide range of English-speaking conspiratorial websites, which we refer to as **gray outlets**, some of which mysteriously operate from Eastern Europe and are curiously led by pro-Russian editors of unknown financing, sensationalize these conspiracies and fake news published by **white outlets**. American-looking social media accounts, hecklers, honeypots, and hackers described earlier, working alongside automated bots, further amplify this Russian propaganda among unwitting Westerners.

Through the end of 2015 and the start of 2016, the Russian influence system began pushing themes and messages seeking to influence the outcome of the US presidential election. Russia's overt media outlets and covert trolls sought to sideline opponents on both sides of the political spectrum with adversarial views toward the Kremlin. They were in full swing during both the Republican and the Democratic primary seasons and may have helped sink the hopes of candidates more hostile to Russian interests long before the field narrowed.

The final piece of Russia's modern active measures surfaced in the summer of 2016 as hacked materials were strategically leaked. The disclosures of WikiLeaks, Guccifer 2.0, and DCLeaks demonstrated how hacks would power the influence system Russia had built so successfully in the previous two years. As an example, on the evening of July 30, 2016, Mr. Watts and his colleagues watched as RT and Sputnik News simultaneously launched false stories of the US air base at Incirlik, Turkey, being overrun by terrorists. Within minutes, pro-Russian social media aggregators and automated bots amplified this false news story. More than 4,000 tweets in the first 78 minutes after launching this false story were traced back to the active measures accounts Foreign Policy Research Institute observers had tracked in the previous two years. These previously identified accounts, almost simultaneously appearing from difficult geographic locations and communities, amplified the fake news story in unison. The hashtags pushed by these accounts were nuclear, media, Trump, and Benghazi. The most common words found in English-speaking Twitter profiles were God, military, Trump, family, country, conservative, Christian, America, and Constitution.[1]

6.2 Social Engineering Patterns in Politics

The Russians, the Republicans, and Donald Trump have been following similar patterns in their social engineering efforts and started blatantly doing so during the 2016 election in the United States. They all work to perpetuate non-truths, ranging from misinformation to blatant lies, and use these statements as click bait in social engineering efforts online and offline. They also all work to discredit the information sources that point out their lies and misstatements about reality. They do these things to help perpetuate their own agendas.

The questions about collusion between the Trump campaign and the Russians will probably remain unanswered forever. But collusion is not necessary in social engineering schemes. All social engineers take advantage of a social context that is comprised of people's beliefs, attitudes, living conditions, expectations, and desires, among other countless factors. The skilled social engineer is able to craft a message that appeals to large populations, specific subpopulations, or even smaller groups. That is an ongoing process in social engineering. Then social engineers can readily play on the efforts of other social engineers by copycatting the already successful ploys of others who share a similar agenda.

Tribalism also plays a role in individual or group responses to social engineering ploys. In the case of US politics and the constant reuse or restatement of lies, people may actually start to believe things that have no basis in reality and help to perpetuate the non-truths. For example, in 2018 and 2019, as caravans of migrants were traveling from Central America through Mexico to the southern US border, one of the fear-generating themes was that the caravans were full of terrorists that wanted to enter the United States to kill its citizens and damage the country. Thus, this socially engineered position on part of the wall supporters played on the social context of fear and xenophobia served with a side dish of racism. The rhetoric helped to create general distrust or confusion over information sources by blurring the lines between fact and fiction.

The Russians, the Republicans, and Donald Trump have also consistently attacked the structure and operations of the US government in order to undermine citizen confidence in democratic governance and foment and exacerbate divisive political fissures. They continuously work to erode trust between citizens and elected officials and their institutions by attacking government agencies like the Department of Justice (DOJ). It is as if they are all attempting to justify overthrowing the government and establishing a dictatorship by creating social unrest and amplifying divisions among democratic populaces. It is all sounding reminiscent of other times and places in history.

6.3 Social Engineering Political Messages

In the realm of politics, social engineers want to influence the outcome of elections and thus their primary goal is to convince people to vote in a particular manner. Since the 2016 election in the United States, there have been numerous congressional hearings addressing how social media was used to influence the election. (See Chapter 1 for an overview of what Facebook reported to Congress.) It is likely that these hearings and investigations will continue. The statements to the US Senate Committee on The Judiciary in The Matter of Cambridge Analytica, by Mr. Christopher Wylie in May 2018, provide considerable insight into the social engineering methods that have come to light as a result of the scandal. Mr. Wylie was the Director of Research for the SCL Group and Cambridge Analytica (CA) from mid-2013 to late 2014. The SCL Group was a UK-based military contractor that worked for the US and UK militaries and also worked at the NATO StratCom Centre in the Baltic region. He told the US Congress several alarming things.

First, Cambridge Analytica was created by the SCL Group with funding from Robert Mercer, an American billionaire based in New York.

Robert Mercer installed Steve Bannon as CA's vice president, with responsibilities to manage the company day-to-day. Mr. Bannon was a follower of the Breitbart Doctrine, which posits that politics flows downstream from culture. Therefore, Mr. Bannon saw cultural warfare as the means to create enduring change in American politics. It was for this reason Mr. Bannon engaged SCL, a military contractor, to build an arsenal of informational weapons he could deploy on the American population. Mr. Bannon wanted to use the same kinds of information operations tactics used by the military for his political aims in the United States and elsewhere. CA was created as the front-facing American brand to allow SCL to work in the United States.

The majority of SCL staff were not American citizens. Although Mr. Bannon was formally warned about the implications of using foreign citizens in US elections in a legal memorandum, the firm disregarded this advice and proceeded to install Alexander Nix, a British national resident in London, as CEO, and sent non-US citizens to play strategic roles embedded in American campaigns.

While at SCL and CA, Mr. Wylie said he was made aware of the firm's black ops capacity, which he understood to include using hackers to break into computer systems to acquire *kompromat* (compromising material) or other intelligence for its clients. The firm referred to these operations as special intelligence services or special information technology (IT) services. He also said he had seen documents relating to several instances where SCL or CA procured hacked material for the benefit of its clients. Some of the targets of these intelligence operations are currently heads of state in various countries.

Of further concern was CA's links to people closely associated with Wikileaks and Julian Assange. The firm hired two senior staff, both of whom were previously aides to John Jones QC in London. Mr. Jones was the British lawyer who represented Julian Assange, Wikileaks, and members of the Gaddafi regime. He later killed himself when he jumped in front of a train in 2016. Although the firm claimed only brief contact with Mr. Assange, recordings of SCL Group's former CEO suggest that contact with Wikileaks began 18 months prior to the US election.

Between 2013 and 2015, CA funded a multimillion dollar operation called Project Ripon. This project was overseen by Mr. Bannon and was based upon research that was originally conducted by psychologists at the University of Cambridge. It should be noted that some of the profiling research used as the basis of CA operations had declared funding from the US Defense Advanced Research Projects Agency (DARPA). The purpose of Ripon was to develop and scale psychological profiling algorithms for use in American political campaigns. To be clear, the work of CA and SCL is not equivalent to traditional marketing, as has been claimed by some. This false equivalence is misleading. CA specialized in disinformation, spreading rumors, *kompromat*, and propaganda. Using machine-learning algorithms, CA worked on moving these tactics beyond its operations in Africa or Asia and into American cyberspace.

Mr. Wylie continued by explaining that CA sought to identify mental and emotional vulnerabilities in certain subsets of the American population and worked to exploit those vulnerabilities by targeting information designed to activate some of the worst characteristics in people, such as neuroticism, paranoia, and racial biases. This was targeted at narrow segments of the population. The Russian-American researcher Dr. Aleksandr Kogan was selected to lead the data harvesting operation, as he offered the use of Facebook apps that he had developed in his academic role in order to collect personal data about Facebook users and their friends. Mr. Wylie later learned that Dr. Kogan did not have permission from Facebook to exploit the apps' privileged access for commercial or political activities. This has been confirmed in legal correspondence with Facebook. Dr. Kogan developed data harvesting applications that would capture not only the original app user but would harvest all the personal data of that user's Facebook friends and connections without their knowledge or explicit consent.

As Facebook has now confirmed, over 80 million data subjects, many of whom were American citizens, had their personal data misappropriated in the Ripon program. Given this scale, Ripon could be one of the largest breaches of Facebook data. CA often stored or transmitted data in insecure formats, including files of hundreds of thousands of Americans' data being passed around via unencrypted emails. CA also allowed access to its American datasets to external contractors, including senior staff from the company Palantir, which is a contractor to the US National Security Agency (NSA). Palantir denies having any formal relationship with CA and states this work was apparently done in a personal capacity.

At the time, Dr. Kogan was also working on Russian state-funded research projects. He was based at times in St. Petersburg and would also fly to Moscow. The Russian team at St. Petersburg were building similar algorithms, using Facebook data for psychological profiling. The Russian project had a particular focus on the dark triad traits of narcissism, Machiavellianism, and psychopathy. The Russian project also conducted behavioral research on online trolling. It should be noted that CA was very much aware of this work going on in Russia, and in fact it sought to pitch the interesting work Alex Kogan had been doing for the Russians to its other clients. Box 6.3 summarizes CA research management activities.

CA did not operate in elections to promote democratic ideals. Oftentimes, CA worked to interfere with voter participation, including by weaponizing fear. In one country, CA produced videos intended to suppress turnout by showing voters sadistic images of victims being burned alive, undergoing forced amputations with machetes, and having their throats cut in a ditch. These videos also conveyed Islamophobic messages. It was created with a clear intent to intimidate certain communities, catalyze religious hatred, portray Muslims as terrorists, and deny certain voters of their democratic rights.

BOX 6.3   CAMBRIDGE ANALYTICA ACTIVITIES SUMMARIZED

Used Russian researchers to gather its data

Openly shared information on rumor campaigns and attitudinal inoculation with Russian companies and executives

Pitched Russian-led profiling projects to other clients

Contracted people who worked for pro-Russian parties in Eastern Europe with suspected Russian intelligence operatives

Referenced the use of former Russian intelligence agents in internal documents

Tested Americans' views on Vladimir Putin's leadership

If it suited the client's objective, the firm was eager to capitalize on discontent and to stoke ethnic tensions. This was not just in its projects in Africa. As the CEO of SCL said in a recorded conversation about the firm's work in the United States in 2016: *It's the things that resonate, sometimes to attack the other group and know that you are going to lose them is going to reinforce and resonate your group. Which is why [...] Hitler attacked the Jews, because he didn't have a problem with the Jews at all, but the people didn't like the Jews [...] So he just leveraged an artificial enemy. Well that's exactly what Trump did. He leveraged a Muslim [...] Trump had the balls, and I mean, really the balls, to say what people wanted to hear.*

Mr. Wylie said he was aware that CA clients requested voter suppression as part of their contracts. CA offered voter disengagement as a service in the United States and there were internal documents that he had seen that made reference to this tactic. His understanding of these projects was that the firm would target African American voters and discourage them from participating in elections.

Facebook was first notified of CA's harvesting scheme in 2015. It did not warn users then, and it only took action to warn affected users three weeks after *The Guardian*, *The New York Times*, and Channel 4 made the story public. Mr. Wylie said that Facebook's behavior before the story broke was to threaten to sue *The Guardian*, and it also tried to intimidate him with aggressive legal notices. Facebook tried to shut down this story from going public when it knew it was true. At the British parliamentary inquiry, the Chief Technology Officer (CTO) of Facebook recently explained, to the surprise of many in the inquiry, that the company had assumed that this was common practice in the United Kingdom. Mr. Wylie said that Facebook also demanded that he hand over his personal computer and phone after the story broke.

Mr. Wylie also said that what he bore witness to at CA should alarm everyone and that CA is the canary in the coal mine to a new Cold War emerging online.[2] The House Committee on the Judiciary and the House Committee on Oversight and Government Reform released what they viewed as the key points about the Wylie testimony, which are shown in Box 6.4.[3]

BOX 6.4   COMMITTEE PERSPECTIVE ON KEY POINTS IN WYLIE TESTIMONY

Cambridge Analytica was an outsourcing company that had none of its own staff or technology, and where all of the work was done by foreign employees and contractors of SCL Elections, a UK company.

Steve Bannon said he wanted to use Cambridge Analytica to discourage specific groups of people from voting—including people likely to vote Democratic.

As early as 2014, Bannon directed Cambridge Analytica to research what types of discontent would influence populations in the US, including testing messaging that was later used by the Trump campaign.

Bannon directed Cambridge Analytica in 2014 to test images and concepts for an American audience relating to Russian President Vladimir Putin and Russian expansion; Putin was the only foreign leader for whom they conducted this testing.

Bannon stated that he did not care if campaign ads created and promoted through Cambridge Analytica promoted incorrect information because was trying to win a culture war and that war is battle.

Wylie called Cambridge Analytica a "full service propaganda machine" that used misappropriated Facebook data to build a psychological profile on the entire US population, map out who was most susceptible to messaging, and then spread that messaging.

Relying on some of the research of CA, bad actors used Facebook ads tools as phishing tools to draw people deeper into the myriad of misinformation and disinformation. Facebook eventually learned about a disinformation campaign run by the Internet Research Agency (IRA), a Russian agency that has repeatedly acted deceptively and tried to manipulate people in the United States, Europe, and Russia. The best estimates are that approximately 126 million people may have been served content from a Facebook page associated with the IRA at some point during the period of the 2016 election.[4]

6.4 Social Engineering People

Today, Russia is not simply targeting computers, but also human beings by weaponizing information in an effort to influence public opinion and encourage particular behavioral actions. These influence campaigns combine the use of cyber technologies to infiltrate computer networks in order to acquire or corrupt data. They combine that with efforts that seek to heighten social discord, amplify Russian produced disinformation, and create distrust of democratic institutions. They particularly fight against a free and fair media and do so via multiple communication technologies and social media platforms.

The Russian influence campaign that occurred during the 2016 US presidential election is a key example of this emerging practice of **soft cyber influence operations**. Russia has used these same tactics in recent years against other democracies, particularly in Europe, including in France, Germany, Ukraine, and Estonia. In the United States, they attempted to penetrate voter databases prior to the 2016 election, successfully penetrated the Democratic National Committee (DNC) network, and accessed state-level Republican organizations and candidates.[5]

There is a storehouse of evidence that points to active measures being deployed from Russia to influence the outcome of the 2016 US presidential election and those measures included a range of socially engineered messaging directed toward US voters. One response on the part of US lawmakers has been to accuse social media providers of malpractice, mismanagement, or political bias. Another response on the part of the Republicans in Congress has been to squash the investigation of Russian involvement and block the release of information and testimony regarding that involvement. It certainly appears that somebody somewhere has something to hide. In addition, the Minority Report lists numerous times that the Republican majority in control of the Congressional investigation ignored numerous Russian active measures and conducted a rather shallow investigation overall.[6]

During Professor Godson's testimony, discussed in the previous section, he provided advice as to how to counter or combat social engineering campaigns such as those mounted by Russia during the 2016 election. He said that one way, which is what the committee is starting to do, would be by educating the American and other populations about the threat of active measures and the price that might need to be paid if they were successful, so that when people heard about such activities they were not taken by them and were not influenced by them.

Professor Godson added that an additional capability needed would be that of reducing the effectiveness of the active measures: Warning, anticipating, education, and what could be done to reduce the effectiveness of the active measures. One of the things that had worked in the past was exposing the perpetrators of the active measures, preferably in real time. Senator Cornyn commented that, as Mr. Watts had pointed out, the advent of social media and the use of social media to move fake stories around the Internet and then get mainstream media to pay attention to them, and, without authenticating the source of the information, repeat them, successfully amplifying those messages, struck him as a huge challenge.

Professor Godson continued, commenting that the third part of this, though really the hard part, was what kind of whole-of-government responses should be developed to actually deal with the problem? He contended that the United States would have to come to grips with this, and that the present committee might not be the only one that would have to deal with this, but the questions have to be asked: What are we willing to tolerate? Are there any red lines for us? If they go over these lines, then will there be these kinds of responses?[2]

Regardless of the direction that Congress may want to take to address the issues that Professor Godson suggested, there are numerous hurdles to regulating and controlling content on the Internet. However, the Federal Communications Commission (FCC) occasionally receives complaints regarding allegedly false information aired on TV or radio. The FCC reviews all complaints for possible violation of its rules, which are narrow in scope. The FCC prohibits broadcasting false information about a crime or a catastrophe if the broadcaster knows the information is false and will cause substantial public harm if aired. The related FCC rules specifically say that the public harm must begin immediately, causing direct and actual damage to property or the health or safety of the general public, or divert law enforcement or public health and safety authorities from their duties.

The FCC is prohibited by law from engaging in censorship or infringing on First Amendment rights of the press. It is, however, illegal for broadcasters to intentionally distort the news, and the FCC may act on complaints if there is documented evidence of such behavior from persons with direct personal knowledge.[7]

6.5 Department of Justice Actions Against Social Engineers

The DOJ has prosecuted numerous social engineers in the past. In February 2018, the Federal Grand Jury indicted 13 Russian individuals and 3 Russian companies for a scheme to interfere in the US political system, including the 2016 presidential election, using social engineering and other methods. The indictment was presented by the Special Counsel's Office. The defendants allegedly conducted what they called information warfare against the United States with the stated goal of spreading distrust toward the candidates and the political system in general. Deputy Attorney General Rod J. Rosenstein commented that this indictment serves as a reminder that people are not always who they appear to be on the Internet. The indictment alleged that the Russian conspirators wanted to promote discord in the United States and undermine public confidence in democracy. Rosenstein also said that the DOJ received exceptional cooperation from private sector companies like Facebook, Oath, PayPal, and Twitter.

According to the allegations in the indictment, 12 of the individual defendants worked at various times for Internet Research Agency LLC, a Russian company based in St. Petersburg, Russia. The other individual defendant, Yevgeniy Viktorovich Prigozhin, allegedly funded the conspiracy through companies known as Concord Management and Consulting LLC, Concord Catering, and many subsidiaries and affiliates. The conspiracy was part of a larger operation called Project Lakhta that included multiple components, some involving domestic audiences within the Russian Federation and others targeting foreign audiences in multiple countries.

The Internet Research Agency allegedly operated through Russian shell companies. It employed hundreds of people for its online operations, ranging from creators of fictitious personas to technical and administrative support, with an annual budget of millions of dollars. The Internet Research Agency was a structured organization headed by a management group and arranged in departments, including graphics, search engine optimization, information technology, and finance departments. In 2014, the agency established a translator project to focus on the US population. In July 2016, more than 80 employees were assigned to the translator project.

Two of the defendants allegedly traveled to the United States in 2014 to collect intelligence for their American political influence operations. To hide the Russian origin of their activities, the defendants allegedly purchased space on computer servers located within the United States in order to set up a virtual private network. The defendants allegedly used that infrastructure to establish hundreds of accounts on social media networks such as Facebook, Instagram, and Twitter, making it appear as if the accounts were controlled by persons within the United States. They used stolen or fictitious American identities, fraudulent bank accounts, and false identification documents. The defendants posed as politically and socially active Americans, advocating for and against particular political candidates. They established social media pages and groups to communicate with unwitting Americans. They also purchased political advertisements on social media.

The Russians also recruited and paid real Americans to engage in political activities, promote political campaigns, and stage political rallies. The defendants and their co-conspirators pretended to be grassroots activists. According to the indictment, the Americans did not know that they were communicating with Russians. After the election, the defendants allegedly staged rallies to support the president-elect while simultaneously staging rallies to protest his election. For example, the defendants organized one rally to support the president-elect and another rally to oppose him, both in New York, on the same day. On September 13, 2017, soon after the news media reported that the Special Counsel's Office was investigating evidence that Russian operatives had used social media to interfere in the 2016 election, one defendant allegedly wrote that they had a slight crisis at work because the FBI busted their activity so they got preoccupied with covering their tracks.

The indictment included eight criminal counts. Count One alleged a criminal conspiracy to defraud the United States by all of the defendants by impairing the lawful functions of the Federal Election Commission, the DOJ, and the US Department of State in administering federal requirements for disclosure of foreign involvement in certain domestic activities. Count Two charged conspiracy to commit wire fraud and bank fraud by the Internet Research Agency and two individual defendants. Counts Three through Eight charged aggravated identity theft by the Internet Research Agency and four individuals. There is no allegation in the indictment that any American was a knowing participant in the alleged unlawful activity. There is no allegation in the indictment that the charged conduct altered the outcome of the 2016 election.

Everyone charged with a crime is presumed innocent unless proven guilty in court. At trial, prosecutors must introduce credible evidence that is sufficient to prove each defendant guilty beyond a reasonable doubt, to the unanimous satisfaction of a jury of twelve citizens. The Special Counsel's investigation was ongoing at the time and they did not provide any comments.[8]

In October 2018, a criminal complaint was unsealed in Alexandria, Virginia, that charged a Russian national with interfering in the US political system, including the 2018 midterm election. The charges alleged that Russian national Elena Alekseevna Khusyaynova conspired with others who were part of a Russian influence campaign to interfere with US democracy, according to Assistant Attorney General Demers. According to US Attorney Terwilliger, the strategic goal of the alleged conspiracy, which continues to this day, is to sow discord in the US political system and to undermine faith in democratic institutions.

According to allegations in the criminal complaint, Elena Alekseevna Khusyaynova, 44, of St. Petersburg, Russia, served as the chief accountant of Project Lakhta, a Russian umbrella effort funded by Russian oligarch, Yevgeniy Viktorovich Prigozhin, and two companies under his control, Concord Management and Consulting LLC and Concord Catering. Project Lakhta includes multiple components, some involving domestic audiences within the Russian Federation and others targeting foreign audiences in the United States, members of the European Union, and Ukraine, among others.

Khusyaynova allegedly managed the financing of Project Lakhta operations, including foreign influence activities directed at the United States. The financial documents she controlled included detailed expenses for activities in the United States, such as expenditure for activists, advertisements on social media platforms, registration of domain names, the purchase of proxy servers, and promoting news postings on social networks. Between January 2016 and June 2018, Project Lakhta's proposed operating budget totaled more than $35 million, although only a portion of these funds were directed at the United States. Between January and June 2018 alone, Project Lakhta's proposed operating budget totaled more than $10 million.

The alleged conspiracy, in which Khusyaynova is alleged to have played a central financial management role, sought to conduct what it called internal information warfare against the United States. This effort was not only designed to spread distrust toward candidates for the US political office and the US political system in general, but also to defraud the United States by impeding the lawful functions of government agencies in administering relevant federal requirements.

The conspirators allegedly took extraordinary steps to make it appear that they were ordinary American political activists. This included the use of virtual private networks and other means to disguise their activities and to obfuscate their Russian origin. They used social media platforms to create thousands of social media and email accounts that appeared to be operated by US persons and used them to create and amplify divisive social and political content targeting US audiences. These accounts were also used to advocate for the election or electoral defeat of particular candidates in the 2016 and 2018 US elections. Some social media accounts posted tens of thousands of messages and had tens of thousands of followers.

The conspiracy allegedly used social media and other Internet platforms to address a wide variety of topics, including immigration, gun control and the Second Amendment, the Confederate flag, race relations, LGBT issues, the Women's March, and the National Football League (NFL) national anthem debate. Members of the conspiracy took advantage of specific events in the United States to anchor their themes, including the shootings of church members in Charleston, South Carolina, and concert attendees in Las Vegas; the Charlottesville Unite the Right rally and associated violence; police shootings of African American men; and the personnel and policy decisions of the current US presidential administration.

The conspirators' alleged activities did not exclusively adopt one ideological view; they wrote on topics from varied and sometimes opposing perspectives. Members of the conspiracy were directed, among other things, to create political intensity through supporting radical groups and to aggravate the conflict between minorities and the rest of the population. The actors also developed tactical playbooks and strategic messaging documents that offered guidance on how to target particular social groups, including the timing of messages, the types of news outlets to use, and how to frame divisive messages.

The criminal complaint does not include any allegation that Khusyaynova or the broader conspiracy had any effect on the outcome of an election. The complaint also does not allege that any American knowingly participated in the Project Lakhta operation.[9]

In October 2018, the DOJ charged officers in the Russian Main Intelligence Directorate (GRU), a military intelligence agency of the General Staff of the Armed Forces of the Russian Federation, with international hacking and related influence and disinformation operations. Conspirators included a Russian Intelligence close access hacking team that traveled abroad to compromise computer networks used by anti-doping and sporting officials and organizations investigating Russia's use of chemical weapons. A grand jury in the Western District of Pennsylvania indicted seven defendants, all officers in the GRU, for computer hacking, wire fraud, aggravated identity theft, and money laundering.

According to the indictment, beginning in or around December 2014 and continuing until at least May 2018, the conspiracy conducted persistent and sophisticated computer intrusions affecting US persons, corporate entities, international organizations, and their respective employees located around the world, based on their strategic interest to the Russian government. Among the goals of the conspiracy was to publicize stolen information as part of an influence and disinformation campaign designed to undermine, retaliate against, and otherwise delegitimize the efforts of international anti-doping organizations and officials who had publicly exposed a Russian state-sponsored athlete doping program, and to damage the reputations of athletes around the world by falsely claiming that such athletes were using banned or performance-enhancing drugs.

The indictment alleged that the defendants Yermakov, Malyshev, Badin, and unidentified conspirators, often using fictitious personas and proxy servers, researched victims, sent spear phishing emails, and compiled, used, and monitored malware command and control servers. When the conspirators' remote hacking efforts failed to capture login credentials, or if the accounts that were successfully compromised did not have the necessary access privileges for the sought-after information, teams of GRU technical intelligence officers, including Morenets, Serebriakov, Sotnikov, and Minin, traveled to locations around the world where the targets were physically located. Using specialized equipment, and with the remote support of conspirators in Russia, including Yermakov, these close access teams hacked computer networks used by victim organizations or their personnel through Wi-Fi connections, including hotel Wi-Fi networks. After a successful hacking operation, the close access team transferred such access to conspirators in Russia for exploitation.

Among other instances, the indictment alleged that, following a series of high-profile independent investigations starting in 2015, which publicly exposed Russia's systematic state-sponsored subversion of the drug-testing processes prior to, during, and subsequent to the 2014 Sochi Winter Olympics (according to one report, known as the McLaren Report), the conspirators began targeting systems used by international anti-doping organizations and officials. After compromising those systems, the defendants stole credentials, medical records, and other data, including information regarding therapeutic use exemptions (TUEs), which allow athletes to use otherwise prohibited substances.

Using social media accounts and other infrastructure acquired and maintained by GRU Unit 74455 in Russia, the conspiracy thereafter publicly released selected items of stolen information, in many cases in a manner that did not accurately reflect their original form, under the false auspices of a hacktivist group calling itself the Fancy Bears' Hack Team. As part of its influence and disinformation efforts, the Fancy Bears' Hack Team engaged in a concerted effort to draw media attention to the leaks through a proactive outreach campaign. The conspirators exchanged emails and private messages with approximately 186 reporters in an apparent attempt to amplify the exposure and effect of their message.

Each defendant was charged with one count of conspiracy to commit computer fraud and abuse, which carries a maximum sentence of five years in prison, one count each of conspiracy to commit wire fraud and conspiracy to commit money laundering, both of which carry a maximum sentence of 20 years. Defendants Yermakov, Malyshev, and Badin were also charged as defendants in federal indictment number CR 18-215 in the District of Columbia, and accused of conspiring to gain unauthorized access into the computers of US persons and entities involved in the 2016 US presidential election, steal documents from those computers, and stage releases of the stolen documents to interfere with the 2016 US presidential election.[10]

6.6 Conclusion

Although there has been considerable debate and speculation regarding the exploitation of social media by foreign organizations to influence the outcome of elections in the United States and Europe during recent elections, the evidence that this occurred has mounted up over time. Analysts contend that Russia has long been involved in active measures and the Russian move into electronic social engineering is not surprising. But the Russians are not alone in their use of social engineering, as the conservative factions and players in the United States have followed similar patterns in their social engineering efforts and started blatantly doing so during the 2016 election in the United States.

6.7 Key Points

Key points covered in this chapter include:

- The Russians have an active measures program that employs social engineering methods combined with numerous other cyber intrusion methods to promote their social and political agenda.
- In the realm of politics, social engineers have the goal of influencing the outcome of elections.
- Facebook has confirmed that over 80 million users, many of whom were American citizens, had their personal data misappropriated in the Ripon program making this probably one of the largest breaches of Facebook's data.
- We need the capability of reducing the effectiveness of the active measures, which could include warning, anticipating, and education.

- The DOJ has taken action against several people who allegedly used social engineering and other methods to interfere in US elections.

6.8 Seminar Discussion Topics

Discussion topics for graduate- or professional-level seminars are:

- What exposure have seminar participants had to political parties, campaigns, supporters, or adversaries using social engineering tactics to support a candidate or proposition?
- What exposure have seminar participants had to political parties, campaigns, supporters, or adversaries using social engineering tactics to oppose a candidate or proposition?
- Have participants discuss why they support or oppose political parties, campaigns, supporters, or adversaries using social engineering tactics in the campaigns or to influence the outcome of an election.

6.9 Seminar Group Issue

Divide participants into multiple groups with each group taking 10 to 15 minutes to develop a list of tactics or methods to educate the public about how social engineering is being used to influence the outcome of an election. Meet as a group and discuss the tactics or methods that were developed by the groups to educate the public about how social engineering is being used to influence the outcome of an election.

Key Terms

Active measures: is the coordinated direction by a centralized authority of overt and covert techniques that propagate Russian ideas and political and military preferences, and undermine those of democratic adversaries.

Domestic anti-social groups: are groups of people or mini-societies that oppose the larger society in which they live and/or work.

Domestic fanatics: are radical groups made up of residents or citizens of the countries in which they kill, sabotage, or spread hate and fear.

Gray outlets: media properties that are established by unknown or obfuscated political, economic, or social powers to disseminate information favorable to their goals or to undermine the activities of their adversaries.

Hate messages: are social media posts that use obnoxious language to ridicule or discriminate against minority or ethnic groups.

Intelligence operations: is the variety of intelligence and counter-intelligence tasks that are carried out by various intelligence organizations, and activities within the intelligence process.

Online alias: is an online identity encompassing identifiers, such as name and date of birth, differing from the employee's actual identifiers, that use a nongovernmental Internet Protocol (IP) address. An online alias may be used to monitor activity on social media websites or to engage in authorized online undercover activity.

Propaganda outlets: media properties that are established by political, economic, or social powers to disseminate information favorable to their goals, or to undermine the activities of their adversaries.

Revanchism: is a policy of seeking to retaliate against political or military adversaries for diplomatic losses or to recover lost territory, reputation, influence, or power.

Soft cyber influence operations: the use of legal but perhaps sinister cyber techniques to influence or persuade target groups to adhere to a particular philosophy or perform desired behaviors.

Spoofing: is an attempt to gain access to a system by posing as an authorized user. Synonymous with impersonating, masquerading, or mimicking.

Synchronized trolling accounts: social media accounts that in unison, or in a carefully timed manner, post or convey the same, similar, or supporting messages.

White outlets: media properties that are established by unknown or obfuscated political, economic, or social powers that are disguised as representing one cause or perspective but may be working on behalf of other parties.

References

1. Disinformation: A Primer in Russian Active Measures and Influence Campaigns. Panel I. Hearing Before the Select Committee on Intelligence of the US Senate One Hundred Fifteenth Congress First Session. March 30, 2017. Accessed February 16, 2019. www.intelligence.senate.gov/sites/default/files/documents/os-trid-033017.pdf
2. Written Statement to the US Senate Committee on the Judiciary in the Matter of Cambridge Analytica and Other Related Issues. Christopher Wylie. May 16, 2018. Accessed February 18, 2019. https://www.judiciary.senate.gov/imo/media/doc/05-16-18%20Wylie%20Testimony.pdf
3. Judiciary and Oversight Committee, Democrats Release Key Takeaways from Interview with Cambridge Analytica Whistleblower. House Committee on the Judiciary and the House Committee on Oversight and Government Reform. April 25, 2018. Accessed February 18, 2019. https://judiciary.house.gov/news/press-releases/judiciary-and-oversight-committee-democrats-release-key-takeaways-interview
4. Facebook at the Hearing before the US House of Representatives Committee on Energy and Commerce. Testimony of Mark Zuckerberg Chairman and Chief Executive Officer. April 11, 2018. Accessed February 2, 2019. www.docs.house.gov/meetings/IF/IF00/20180411/108090/HHRG-115-IF00-20180411-SD002.pdf
5. Old Tactics, New Tools: A Review of Russia's Soft Cyber Influence Operations. A Minority Staff Report Prepared for Democratic Members of the Subcommittee on Oversight, Committee on Science, Space & Technology. November 2017. Accessed February 19, 2019. https://science.house.gov/sites/democrats.science.house.gov/files/documents/Russian%20Soft%20Cyber%20Influence%20Operations%20-%20Minority%20Staff%20Report%20-%20November%202017.pdf
6. Minority Views. March 26, 2018. Accessed February 19, 2019. https://intelligence.house.gov/UploadedFiles/MinorityViews.pdf
7. Broadcasting False Information. FCC. January 5, 2018. Accessed February 19, 2019. https://www.fcc.gov/consumers/guides/broadcasting-false-information
8. Grand Jury Indicts Thirteen Russian Individuals and Three Russian Companies for Scheme to Interfere in the United States Political System. Department of Justice Office of Public Affairs. February 16, 2018. Accessed February 19, 2019. https://www.justice.gov/opa/pr/grand-jury-indicts-thirteen-russian-individuals-and-three-russian-companies-scheme-interfere
9. Russian National Charged with Interfering in US Political System. Department of Justice Office of Public Affairs. October 19, 2018. Accessed February 19, 2019. https://www.justice.gov/opa/pr/russian-national-charged-interfering-us-political-system

10. US Charges Russian GRU Officers with International Hacking and Related Influence and Disinformation Operations. Department of Justice Office of Public Affairs. October 4, 2018. Accessed February 19, 2019. https://www.justice.gov/opa/pr/us-charges-russian-gru-officers-international-hacking-and-related-influence-and

7

SOCIALLY ENGINEERED ATTACKS BY INSIDERS

Social engineering attacks have damaged US National Security and compromised intelligence and military operations for several decades. Many of those attacks were perpetrated by insiders who engineered their way into government agencies only to end up walking away with sensitive and classified materials. It is just not the government that is at risk, all organizations face some level of threat from insiders, and the possibility that an insider may collaborate and conspire with an outsider to steal, sabotage, or humiliate their employees. Managers and security personnel need to be just as concerned about insiders utilizing social engineering tactics as they are about outside social engineers working to compromise systems employees and suppliers. In this chapter, we turn our attention to the efforts of social engineering attacks by insiders.

7.1 The Nature of the Insider Threat

Insiders who do steal data or information usually have an idea of what they will do with them, or who outside the organization considers the data to be of value enough for somebody to steal. There are numerous potential scenarios that can lead the insider to steal data and information. They could already have a buyer and could be conspiring with an outsider to illegally transfer the material. They also may be seeking a new job and intend to use the information and data as leverage to gain new employment by offering it to companies that may hire them. In some cases they may want to make an organization's data and information public by posting it on the Internet in order to reveal things about the business or government agency that may disrupt processes and jeopardize business relationships, or attract people who want to embarrass an organization or expose activity that they and others considered unethical or illegal. No matter why the theft occurs, organizations need to take steps to be sure that they are protected.

Over the last couple of decades, there have been several trends that have made organizations more vulnerable to insider offenses. Many organizations have gone through some sort of downsizing reducing their headcount and often combining job functions with an eye on financial savings and without any specific regard for security. There has also been a trend toward having more **open organizations** and providing employees with access to more tools, resources, and data in the hope that the new leaner organizations will become more productive by empowering employees. In addition, the information technology (IT) industry has greatly focused on bringing products to market that are advertised to provide employees with more tools so they can have more access and be more productive. All of these trends were based more on hope than they were on proven results.

At the societal level, more people have greater access to **personal technologies,** such as smartphones, flash drives, and other devices that better enable them to spy or steal intellectual property. The Internet allows insiders to quickly move data or information out of an organization's facility. The Internet can also provide a communication platform for insiders to stay in contact with outside co-conspirators regarding their actions or the types of information they should look for and misappropriate. This communication can also aid insiders in providing outsiders with access to internal resources or make it easier to access physical properties or assets that could be the target of theft or destruction. Protecting against such threats is an absolute necessity in all security efforts.

There have been numerous incidents of insiders attacking information systems. Some attacks occur for revenge or out of anger against the organization or managers and staff. Other attacks involving theft of data or trade secrets often happen for financial gain. The FBI contends that insiders do not need to know how to hack information systems from the outside because they already have some knowledge, and at times extensive knowledge, of an organization's information systems and the **access control for computer systems**. They also may have very few restrictions to their access privileges and therefore can cause extensive damage to the system or steal system data.[1]

Insider threats, including sabotage, theft, espionage, fraud, and competitive advantage, are often carried out through abusing access rights, theft of materials, and mishandling physical devices or improperly configured **access control systems**. Insiders do not always act alone and may not be aware they are aiding a threat actor (i.e., the unintentional insider threat). It is vital that organizations understand normal employee baseline behaviors and also ensure employees understand how they may be used as a conduit for others to obtain information. Types of crimes perpetrated by insiders are shown in Box 7.1.

Every organization is always at risk of having trade secrets compromised, intellectual property stolen, and business plans revealed in an untimely manner. Industrial espionage and spying remain at a high level and are practiced on an international scale. An organization's data security and privacy planning process need to take these threats into consideration and carefully control **authorized logical access** and **authorized physical access**.

BOX 7.1   TYPES OF CRIMES PERPETRATED BY INSIDERS

Theft by employees
Deposit fraud or alterations of deposit instruments
Misappropriation, disappearance or destruction of money and securities
Robbery, safe or secure storage burglary
Computer crimes (theft, funds transfer fraud)
Intellectual property theft
Theft of information to access computer systems from the outside
Personally Identifiable Information (PII) of employees and corporate officers
Information to access computer systems in the supply chain and distribution channels

7.2 National Security and Social Engineering Threats

There have been several high-profile insider attacks on government agencies during the last decade. The top areas for potential risk include criminals, industrial competitors, insider threats, and state-sponsored adversaries. All can be equally effective and damaging. Experts agree that traditional security measures are not sufficient for the rapidly shifting threat landscape. Security education and awareness programs that are transparent and communicated to the workforce are critical to alleviating security risks caused by social engineering and insider threats.[2] Social engineering is a favored tool of these adversaries, especially insiders who practice the craft of social engineering every minute of every day in their efforts compromise systems, data, trade secrets, and more.

Many security professionals contend that the biggest modern-day threat against sensitive computer systems, networks, and data is the insider threat. An insider is an individual who possesses a certain level of access, privilege, and trust within an organization due to their position, role, or task within that organization. The Department of Defense (DoD) defines an insider as anyone who uses authorized credentials to access a DoD computer and/or network, regardless of whether or not those credentials were acquired through legal channels. While an outsider must gain access and privilege to a system using social engineering or some other method in order to damage that system, an insider generally inherits those capabilities by default. At this point, the only thing that separates an insider employee from an insider threat is their actions and intentions. Each insider poses the threat of malicious activity. Most organizations assume an insider is honest and is operating in the best interests of the organization. However, what if an insider's intentions change from benign to malicious?

Government agencies and military commands constantly need to address how they detect malicious behavior from within their own walls? Modern-day computer defenses range from firewalls to intrusion detection systems (IDS) to access control lists (ACL), but their primary focus of mitigating the outsider threat remains the same. An insider is given a natural migration path inside the perimeter of enterprise security controls. Efforts to incorporate these same defenses against insiders have thus far been fruitless. A great need still exists for a real-time, lightweight detection and mitigation systems for insider misuse. Access control is the fundamental basis of computer security, but still remains a relative weakness in dealing with everyday threats, especially those posed by insiders. Authentication, authorization, and audit are the three primary components of access control, which can be observed in countless mainstream implementations, including firewalls, virtual private networks, and file permissions.

Virtually every security-related process or product is some flavor of access control. In Discretionary Access Control (DAC), the owner of an object can assign access to other users. In Mandatory Access Control (MAC), access is granted to users based on security policy. Unfortunately, current access control mechanisms are too coarse-grained, complex, and non-scalable to oppose the insider threat. Modern-day operating systems enforce access control at the granularity level of a file, but that does little to stop an insider who already has access to that file based on their position within the organization. The insider threat is minimally addressed by current information security practices, yet the insider poses the most serious threat to the organization for various reasons, which are shown in Box 7.2.

A **comprehensive security plan** to address insider threats against critical information systems will include an advanced access control approach, which is needed to support fine-grained, active, and scalable access control services. This will prevent insider threats in

BOX 7.2   VARIOUS REASONS INSIDERS POSE SEVERE THREATS

Insiders are given a high level of trust.

It is easy for an insider to establish unauthorized entry points and anomalous channels into information systems.

More advanced forms of security such as encryption do not deal directly with the concept of access control.

Current access control methods are too coarse-grained to look inside the box and prevent an insider from abusing his privileges.

Methods of auditing and forensics are generally after the fact and do little to prevent an insider from doing damage.

terms of over-privileges based on the least-privilege principle, but cannot prevent the privilege-abuse problem. Applied computer forensic approaches are necessary to thwart the privilege-abuse problems where an insider does not have to violate access controls to perform malicious acts, as well as privilege escalation issues, where an insider would use various approaches to gain additional privileges such as root access. When used in combination, strong access control and applied computer forensics will serve to mitigate the threats posed by malicious insiders. The primary objective of current research is to develop applied computer forensic approaches for preventing and detecting insider threats in sensitive organizations in conjunction with advanced access control systems such as FASAC (Fine-Grained, Active, and Scalable Access Control).[3]

A high-profile contemporary example of an insider using social engineering to steal classified information is Edward J. Snowden. Upon discovery of his actions, he fled to Hong Kong. The US Department of Justice (DOJ) was in continual contact with their Hong Kong counterparts starting on June 10, 2013, when they learned that Snowden was in Hong Kong. Attorney General Eric Holder placed a phone call on June 19 EDT, with his counterpart, Hong Kong Secretary for Justice Rimsky Yuen, stressing the importance of the matter and urging Hong Kong to honor the request for Snowden's arrest. Snowden was being charged with violations of:

- 18 USC § 793(d) (Unauthorized Disclosure of National Defense Information);
- 18 USC § 798(a)(3) (Unauthorized Disclosure of Classified Communication Intelligence); and
- 18 USC § 641 (Theft of Government Property).

On June 15, 2013, the United States requested pursuant to the US/HK Surrender Agreement that Hong Kong Special Administrative Region (HKSAR) authorities provisionally arrest the fugitive for purposes of extradition. The US request complied with all aspects of the treaty in force between the US and the HKSAR containing all documents and information required for HKSAR to provisionally arrest Snowden.

On June 17, 2013, the Hong Kong authorities acknowledged receipt of the US request. Despite repeated inquiries, the Hong Kong authorities did not respond with any requests for additional information or documents, stating only that the matter was under review and refusing to elaborate. Then on June 21, 2013, the Hong Kong authorities requested additional information concerning the US charges and evidence. The US had been in communication with the Hong Kong authorities on their inquiries. The US authorities were in the process of responding to the request when they learned that the Hong Kong authorities had allowed the fugitive to leave Hong Kong. He eventually ended up in Russia and is still being pursued by the US government.[4]

Some people viewed Snowden as a hero for exposing surveillance programs of the US government, while others called for his vigorous prosecution. Following continued national security leaks by Edward Snowden, Congressman John Conyers, Jr. (D-Mich.) stated that it was unfortunate that so much of the Congress' and the media's focus were on the whereabouts of Edward Snowden. He contended that the United States should focus time and attention on ensuring that law-abiding Americans were not unnecessarily subject to intrusive surveillance; making sure US media organizations were not targeted merely for informing the public; closing Guantanamo and releasing those individuals who posed the United States no harm; and demanding that legal safeguards were in place with respect to the US government's shortsighted use of drones. In June 2013 Conyers contended that these were the overriding, critical issues facing the Congress, not the whereabouts or motives of Edward Snowden. Revelations over the previous several weeks by Edward Snowden and others made clear that the United States was at a crossroads. Congress needed to choose how to respond, not to Edward Snowden, but to the strain that this never-ending war about Snowden and security leaks placed on the United States' principles and laws.[5]

7.3 The National Insider Threat Task Force

The National Insider Threat Task Force (NITTF) was established after the WikiLeaks release of thousands of classified documents through the global media and the Internet. Its mission is to deter, detect, and mitigate actions by employees who may represent a threat to national security by developing a national insider threat program with supporting policy, standards, guidance, and training.

Under Executive Order (EO) 13587, the NITTF is co-chaired by the US Attorney General and the Director of National Intelligence. They, in turn, designated the Federal Bureau of Investigation (FBI) and the National Counterintelligence Executive to co-direct the daily activities of the NITTF. The NITTF comprises employees and contractors from a variety of federal departments and agencies (D/As), and its work impacts more than 99 federal D/As that handle classified material. The following D/As have representatives on the NITTF: The FBI, National Counterintelligence and Security Center (NCSC), Defense Intelligence Agency (DIA), Central Intelligence Agency (CIA), and Transportation Security Administration.

The NITTF responds directly to the Senior Information Sharing and Safeguarding Steering Committee, which was also established under EO 13587. The steering committee comprises representatives from largely intelligence community agencies with extensive access to classified networks and materials, including the departments of State, Energy, Justice, Defense, and Homeland Security, CIA, FBI, Office of the Director of National Intelligence, NCSC, National Security Agency, DIA, the Program Manager (Information Sharing Environment), Office of Management and Budget, National Security Council Staff, and Information Security Oversight Office.

The NITTF sees the insider threat as a threat posed to US national security by someone who misuses or betrays, wittingly or unwittingly, their authorized access to any US government resource. This threat can include damage through espionage, terrorism, unauthorized disclosure of national security information, or through the loss or degradation of departmental resources or capabilities. This can easily happen when there are **gaps in security**.

The NITTF has drawn together expertise from across the government in areas of security, counterintelligence, and information assurance to develop the policies and standards necessary for individual D/As to implement insider threat programs. Part of the NITTF effort involves hosting training and providing D/As with assistance to better educate their workforces to recognize potential insider threat activity, without creating an atmosphere of distrust. The NITTF conducts assessments of the adequacy of insider threat programs within individual D/As. Through its interface with individual D/As, the NITTF identifies and circulates best practices for detecting, deterring, and mitigating emerging threats, and continues to assist D/As in trouble-shooting issues.

The detection of potentially malicious behavior involves authorized insider threat personnel gathering information from many sources and analyzing that information for clues or behaviors of concern. A single indicator may say little; however, if taken together with other indicators, a pattern of concerning behavior may arise that can add up to someone who could pose a threat. It is important to consider relevant information from multiple sources to determine if an employee's behavior deserves closer scrutiny, or whether a matter should be formally brought to the attention of an investigative or administrative entity, such as the FBI or an agency's Inspector General. It is also possible that the individual has no malicious intent, but is in need of help. In either case, the individual may pose a threat to national security, and the situation requires further inquiry.

It is critically important to recognize that an individual may have no malicious intent, but is in need of help. The United States has invested a tremendous amount in its national security workforce and it is in everyone's interest to help someone who may feel he or she has no other option than to commit an egregious act such as espionage, unauthorized disclosure, suicide, workplace violence, or sabotage. Intervention prior to the act can save an employee's career, save lives, and protect national security information. This can be addressed in part by conducting **individual assessments** of employees.

There are also unwitting insiders who can be exploited by others. The nation's adversaries have become increasingly sophisticated in targeting US interests, and an individual may be deceived into advancing those adversaries' objectives without knowingly doing so.

Taken together, the national policy mandates that every executive branch agency with access to classified information establishes an insider threat program in line with standards and guidance from the NITTF. However, there is a recognition of differing levels of risk and, therefore, differing levels of protection required based on such things as size of cleared population, extent of access to classified computer systems, and amount of classified information maintained by the D/A. The national insider threat policy directs heads of D/As to develop their programs using risk management principles. The NITTF is working with D/As, as well as the Classified Information Sharing and Safeguarding Office, to assess the extent of applicability of the minimum standards to each of the 99+ executive branch D/As with access to classified information based on the associated risk.

Insider threat programs are developed and operated in coordination with an agency's records management office, legal counsel, and civil liberties and privacy officials to build in protections against infringing upon employees' civil liberties/civil rights, privacy, or whistleblower protections. Departments and agencies are required to provide training in these areas to program personnel, as well as the general workforce. Department and agency heads also have a responsibility to ensure these protections are maintained through oversight of their insider threat programs.

Insider threat programs target anomalous behaviors, not individuals. Additionally, government employees who handle classified information understand that, to hold a security clearance, they accept additional oversight of their workplace activities. Employees sign authorizations for the conduct of investigations to obtain and retain security clearances and there are warning banners on computers and in certain areas of facilities that alert people that they have a lower expectation of privacy.

When classified information is divulged in an unauthorized manner outside the confines of the US government national security structure, that information can create situations that are harmful to US interests and, in some cases, could be life-threatening. Classified information in the wrong hands can provide a unique and potentially dangerous advantage to those state and non-state actors whose interests are opposed to those of the United States. For example, the unauthorized release of classified information could: Provide details about weapons systems the country relies on to defend itself; expose overseas intelligence operations and personnel; identify critical vulnerabilities in the US national infrastructure that, if exploited, could damage internal US defense, transportation, health, financial, and/or communication capabilities.[6] The NITTF defines five main categories of insider threat, which are shown in Box 7.3.

BOX 7.3   NITTF CATEGORIES OF INSIDER THREATS

Leaks are the intentional, unauthorized disclosure of classified or proprietary information to a person or an organization that does not have a need to know.

Spills are the unintentional transfer of classified or proprietary information to unaccredited or unauthorized systems, individuals, applications, or media.

Espionage is the unauthorized transmittal of classified or proprietary information to a competitor, foreign nation or entity with the intent to harm.

Sabotage means to deliberately destroy, damage, or obstruct, especially for political or military advantage.

Targeted violence represents any form of violence that is directed at an individual or group, for a specific reason.

An example of a leak is like the story about *PlayStation All-Stars Battle Royale*. This leak involved a mascot fighting game: *Super Smash Brothers* for Wii-U. While the video games themselves are similar, the circumstances behind their leaks are not. Whereas Sony accidentally leaked its own private information in a beta download, Nintendo's leak came from an employee who had access to a camera and an unreleased version of the game.

Posting anonymously on 4chan's video games board, the leaker shared images of multiple unconfirmed characters along with screenshots of different game modes that had not yet been shown to the public. At first, the leak was deemed to be a hoax due to the outrageous claim that one of the characters was the dog from the popular '80s game *Duck Hunt*. But within hours, the leaker had posted videos of themselves playing as all of the characters that had yet to be announced, along with pictures of different collectibles that didn't make it into the main game. There are unconfirmed reports that Nintendo had figured out which employee leaked all of this sensitive information and had dealt with them.

Harry Potter and the Tale of $20 million Down the Drain: With the release of the final Harry Potter book on the horizon, tensions were high in the Bloomsbury offices. After dealing with nightmarish leaks a few years prior, where people actually took time out of their day to ruin the story for others by yelling out death spoilers for *Harry Potter and the Half-Blood Prince* in public before the book's release, Bloomsbury wasn't taking any chances on letting the final book in the series be spoiled in the same manner.

In an attempt to block spoilers and leaks, the company proceeded to spend upward of $20 million on security measures for the book shipments going out to retailers and threaten any store that even dared to open the containers holding the precious books. In the end, this was all for nothing, as someone still managed to get a copy of the book days before its release. Much to the horror of Bloomsbury, the person proceeded to take pictures of every single page in the book and post them online for everyone to see. The big finale was spoiled, and Bloomsbury was out a huge chunk of money for its troubles.

Spills are the unintentional transfer of classified or proprietary information to unaccredited or unauthorized systems, individuals, applications, or media. The most common form of insider threat is a spill. Spills remind us that you don't have to have malicious intent to cause damage. Most people think of data spills from computer systems or over the Internet. Spills, however, are not limited to the cyber realm. They can occur when a book is published or when a public presentation or interview is given.

Espionage is the unauthorized transmittal of classified or proprietary information to a competitor, foreign nation, or entity with the intent to harm. Example: Gregory Allen Justice, was convicted of economic espionage for selling sensitive satellite information to a person he believed to be an agent of a Russian intelligence service. Justice was an engineer who worked for a cleared defense contractor. Specifically, he worked on military and commercial satellite programs.

In exchange for providing these materials during a series of meetings between February and July of 2016, Justice sought and received thousands of dollars in cash payments. During one meeting, Justice discussed developing a relationship like one depicted on the television show *The Americans*, and during their final meeting, Justice offered a tour of his employer's production facilities where Justice said all military spacecraft were built.

Sabotage means to deliberately destroy, damage, or obstruct, especially for political or military advantage. Although sabotage is often conducted for political or military reasons, other motivations can include personal disgruntlement. Example: A systems administrator granted developer testers local administrative access on their system. The testers created five more administrator accounts, which were never noticed, and backdoors were created into different databases. When one of the developers found out he was going to be fired, he accessed the system through one of the backdoors and shut the system down.

Targeted violence represents any form of violence that is directed at an individual or group, for a specific reason. In other words, not a random act of violence. Example: An employee overheard his co-worker make a threatening statement involving a firearm. The co-worker was reported to have been upset regarding an issue that occurred in the workplace, and made the comment, if I had a gun, I would shoot them. Following an investigation, the co-worker admitted to making those remarks and stated that he did not intend to act on the comment he made. The co-worker admitted to having a temper, but had no intentions of shooting anyone.[7]

7.4 Social Engineering Attacks on Businesses

During the last several years, there have been numerous breaches of large databases maintained by name brand companies. Many of these cases have gone on to be solved but millions of identities were compromised in the process, which helps to illustrate the need for much better security than currently exists to protect personal and financial data. However, many cases of security breaches of customer data or PII go unsolved and are never prosecuted.

Marriott International said that a breach of its Starwood guest reservation database exposed the personal information of up to 500 million people. According to Marriott, the hackers accessed people's names, addresses, phone numbers, email addresses, passport numbers, dates of birth, gender, Starwood loyalty program account information, and reservation information. For some, they also stole payment card numbers and expiration dates. Marriott said the payment card numbers were encrypted, but it did not yet know if the hackers also stole the information needed to decrypt them. The hotel chain said the breach began in 2014 and anyone who made a reservation at a Starwood property on or before September 10, 2018, could be affected. Starwood brands include W Hotels, St. Regis, Sheraton Hotels & Resorts, Westin Hotels & Resorts, Le Méridien Hotels & Resorts, and other hotel and timeshare properties.[8]

There's a good chance that any one of the 143 million American consumers' sensitive personal information was exposed in a data breach at Equifax, one of the three major credit reporting agencies in the United States. According to Equifax, the breach lasted from mid-May through July of 2017. The hackers accessed people's names, social security numbers (SSNs), birth dates, addresses, and, in some instances, driver's license numbers. They also stole credit card numbers for about 209,000 people and dispute documents with personal identifying information for about 182,000 people. In addition, they grabbed personal information of people in the United Kingdom and Canada.[9]

In 2015, the Office of Personnel Management (OPM) announced two separate but related cybersecurity incidents that impacted the data of federal government employees, contractors, and others. In June 2015, the OPM discovered that the background investigation records of current, former, and prospective federal employees and contractors had been stolen. The OPM and the interagency incident response team concluded with high confidence that sensitive information, including the SSNs of 21.5 million individuals, was stolen from the background investigation databases. This includes 19.7 million individuals that applied for a background investigation, and 1.8 million non-applicants, primarily spouses or co-habitants of applicants. Some records also include findings from interviews conducted by background investigators and approximately 5.6 million include fingerprints. Usernames and passwords that applicants used to fill out their background investigation forms were also stolen. While background investigation records do contain some information regarding mental health and financial history provided by applicants and people contacted during the background investigation, there is no evidence that health, financial, payroll, and retirement records of federal personnel or those who have applied for a federal job were impacted by this incident (e.g., annuity rolls, retirement records, USA JOBS, Employee Express). In 2015, the OPM discovered that the personnel data of 4.2 million current and former federal government employees had been stolen. This meant that information such as full name, birth date, home address, and SSNs were affected.

For people who underwent a federal background investigation in 2000 or afterward (which occurs through the submission of forms SF-86, SF-85, or SF-85P for either a new investigation or a reinvestigation), it was highly likely that they were impacted by the incident involving background investigations. If people had undergone a background investigation prior to 2000, they may still have been impacted, but it was less likely. Current or former federal employees could also have been impacted by the separate but related incident involving personnel records.[10]

Fresenius Medical Care North America (FMCNA) agreed to pay $3.5 million to the US Department of Health and Human Services (HHS) Office for Civil Rights (OCR), and to adopt a comprehensive corrective action plan, in order to settle potential violations of the Health Insurance Portability and Accountability Act (HIPAA) Privacy and Security Rules. FMCNA is a provider of products and services for people with chronic kidney failure. They have over 60,000 employees and serve over 170,000 patients. On January 21, 2013, FMCNA filed five separate breach reports for separate incidents occurring between February 23, 2012 and July 18, 2012, implicating the electronic protected health information (ePHI) of five separate FMCNA-owned covered entities (FMCNA covered entities).

The five locations of the breaches were Bio-Medical Applications of Florida, Inc. d/b/a Fresenius Medical Care Duval Facility in Jacksonville, Florida (FMC Duval Facility); Bio-Medical Applications of Alabama, Inc. d/b/a Fresenius Medical Care Magnolia Grove in Semmes, Alabama (FMC Magnolia Grove Facility); Renal Dimensions, LLC d/b/a Fresenius Medical Care Ak-Chin in Maricopa, Arizona (FMC Ak-Chin Facility); Fresenius Vascular Care Augusta, LLC (FVC Augusta); and WSKC Dialysis Services, Inc. d/b/a Fresenius Medical Care Blue Island Dialysis (FMC Blue Island Facility).

The OCR's investigation revealed that FMCNA covered entities failed to conduct an accurate and thorough risk analysis of
potential risks and vulnerabilities to the confidentiality, integrity,
and availability of all of its ePHI. The FMCNA covered entities
impermissibly disclosed the ePHI of patients by providing unauthorized access for a purpose not permitted by the Privacy Rule.
In addition to a $3.5 million monetary settlement, a corrective
action plan required the FMCNA covered entities to complete a
risk analysis and risk management plan, revise policies and procedures on device and media controls as well as facility access controls, develop an encryption report, and educate its workforce on
policies and procedures.[11]

In April 2018, the Securities and Exchange Commission (SEC)
announced that the entity formerly known as Yahoo! Inc. had agreed
to pay a $35 million penalty to settle charges that it misled inves-
tors by failing to disclose one of the world's largest data breaches in
which hackers stole personal data relating to hundreds of millions
of user accounts. According to the SEC's order, within days of the
December 2014 intrusion, Yahoo's information security team learned
that Russian hackers had stolen what the security team referred to
internally as the company's crown jewels: Usernames, email addresses,
phone numbers, birth dates, encrypted passwords, and security questions and answers for hundreds of millions of user accounts. Although
information relating to the breach was reported to members of Yahoo's
senior management and legal department, Yahoo failed to properly
investigate the circumstances of the breach and to adequately consider
whether the breach needed to be disclosed to investors. The fact of
the breach was not disclosed to the investing public until more than
two years later; that is, when Yahoo was in the process of closing the
acquisition of its operating business by Verizon Communications, Inc
in 2016.

The SEC's order found that when Yahoo filed several quarterly and
annual reports during the two-year period following the breach, the
company failed to disclose the breach or its potential business impact
and legal implications. Instead, the company's SEC filings stated that
it faced only the risk of, and negative effects that might flow from,
data breaches. In addition, the SEC's order found that Yahoo did not

share information regarding the breach with its auditors or outside counsel in order to assess the company's disclosure obligations in its public filings. Finally, the SEC's order found that Yahoo failed to maintain disclosure controls and procedures designed to ensure that reports from Yahoo's information security team concerning cyber breaches, or the risk of such breaches, were assessed properly and in a timely manner for potential disclosure.

Verizon acquired Yahoo's operating business in June 2017. Yahoo has since changed its name to Altaba Inc. Yahoo neither admitted nor denied the findings in the SEC's order, which required the company to cease and desist from further violations of Sections 17(a)(2) and 17(a)(3) of the Securities Act of 1933 and Section 13(a) of the Securities Exchange Act of 1934 and Rules 12b-20, 13a-1, 13a-11, 13a-13, and 13a-15. The SEC's investigation was continuing in 2019.[12]

Additional data breaches have occurred at Lord & Taylor, Saks Fifth Avenue, Saks OFF 5TH, and Under Armour's MyFitnessPal, as well as other businesses and government entities. Comprehensive data on breaches is not readily available for all sectors but Table 7.1 shows the number of people affected by breaches involving health-related information from 2010 to 2015; Table 7.2 shows the number of people per source of protected health information breaches from 2010 to 2015; Table 7.3 shows the number of reported protected health information breaches from 2010 to 2015; and Table 7.4 shows the sources of protected health information breaches from 2010 to 2015.

Table 7.1 Number of People Affected by Protected Health Information Breaches 2010–2015

TYPE OF BREACH	2010	2011	2012	2013	2014	2015
Hacking/IT incident	568,358	297,269	900,684	236,897	1,786,630	111,812,172
Improper disposal	34,587	63,948	21,329	526,538	93,612	82,421
Loss	924,909	6,019,578	95,815	142,411	243,376	47,214
Theft	3,691,460	4,720,129	927,909	5,397,989	7,058,678	740,598
Unauthorized access/disclosure	130,106	118,444	338,767	383,759	3,019,284	572,919
Other breach	158,593	13,981	503,900	254,305	413,878	N/A

Source: US Department of Health and Human Services, Office for Civil Rights. Breaches Affecting 500 or More Individuals. February 1, 2016.[13]

Table 7.2   Number of People per Source of Protected Health Information Breaches 2010–2015

SOURCE OF BREACH	2010	2011	2012	2013	2014	2015
Desktop computer	246,643	2,042,186	81,385	4,348,129	2,378,304	316,226
Electronic medical record	803,600	1,720,064	136,751	40,196	121,845	3,948,985
Email	8,050	3,111	294,308	58,847	519,625	583,977
Laptop	1,507,914	405,873	575,529	1,023,181	1,273,612	391,830
Network server	665,123	613,963	921,335	320,127	7,253,441	107,252,466
Paper/film	204,966	103,711	198,409	575,076	590,352	229,743
Portable electronic device	29,714	1,516	124,978	154,877	141,110	209,558
Other source	2,058,166	8,259,368	455,709	422,381	343,537	322,539

Source: US Department of Health and Human Services (HHS) Office for Civil Rights. Breaches Affecting 500 or More Individuals. February 1, 2016.[13]

Table 7.3   Number of Reported Protected Health Information Breaches 2010–2015

TYPE OF INFORMATION BREACH	2010	2011	2012	2013	2014	2015
Hacking/IT incident	10	16	16	23	32	57
Improper disposal	10	7	7	13	11	6
Loss	18	17	19	24	28	22
Theft	127	118	117	124	113	80
Unauthorized access/disclosure	7	26	25	63	72	100
Other breach	22	2	18	24	28	0

Source: US Department of Health and Human Services, Office for Civil Rights. Breaches Affecting 500 or More Individuals. February 1, 2016.[13]

Table 7.4   Number of Protected Health Information Breaches by Source 2010–2015

SOURCE OF INFORMATION BREACH	2010	2011	2012	2013	2014	2015
Desktop computer	28	35	23	39	29	29
Electronic medical record	3	6	6	14	14	16
Email	5	2	10	20	36	37
Laptop	50	38	51	67	42	38
Network server	17	16	20	30	46	41
Paper/film	46	45	47	53	62	67
Portable electronic device	6	2	19	20	22	15
Other source	42	50	26	24	34	22

Source: US Department of Health and Human Services, Office for Civil Rights. Breaches Affecting 500 or More Individuals. February 1, 2016.[13]

7.5 Basic Steps to Protect Against Insider Threats

There are many off-the-shelf recommendations to help secure finan-cial instruments and prevent **insider misconduct,** including fraud and abuse. However, these steps within themselves will not guarantee that an organization is safe. The US Small Business Administration (SBA) provides a list of recommendations that are generally consistent with those provided by several different organizations. Those recommen-dations include:

- Conducting background checks when hiring employees.
- Protecting bank accounts and credit cards by limiting and auditing their use.
- Securing information systems and computers.
- Using a dedicated computer for banking.
- Educating employees about security.
- Having **appropriate separation of duties** for financial pro-cesses and instruments.
- Having adequate insurance coverage against insider theft.[14]
- Having Fidelity Bonds or Commercial Crime Policies that are specifically designed to protect organizations from the financial impact of dishonest acts committed by employees.

Protecting against insider threats is challenging in any situation but even more so when the insider that can do the most damage is generally already in a trusted position. Defending against the **insider-outsider threat** is also challenging but protecting against and **insider-outsider team** may be the most difficult of all situations when it comes to maintaining security.

The insider may recruit outside help if they need to supplement their capabilities. If the insider needs a truck, needs to have some heavy lifting done, or needs to augment their computer skills in order to perpetrate a fraud scheme they may team up with an outsider. Outside help may be seen as safer for the insider because they do not need to reveal to other employees that they are working on commit-ting a crime.

Conversely, the outsider may recruit the insider if the out-sider is attempting to increase their access to a facility or to a com-puter system and the insider can provide assistance in that effort. The insider can provide the outsider with physical help or just with information that makes it easier to enter a facility and perpetrate a crime. The deliberate actions on the part of an insider-outsider team can cause considerable damage and cost large sums of money.

Building an insider threat program can help organizations detect, deter, and respond to threats resulting from malicious and unintentional insiders. It is important to acknowledge that program development and scope may vary based on an organization's size, budget, culture, and industry. Definitely include key staff and personnel from across the organization including:

- Human resources
- Physical security
- Information security
- Information technology
- Data owners
- Business continuity planners
- Legal counsel (ethics and privacy)

The insider threat working group should be responsible for developing and implementing a comprehensive insider threat program to reduce risk to people, data, systems, and facilities. It is best to consider a phased approach to control cost and minimize the impact on operations (pilot, limited scope, entire organization) and apply risk-based methods that leverage business continuity plans and risk assessments to prioritize asset protection. It is important to appropriately:

- Incorporate legal and regulatory requirements
- Identify data sources that monitor behavior
- Integrate human resources management systems into the process
- Select video surveillance cameras
- Establish entry/exit tracking systems
- Implement a network user activity monitoring system
- Establish a financial fraud detection system
- Collaborate with data owners to ensure information sharing
- Safeguard privacy, civil rights, and civil liberties
- Account for organizational culture during planning and execution

It is a critical step to establish an ongoing training program that encourages executive leadership attendance and:

- Incorporates training during **onboarding**
- Requires annual refresher training
- Reinforces program objectives during voluntary and involuntary departures
- Tailors training to address unique mitigation roles and responsibilities[15]

7.6 Conclusion

The biggest modern-day threat against sensitive computer systems, networks, and data is the insider threat. There are numerous potential scenarios that can lead the insider to steal data and information. All organizations face some level of threat from insiders and the possibility that an insider may collaborate and conspire with an outsider to steal, sabotage, or humiliate their employees.

7.7 Key Points

Key points covered in this chapter include:

- At the societal level, more people have greater access to personal technologies, such as smartphones, flash drives, and other devices that better enable them to spy or steal intellectual property.
- There have been several high-profile insider attacks on government agencies during the last decade. The top areas for potential risk include criminals, industrial competitors, insider threats, and state-sponsored adversaries.
- The detection of potentially malicious behavior involves authorized insider threat personnel gathering information from many sources and analyzing that information for clues or behaviors of concern.
- There are also unwitting insiders who can be exploited by the nation's adversaries, who have become increasingly sophisticated in targeting US interests, and an individual may be

deceived into advancing those adversaries' objectives without knowingly doing so.

- Building an insider threat program can help organizations detect, deter, and respond to threats resulting from malicious and unintentional insiders.
- During the last several years, there have been numerous breaches of large databases maintained by name brand companies. Many of these cases have gone on to be solved but millions of identities were compromised in the process, which helps to illustrate the need for much better security than what currently exists in order to protect personal and financial data.
- Sabotage means to deliberately destroy, damage, or obstruct, especially for political or military advantage. Although it is often conducted for political or military reasons, other motivations can include personal disgruntlement.

7.8 Seminar Discussion Topics

Discussion topics for graduate- or professional-level seminars are:

- What experience have seminar participants had in situations where there was a breach of security by an insider or an insider-outsider team?
- What security plans or procedures do the organizations at which participants are employed have in place to prevent insider incidents and security breaches?
- What are the procedures in the organizations at which participants are employed for reporting suspected or possible insider misconduct?

7.9 Seminar Group Project

Divide participants into multiple groups with each group taking 10 to 15 minutes to develop a list of behaviors that an employee may have that could indicate that they are going to commit a security violation or launch an insider attack against the organization. Meet as a group and discuss the list of behaviors identified by the groups.

Key Terms

Access control for computer systems: is a process that either allows
or disallows individual users to have access to specific computer applications and computer datasets including what the
user is allowed to do on the systems with their level of access.

Access control systems: are those automated and human functions
that allow a properly identified person or logical entity access
to an organization's facilities or computer systems.

Appropriate separation of duties: is an organization structure that
prevents individual employees or agents from having access
to or control of work functions in a manner that would allow
them to independently misappropriate corporate assets with
little chance of detection.

Authorized logical access: is the access that an insider is allowed to
have to an organization's computer and communication systems that an employee may need to perform their job duties.

Authorized physical access: is the access that an insider is allowed
to have to an organization's property, buildings, and areas of
buildings that an employee may need to perform their job
duties.

Comprehensive security plan: covers all security needs of an organization from the ground up and is designed to mitigate known
security threats.

Gaps in security: are security measures or mitigation methods that
are inadequate to protect an asset or do not thoroughly protect
the asset that they were deployed to protect.

Individual assessments: are designed to evaluate how well an individual employee is performing a specific task or types of tasks
necessary to fulfill their job responsibilities.

Insider misconduct: conduct by an employee that is against organization policies or procedures or that can otherwise harm the
employing organization.

Insider-outsider team: is two or more people that jointly conspire
to act maliciously against an organization with which one of
them (the insider) is employed or has privileged access.

Insider-outsider threat: is a threat that emerges as a result of a relationship between one of an organization's employees and a

person working for an outside organization or who is otherwise not related to the employee's organization.

Onboarding: a process that integrates the new hire into the social and cultural aspects of an organization.

Open organizations: tend to be more informal and not highly structured—they often lack strict hierarchal communication structures, project teams are fluid, information flows freely, and employees have extensive access to information, systems, and people.

Personal technologies: include employee-owned devices such as cell phones, tablets, laptops, and digital media that can be used to inappropriately record and remove propriety information from an employer's facilities.

References

1. Testimony of Ronald L. Dick, Director, National Infrastructure Protection Center, Before the House Energy and Commerce Committee, Oversight and Investigation Subcommittee Washington, DC. United States Department of Justice, Federal Bureau of Investigation. April 5, 2001. Retrieved February 22, 2019. https://www.fbi.gov/news/testimony/issue-of-intrusions-into-government-computer-networks
2. Defense Community Discusses Cyber Challenges at Industrial Security Seminar. Space and Naval Warfare Systems Command Public Affairs. Stillions, Tina C. May 16, 2014. Accessed February 22, 2019. https://www.navy.mil/submit/display.asp?story_id=81058#
3. Countering Insider Threats—Handling Insider Threats Using Dynamic, Run-Time Forensics. Air Force Research Laboratory Information Directorate Rome Research Site, Rome, New York. Hallahan, Jason. October 2007. Accessed February 22, 2019. apps.dtic.mil/dtic/tr/fulltext/u2/a473440.pdf
4. Justice Department Statement on the Request to Hong Kong for Edward Snowden's Provisional Arrest. Department of Justice Office of Public Affairs. June 26, 2013. Accessed February 23, 2019. https://www.justice.gov/opa/pr/justice-department-statement-request-hong-kong-edward-snowden-s-provisional-arrest
5. Conyers Statement on Edward Snowden Disclosures. US House Committee on the Judiciary. June 24, 2013. Accessed February 23, 2019. https://judiciary.house.gov/press-release/conyers-statement-edward-snowden-disclosures
6. National Insider Threat Task Force (NITTF) Mission. National Counterintelligence and Security Center. Accessed February 22, 2019. https://www.dni.gov/index.php/ncsc-who-we-are

7. Stand Alone. National Insider Threat Task Force (NITTF). Accessed February 22, 2019. https://www.dni.gov/ncsc/Insider-Threat/main.html?mode=browse#
8. The Marriott Data Breach. FTC. Gressin, Seena. December 4, 2018. Accessed February 23, 2019. https://www.consumer.ftc.gov/blog/2018/12/marriott-data-breach
9. The Equifax Data Breach: What to Do. FTC. Gressin, Seena. September 8, 2017. Accessed February 23, 2019. https://www.consumer.ftc.gov/blog/2017/09/equifax-data-breach-what-do
10. What Happened? US Office of Personnel Management. 2015. Accessed February 23, 2019. https://www.opm.gov/cybersecurity/cybersecurity-incidents/
11. Five Breaches Add Up to Millions in Settlement Costs for Entity that Failed to Heed HIPAA's Risk Analysis and Risk Management Rules. US Department of Health and Human Services. February 1, 2018. Accessed February 23, 2019. https://www.hhs.gov/about/news/2018/02/01/five-breaches-add-millions-settlement-costs-entity-failed-heed-hipaa-s-risk-analysis-and-risk.html
12. Altaba, Formerly Known as Yahoo!, Charged with Failing to Disclose Massive Cybersecurity Breach; Agrees To Pay $35 Million. FTC. April 24, 2018. Accessed February 23, 2019. https://www.sec.gov/news/press-release/2018-71
13. Breaches of Unsecured Protected Health Information. The Office of the National Coordinator for Health Information Technology. February 2016. Accessed February 23, 2019. https://dashboard.healthit.gov/quickstats/pages/breaches-protected-health-information.php
14. 7 Ways to Protect Your Small Business from Fraud and Cybercrime United States Small Business Administration. Beesley, Caron. May 8, 2013. Retrieved May 25, 2016. https://www.sba.gov/blogs/employee-fraud-what-you-can-do-about-it
15. Establish a Comprehensive Insider Threat Program. US DHS. August 16, 2018. Accessed February 24, 2019. https://www.dhs.gov/establish-program

8

EDUCATING PEOPLE TO PREVENT SOCIAL ENGINEERING ATTACKS

When it comes to preventing social engineering attacks, the main defenses are preventing spam, requiring permissions for code to run a system, and a collection of tips sheets offered up by various organizations and government agencies. Hopefully these efforts have been helpful in reducing the number and the effectiveness of social engineering attacks, but the attacks continue and people continue to be victimized at the cost of billions of dollars every year. Thus, the efforts to educate the public on prevention need to be greatly expanded and, above all, should include accurate information to fight against disinformation, misinformation, and fake news, and do this with unbiased and accurate information. This will require the use of all communication tools in order to inform people about inaccurate or malicious material being circulated through all media. This chapter examines many of the challenges that defenders face when trying to prevent damage from social engineering attacks whether they originate in St. Petersburg or Washington, DC.

8.1 Social Engineering Attacks Come in Many Shapes and Sizes

A review of the tips sheets and advice offered up on many websites to help protect consumers clearly shows that greater effort is needed to make this information more useful and to get it more widely distributed. In addition to usefulness and distribution shortcomings, most tips and advice on social engineering is rather flat and shallow. There is more than one type of social engineering attack that needs to be defended against and a one-size-fits-all approach to education and awareness building is not adequate. Figure 8.1 shows four types of

Quick hits resulting in malicious code through a payload or link to infected website	Scheme bait that draws people deeper into financial fraud schemes or extracts more information and greater access
Persuasion and sway campaigns that keep users engaged and moves them toward specific actions	Radicalization of individuals politically, socially, or behaviorally

Figure 8.1   Types of social engineering attacks.

social engineering attacks that people can fall victim to, only to end up with a myriad of problems in their lives.

Earlier chapters in this book examine many of the various types of social engineering attacks and motivations. To help plan awareness and education programs the four categories of social engineering attacks shown in Figure 8.1 can serve as a planning and guidance tool for educators. The quick hit attack through email or links to malicious websites is certainly the easiest attack to explain and to defend against, the issue that remains is why so many people still become victims of such attacks.

The scheme bait attacks that draw people deeper into fraud schemes or extract more information and greater access to systems is effective because people either pay little attention to the security issues involved in such attacks or they fall prey to false promises, greed, or some primal desire to see the prize that the click on a link is supposed to provide. In spite of thousands of warnings about such attacks, people keep getting caught in the trap year after year.

Persuasion and sway campaign attacks are more complex and the social engineering is more sophisticated. The promise of an inside scoop on a conspiracy, or malicious text about or photos of celebrities or politicians, keeps users engaged and moves them toward more specific actions. This includes continuing to follow the posts or emails to find out or see more, especially when it comes to emotional topics like Islamophobia, xenophobia, racism, sexism, or hatred of liberals. These attacks are designed to keep people engaged as long as possible and when possible recruit them into a symbolic clan or tribe of like thinkers. This type of attack is more complex to explain because people are responding to their beliefs and are drawn in by what they want to hear or see as opposed to a more balanced perspective.

The social engineering attacks designed toward **radicalization** of individuals politically, socially, or behaviorally is more complex than the persuasion attack and it is also more effective on people who have a predisposition toward hatred, racism, anarchy, violence, and anti-social behavior in general. These campaigns were made famous by the Islamic State of Iraq and Syria, Islamic State of Iraq and the Levant, the Islamic State, or Daesh (ISIS) over the last several years as the organization worked to recruit people into the cause as supporters or fighters, but the Russian social engineering attacks on the United States before and during the 2016 election were equally as complex and certainly just as dastardly.

In addition to understanding the types of social engineering attacks, it is also important to understand how the population of Internet users is divided by many social, economic, and educational characteristics. These segments learn differently, they retain information differently, and they have varying levels of concern toward security. Many of them just totally ignore security when working online.

8.2 The Diversity in Electoral Populations that Need Education

One of the dynamics that makes the one-size-fits-all awareness or education campaign ineffective is the diversity in the population. The persuasion and divisiveness attack was used heavily during the 2014 to 2020 elections in several countries. These attacks were very effective among some segments of the population and less effective with other segments. In the United States, voting and registration rates tend to increase with education. In 2016 in the United States the voting rate for citizens with at least a bachelor's degree was 76.3% compared to 34.3% for those who had not received a high school diploma. Table 8.1 shows the diverse education levels of US voters in the 2016 election, while Table 8.2 shows voting and registration among native and naturalized citizens, by race, Hispanic origin, and region of birth, during the 2016 election.[1,2]

This data illustrates diversity in learning styles that cannot be met with a singular one-size-fits-all awareness or education program. To effectively communicate with these diverse population segments will require a multitude of communication styles and will perhaps require communication in multiple languages, dialects, and mediums.

Table 8.1   Diversity in Education Levels Among US Voters 2016

US POPULATION OVER 18 YEARS OLD	TOTAL CITIZEN POPULATION (THOUSANDS)	REPORTED REGISTERED 2016 ELECTION		REPORTED VOTED 2016 ELECTION	
		NUMBER (THOUSANDS)	PERCENT	NUMBER (THOUSANDS)	PERCENT
Total	224,059	157,596	70.3	137,537	61.4
Less than 9th grade	5,643	2,389	42.3	1,788	31.7
9th to 12th grade, no diploma	14,715	6,906	46.9	5,202	35.3
High school graduate	65,518	40,983	62.6	33,774	51.5
Some college or associate's degree	66,809	48,845	73.1	42,296	63.3
Bachelor's degree	46,317	37,270	80.5	34,364	74.2
Advanced degree	25,057	21,203	84.6	20,113	80.3

Source: Voting and Registration 2016. US Census Bureau.

The census data shows numerous population segments that may require specialized awareness programs to be developed.

Beyond the need to develop a multitude of approaches to educate voters on how to identify reliable objective information being emitted from campaign sources, there is a need to teach voters how to identify socially engineered biased news media and social media activity. Politicians will hide behind the First Amendment to justify the use of **disinformation**, along with their misleading statements and their blatant lies and false claims about their talents and motivations and the weaknesses of their opponents. The conservatives confess they are fighting a culture war for power and do not care if they lie, cheat, steal, or desecrate American democracy to achieve victory. Thus independent organizations are needed to lead education efforts to combat socially engineered political messaging with **counter-messaging** and provide **alternative master narratives**.

The US Election Assistance Commission has collaborated with local election officials to develop a series of helpful tips for election management. This series provides tips and suggests best practices to help people run efficient and effective elections. Voter education programs impact voter turnout. Well-planned programs can motivate and encourage citizens to participate in the voting process. Above all, as part of the education effort accurate information should be included in order to fight against disinformation, misinformation, and

Table 8.2 Voting and Registration Among Native and Naturalized Citizens, by Race, Hispanic Origin, and Region of Birth 2016

US POPULATION OVER 18 YEARS OLD		TOTAL CITIZEN POPULATION (THOUSANDS)	REPORTED REGISTERED 2016 ELECTION		REPORTED VOTED 2016 ELECTION	
			NUMBER (THOUSANDS)	PERCENT	NUMBER (THOUSANDS)	PERCENT
Total population	All races	224,059	157,596	70.3	137,537	61.4
	White alone	177,865	127,463	71.7	111,891	62.9
	White non-Hispanic alone	154,450	114,151	73.9	100,849	65.3
	Black alone	28,808	19,984	69.4	17,119	59.4
	Asian alone	10,283	5,785	56.3	5,043	49.0
	Hispanic (of any race)	26,662	15,267	57.3	12,682	47.6
	White alone or in combination	181,238	129,664	71.5	113,707	62.7
	Black alone or in combination	30,326	20,935	69.0	17,875	58.9
	Asian alone or in combination	11,118	6,369	57.3	5,542	49.9
Native citizen	All races	204,212	145,351	71.2	126,763	62.1
	White alone	157,069	120,760	72.3	106,047	63.5
	White non-Hispanic alone	149,815	111,095	74.2	98,255	65.6
	Black alone	26,597	18,512	69.6	15,756	59.2
	Asian alone	3,976	2,046	51.5	1,778	44.7
	Hispanic (of any race)	19,848	11,198	56.4	9,040	45.5
	White alone or in combination	170,288	122,837	72.1	107,748	63.3
	Black alone or in combination	28,037	19,428	69.3	16,477	58.8
	Asian alone or in combination	4,750	2,586	54.4	2,238	47.1

(Continued)

Table 8.2 (Continued) Voting and Registration Among Native and Naturalized Citizens, by Race, Hispanic Origin, and Region of Birth 2016

US POPULATION OVER 18 YEARS OLD		TOTAL CITIZEN POPULATION (THOUSANDS)	REPORTED REGISTERED 2016 ELECTION		REPORTED VOTED 2016 ELECTION	
			NUMBER (THOUSANDS)	PERCENT	NUMBER (THOUSANDS)	PERCENT
Naturalized citizen	All races	19,847	12,245	61.7	10,774	54.3
	White alone	10,796	6,704	62.1	5,844	54.1
	White non-Hispanic alone	4,635	3,056	65.9	2,594	56.0
	Black alone	2,210	1,472	66.6	1,363	61.7
	Asian alone	6,307	3,738	59.3	3,265	51.8
	Hispanic (of any race)	6,815	4,070	59.7	3,642	53.4
	White alone or in combination	10,981	6,827	62.2	5,959	54.3
	Black alone or in combination	2,290	1,507	65.8	1,398	61.1
	Asian alone or in combination	6,367	3,783	59.4	3,305	51.9

Source: Voting and Registration 2016. US Census Bureau.

fake news with the support of **credible voices**. All the communication tools should be used in order to inform people about inaccurate material being circulated through all media. The following seven tips should help strengthen voter education efforts.[3]

Tip #1: Use data to guide your approach to planning voter education efforts. The more you know about your voters, the more effective your approach will be. Remember different voters have different learning styles. Understand how to best reach the voting public to counter **deceptive marketing**, including **news feeds**, websites, social media, print media, radio, television, or in person. Gain insight into voters by gathering and reviewing data from past elections on:
- Undervotes
- Spoiled ballots
- Errors on provisional ballots
- Absentee voting by precinct

Tip#2: Keep your website current; review and evaluate it frequently. Keep it fresh and accessible with a prominent front page. To keep your website user friendly, make sure you have a clean, simple, visually appealing presentation, avoiding crowding content with too many graphics and photographs. Write in plain language and link to a frequently asked questions section (FAQs) and highlight the FAQs of most interest to voters. In addition:
- Include registration requirements, polling locations, and early and absentee voting in the FAQ section.
- Highlight any new laws or information that affect voters.
- Post a simple version of your operations calendar that includes deadlines and dates of specific interest to voters.
- Link to sites that offer thorough explanations about complex topics specific to various types of voters.
- Include a directory of election officials.
- Provide contact information for your help desk.
- Link to candidate and political party websites if your statutes permit doing so.
- Ask nonpartisan civic and advocacy groups, schools, and colleges or universities to link to your website.

- Create a press kit for media. Include press releases, social media posts, stock photos, and any videos you have about election preparation activities.
- Link to historical data on turnout trends and on registration.
- Publicize your voter education activities. Invite the media to attend.
- Use adaptive communication tools, such as enhanced fonts and audio formats of all materials for visually impaired voters.
- Remember to update your website frequently.
- Assign a knowledgeable staff member to be your online manager.
- Create teletypewriter (a communication device used by people who are deaf, hard-of-hearing, or have severe speech impairment) (TTY) formats of all materials for hearing-impaired voters.
- Make all information on your website available to minority language groups in your jurisdictions and provide written and audio translations.
- Consider hiring a web design firm to evaluate the site's usability.

Tip#3: Try social media as an education tool including Twitter, Facebook, YouTube, mobile apps, and email, which can help you reach young and first-time voters. An effective **social media presence** requires a significant time commitment from staff but offers substantial cost savings over traditional media methods. Dedicate knowledgeable and enthusiastic staff to listen and respond appropriately to direct voter questions and comments. It is also helpful to develop an electronic I Voted sticker for Facebook pages and encourage followers to use it and contact their followers on Election Day. Lastly, ask nonpartisan civic and advocacy groups, schools, and colleges or universities to include a link on their websites to follow your office on Facebook and Twitter.

Tip#4: Rely on a variety of media because many voters will retain information better when it comes from print, TV, radio, or advertising. Encourage local media to devote prominent coverage to your voter education events. Issue frequent press releases, ask local newspapers to print your voter guide as an insert, and practice **political correctness** to help your campaign gain more positive coverage. Also contact local radio, television, and public broadcast stations to arrange public service announcements on timely **positive message promotional activities** of interest to voters. It also helps to use educational billboards or to partner with public transportation officials to place signs on public transport. Other helpful actions include:

- Consulting local utility companies and government offices about placing voter education inserts into their regular mailings.
- Issuing routine mailings in several languages of voter informational brochures, palm cards, or bookmarks.
- Soliciting advice from your state's disability advocacy office and from organizations that represent differently abled citizens about how best to reach disabled citizens.
- Getting input from tribal governors and from minority voter and minority language advocacy groups on appropriate methods for providing voter education in culturally relevant formats.

Tip#5: Give voters personal attention and keep yourself and your staff current on all election laws, dates, and procedures to best help voters who contact your project directly. You can assist voters through personal interactions by assigning knowledgeable staff members to help voters who visit your office in person; and have a good supply of voter education brochures, palm cards, and bookmarks updated, available, and prominently displayed in your office.

It is helpful to establish a community outreach program for civic groups, senior centers, and retirement homes and arrange to visit senior centers with registration forms, educational brochures, election calendars, and voting system demonstrations. Do this on an ongoing basis by developing programs at long-term care facilities that help the residents remain engaged and keep their voter registration information current, and partner with local business and trade organizations, government offices, and nonpartisan advocacy groups to help take education to the voters.

Have as much interaction as possible and offer to help schools, colleges, and universities conduct mock elections, send volunteer guest speakers during voter registration drives and offer your voting equipment, privacy booths, and trouble-shooters for demonstrations to other groups that sponsor voter education events at your location or at their locations. This can also help to establish temporary satellite locations that offer voter information and services in the weeks before registration closes. If possible, use a mobile office to visit high-traffic areas such as shopping malls, senior centers, libraries, and colleges before each election.

Tip #6: Create a voter toolkit with essential information for voters in your jurisdiction. Include in the voter toolkit information on how to register and deadlines for registration along with voter identification requirements. Also include voting dates, hours, and times, sample ballots, a voter guide, absentee and vote-by-mail options, contact information for your help desk and staff, your website address, and Facebook and Twitter account names.

Tip #7: Coordinate education across platforms and utilize many voter education tools in several different formats. For example, provide your voter toolkit online and in brochure format, deliver regular newsletters featuring timely articles and voter-relevant deadlines via print, email, social media, and mobile apps. Remind voters of upcoming dates via email, Twitter and Facebook posts, and mailings. Also, on your website, provide electoral district maps and maps with driving directions to polling places, through mobile apps and link to mapping software on all platforms.

If possible, offer demonstration or educational videos on how to vote, how to use technology, and how your office makes the election results secure and accurate. Upload these presentations to YouTube and other electronic outlets.[3]

8.3 Neutralizing Click Bait by Educating Internet Users

Phishing or the use of scheme bait that draws people deeper into financial fraud schemes or extracts more information and greater access to systems remains one of the leading social engineering methods used to perpetrate Internet crime. There are numerous websites that offer fraud prevention tips, all reiterating a basic theme. Box 8.1 shows a typical message to consumers to combat online fraud schemes.[4]

The basic message is usually followed with tips on how Internet users should be cautious. Although the standard message is clearly stated, the delivery is obviously not effective enough. If the United States, and, in fact, the world, is really going to make a more successful effort to fight back against social engineering attacks, there will need to be considerably more effort put forth in the education endeavor. It may require a campaign on the scale of convincing people to use seat belts in their automobiles that occurred in the 1950s and 1960s and continues today. Other large-scale education efforts have included anti-smoking, environmental protection, such as "Don't litter and Don't pollute," and "Don't consume alcohol when pregnant."

The National Education Technology Plan of the US Department of Education Office of Educational Technology (OET) may be part of the solution. The OET develops national educational technology policy and establishes the vision for how technology can be used to transform teaching and learning and how to make everywhere, all-the-time learning possible for early learners through K-12, higher education, and adult education.

BOX 8.1   TYPICAL PUBLIC SERVICE MESSAGE TO COMBAT INTERNET CRIME

Phishing is when a scammer uses fake email, text messages, or copycat websites to try to steal a person's identity or personal information, such as credit card numbers, bank account numbers, debit card PINs, and account passwords. The scammer may state that the user's account has been compromised or that one of the user's accounts was charged incorrectly.

The OET proposes that technology can be a powerful tool for transforming learning. It can help affirm and advance relationships between educators and students, reinvent our approaches to learning and collaboration, shrink long-standing equity and accessibility gaps, and adapt learning experiences to meet the needs of all learners. The OET contends that education leaders should set a vision for creating learning experiences that provide the right tools and support for all learners to thrive. Furthermore, education stakeholders should commit to working together across organizational and geographic boundaries to use technology to improve American education. The OET carries out its mission by:

- Promoting equity of access to transformational learning experiences enabled by technology;
- Supporting personalized professional learning for state, district, and school leaders and educators;
- Ensuring all learners are connected to broadband Internet in their classrooms and have access to high-quality, affordable digital learning resources at school and at home;
- Fostering a robust ecosystem of entrepreneurs and innovators; and,
- Leading cutting-edge research to provide new types of evidence and to customize and improve learning.

The National Education Technology Plan (NETP) sets out a national vision and plan for learning, enabled by technology through building on the work of leading education researchers; district, school, and higher education leaders; classroom teachers; developers; entrepreneurs; and nonprofit organizations. The principles and examples provided in the plan align with the Activities to Support the Effective Use of Technology (Title IV A) of the Every Student Succeeds Act, as authorized by Congress in December 2015. Since the 2010 NETP, the United States has made significant progress in leveraging technology to transform learning in a variety of ways:

- The conversation has shifted from whether technology should be used in learning to how it can improve learning to ensure that all students have access to high-quality educational experiences.

- Technology is increasingly being used to personalize learning and give students more choice over what and how they learn and at what pace, preparing them to organize and to direct their own learning for the rest of their lives.

- Advances in the learning sciences have improved our understanding of how people learn and illuminated which personal and contextual factors impact their success the most.

- Research and experience have improved our understanding of what people need to know and the skills and competencies they need to acquire for success in life and work in the 21st century. Through pre-service teacher preparation programs and professional learning, educators are gaining experience and confidence in using technology to achieve learning outcomes.

- Sophisticated software has begun to allow us to adapt assessments to the needs and abilities of individual learners and provide near real-time results.

- Nationally, progress has been made toward ensuring that every school has high-speed classroom connectivity as a foundation for other learning innovations.

- The cost of digital devices has decreased dramatically, while computing power has increased, along with the availability of high-quality interactive educational tools and apps.

- Technology has allowed us to rethink the design of physical learning spaces to accommodate new and expanded relationships among learners, teachers, peers, and mentors.[5]

8.4 Rethinking How to Package the Social Engineering Prevention Message

One of the biggest challenges in teaching people is understanding that people learn differently. There is more than one way people learn, which means that there must be multiple ways to teach the same message to effectively reach a greater number of people. There are several models of learning that the NETP is working to enable with technology.

Personalized learning refers to instruction in which the pace of learning and the instructional approach are optimized for the needs of each learner. Learning objectives, instructional approaches, and instructional content (and its sequencing) all may vary based on learner needs. In addition, learning activities are meaningful and relevant to learners, driven by their interests, and often self-initiated.

In a blended learning environment, learning occurs online and in person, augmenting and supporting teacher practice. This approach often allows students to have some control over time, place, path, or pace of learning including the use of **visual content**. In many blended learning models, students spend some of their face-to-face time with the teacher in a large group, some face-to-face time with a teacher or tutor in a small group, and some time learning with and from peers. Blended learning often benefits from a reconfiguration of the physical learning space to facilitate learning activities, providing a variety of technology-enabled learning zones optimized for collaboration, informal learning, and individual-focused study.

Increased connectivity also increases the importance of teaching learners how to become responsible digital citizens. We need to guide the development of competencies to use technology in ways that are meaningful, productive, respectful, and safe. For example, helping students learn to use proper online etiquette, to recognize how their personal information may be collected and used online, and to leverage access to a global community to improve the world around them can help prepare them for successfully navigating life in a connected world. Mastering these skills requires a basic understanding of the technology tools and the ability to make increasingly sound judgments about the use of them in learning and daily life.

It is important to note the research being done on early stage educational technology and how this research might be applied more widely to learning in the future. As part of their work in cyber learning, the National Science Foundation (NSF) is researching opportunities offered by integrating emerging technologies with advances in the learning sciences. Following are examples of the projects being funded by the NSF as part of this effort.

- Increased use of games and simulations to give students the experience of working together on a project without leaving their classrooms: Students are actively involved in a situation that feels urgent and must decide what to measure and how to analyze data in order to solve a challenging problem. In one example, an entire classroom becomes a scaled-down simulation of an earthquake. As speakers play the sounds of an earthquake, the students can take readings on simulated seismographs at different locations in the room, inspect an emerging fault line, and stretch twine to identify the epicenter. Another example is Robot-Assisted Language Learning in Education (RALL-E), in which students learning Mandarin converse with a robot that exhibits a range of facial expressions and gestures, coupled with language dialogue software. Such robots will allow students to engage in a social role-playing experience with a new language without the usual anxieties of speaking a new language. The RALL-E also encourages cultural awareness while encouraging good use of language skills and building student confidence through practice.

- New ways to connect physical and virtual interactions with learning technologies that bridge the tangible and the abstract: For example, there is a molecules project that has students manipulate a physical ball-and-stick model of a molecule, while a camera senses the model and visualizes it with related scientific phenomena, such as the energy field around the molecule. Students' tangible engagement with a physical model is connected to more abstract, conceptual models, supporting students' growth of understanding. Toward a similar goal, elementary school students sketch pictures of mathematical situations by using a pen on a tablet surface with representational tools and freehand sketching, much as they would on paper. Unlike with paper, they easily copy, move, group, and transform their pictures and representations in ways that help them to express what they are learning about mathematics. These can be shared with the teacher, and, via artificial intelligence, the computer can help the teacher see patterns in the sketches and support the teacher's use of student expression as a powerful instructional resource.
- Interactive three-dimensional imaging software is creating potentially transformational learning experiences: With three-dimensional glasses and a stylus, students are able to work with a wide range of images from the layers of the Earth

to the human heart. This type of versatile technology allows students to work with objects schools typically would not be able to afford, thereby providing a richer, more engaging learning experience.

- Augmented reality (AR) as a new way of investigating our context and history: The Transforming Education Exploratory project researchers addressed how and for what purposes AR technologies can be used to support the learning of critical inquiry strategies and processes. Students can use a mobile device with AR to augment their field experience at a local historical site. In addition to experiencing the site as it exists, AR technology allows students to view and experience the site from several social perspectives and to view its structure and uses across several time periods. Research focuses on the potential of AR technology in inquiry-based fieldwork for disciplines in which analysis of change across time is important to promote understanding of how very small changes across long periods of time may add up to very large changes.[6]

The partnerships between teacher preparation programs and school districts are emblematic of the types of partnerships we will need to build across all education groups if we hope to increase the use of technology in learning from an add-on to an integral and foundational component of the education system. Technology should not be separate from content area learning but used to transform and expand pre- and in-service learning as an integral part of teacher learning. Our education system continues to see a marked increase in online learning opportunities and blended learning models. Institutions of higher education, school districts, classroom educators, and researchers need to come together to ensure practitioners have access to current information regarding research-supported practices and an understanding of the best use of emerging online technologies to support learning in online and blended spaces.[5]

8.5 Preventing Radicalization of Individuals

The most complex model of social engineering on the Internet has been the radicalization of individual citizens against their people or their government and their recruitment to violent extremism.

The ISIS model of recruitment and radicalization is a historically extreme example of how social engineering has been used by **international fanatics** to turn people into violent extremists who perform heinous acts of violence and crimes against humanity.

Successes in the war on terrorism and the arrests of many key al-Qaeda leaders diminished the ability of the group to attack the US homeland, but a Sunni extremist movement evolved from being run entirely by al-Qaeda central to a broader movement. Al-Qaeda and other groups remained committed to attacking the United States and are also attempting to broaden their appeal to English-speaking Western Muslims by disseminating socially engineered, violent, Islamic, extremist propaganda via media outlets and the Internet. The Islamic radicalization of US persons, whether foreign-born or native, has become an increasing concern. Radicalization by Islamic groups as well as white supremacy and other domestic hate and terror groups in the United States exist nationwide. Key to the success of stopping the spread of radicalization is identifying patterns and trends in the early stages.

The FBI defines domestic extremists as US persons who appeared to have assimilated, but in reality rejected the cultural values, beliefs, and environment of the United States. The threat from homegrown extremists is likely smaller in scale than that posed by overseas terrorist groups such as al-Qaeda but is potentially larger in psychological impact. Since 2005 the FBI, other federal agencies, and foreign partners have dismantled a global network of extremists who are operating independently of any known terrorist organization. Several individuals affiliated with this network were arrested for providing material support in connection with the plotting of a terrorist attack in the United States and other countries. The apparent increase of cases involving homegrown extremists may represent an increased sensitivity of law enforcement to activities not previously regarded as terrorism, but we cannot rule out the possibility that both the homegrown phenomenon and the increasing popularity of **domestic anti-social groups** and **domestic fanatics** are growing.

The Internet is a venue for the radicalization of young, computer-savvy Westerners (both male and female) who identify with the **hate messages** of extremist ideology and are sometimes eager to get involved in **ideological conflict**. An older generation of supporters and sympathizers of violent extremism, in the post-9/11 environment of increased law enforcement scrutiny, have migrated their radicalization, recruitment, and material support activities online. Radicalization via the Internet is participatory, and individuals are actively engaged in exchanging extremist propaganda and rhetoric online, which may facilitate the violent extremist cause and **ideologically motivated violence**. These online activities further their indoctrination, create links between extremists located around the world, and may serve as a springboard for future terrorist activities.[7]

Domestic terrorism is perpetrated by individuals and/or groups inspired by or associated with primarily US-based movements, such as the **sovereign citizens** that espouse extremist ideologies of a political, religious, social, racial, or environmental nature. For example, the June 8, 2014, Las Vegas shooting, during which two police officers inside a restaurant were killed in an ambush-style attack, was committed by a married couple who held anti-government views and who intended to use the shooting to start a revolution. The threat of domestic terrorism also remains persistent overall, with actors crossing the line from First Amendment protected rights to committing crimes to further their political agenda. Three factors have contributed to the evolution of the terrorism threat landscape:

- The Internet: International and domestic actors have developed an extensive presence on the Internet through messaging platforms and socially engineered online images, videos, and publications, which facilitate the groups' abilities to radicalize and recruit individuals receptive to extremist messaging. Such messages are constantly available to people participating in social networks dedicated to various causes, particularly younger people comfortable with communicating in the social media environment.
- Use of social media: In addition to using the Internet, social media has allowed both international and domestic terrorists to gain unprecedented, virtual access to people living in the United States in an effort to enable homeland attacks and support **recruiting and indoctrination** efforts. ISIS, in particular, encouraged sympathizers to carry out simple attacks where they were located against targets, and soft targets in

particular, or to travel to ISIS-held territory in Iraq and Syria and join its ranks as foreign fighters. This message has resonated with supporters in the United States and abroad, and several recent attackers have claimed to be acting on ISIS' behalf.

- Homegrown violent extremists (HVEs): The FBI must identify those sympathizers who have radicalized and become HVEs within the United States and who aspire to attack the nation from within. HVEs are defined by the Bureau as global-jihad-inspired individuals who are based in the United States, have been radicalized primarily in the United States, and are not directly collaborating with a foreign terrorist organization. Currently, the FBI is investigating suspected HVEs in every state.[8]

A February 2019 policy statement released from the White House recognized that the American public increasingly relies on the Internet for socializing, business transactions, gathering information, entertainment, and creating and sharing content. The rapid growth of the Internet has brought opportunities but also risks, and the federal government is committed to empowering members of the public to protect themselves against the full range of online threats, including online radicalization to violence.

Violent extremist supremacist groups and violent sovereign citizens are leveraging online tools and resources to propagate socially engineered messages of violence and division. These groups use the Internet to disseminate propaganda, identify and groom potential recruits, and supplement their real-world recruitment efforts. Some members and supporters of these groups visit mainstream social media websites to see whether individuals might be recruited or encouraged to commit acts of violence, look for opportunities to draw targets into private exchanges, and exploit popular media such as music videos and online video games. Although the Internet offers countless opportunities for Americans to connect, it has also provided violent extremists with access to new audiences and instruments for radicalization.

As a starting point to prevent online radicalization to violence in the homeland, the federal government will focus on raising awareness about the threat and providing communities with practical information and tools for staying safe online. In this process, the US government plans to work closely with the technology industry to consider policies, technologies, and tools that can help counter violent extremism online. Companies already have developed voluntary measures to promote Internet safety such as fraud warnings, identity protection, and Internet safety tips.

This approach is consistent with Internet safety principles that have helped keep communities safe from a range of online threats, such as cyber bullies, scammers, gangs, and sexual predators. While each of these threats is unique, experience has shown that a well-informed public, armed with tools and resources to stay safe online, is critical to protecting communities. Pursuing such an approach is also consistent with the community-based framework outlined in Empowering Local Partners to Prevent Violent Extremism in the United States and the Strategic Implementation Plan for Empowering Local Partners to Prevent Violent Extremism in the United States.

To organize efforts more effectively, the US government plans an Interagency Working Group to Counter Online Radicalization to Violence, established in early 2013 chaired by the National Security Staff at the White House and involving specialists in countering violent extremism, Internet safety experts, and civil liberties and privacy practitioners from across the US government. This working group is to be responsible for developing plans to implement an Internet safety approach to address online violent extremism, coordinating the federal government's activities, assessing progress against these plans, and identifying additional activities to pursue for countering online radicalization to violence. The working group will coordinate with federal departments and agencies to raise awareness and disseminate tools for staying safe from online violent extremism primarily through three means.

First, information about online violent extremism will be incorporated into existing federal government Internet safety initiatives. Internet safety initiatives at the Department of Education, the Federal Bureau of Investigation (FBI), the Federal Trade Commission (FTC), the Department of Homeland Security (DHS), and other agencies provide platforms that already reach millions of Americans, and relevant departments and agencies will work to add materials related to online radicalization.

The primary government platform for raising awareness about Internet safety is OnGuard Online, managed by the FTC and involving 16 departments and agencies, including the DHS, the Department of Justice (DOJ), and the Department of Education. OnGuard Online, in addition to other federal government Internet safety platforms like Stop.Think.Connect and Safe Online Surfing (SOS) will begin including information about online violent extremism. This information will also be posted on the Countering Violent Extremism home page on the Department of Homeland Security's website and updated to reflect new best practices and research.

Second, the federal government will work with local organizations throughout the country to disseminate information about the threat. One reason for the success of federal government Internet safety awareness efforts is that they work closely with local organizations such as school districts, parent teacher associations, local government, and law enforcement to communicate to communities. Law enforcement is a particularly important partner in raising awareness about radicalization to violence and is already developing materials with support from the DOJ. Law enforcement departments and agencies have established Internet safety programs and relationships with community members and local organizations that can reach multiple audiences with critical information about the threat of online violent extremism and recruitment. Departments and agencies will provide the latest assessments of this threat to local partners and encourage them to incorporate this information into their programs and initiatives.

Third, departments and agencies will use pre-existing engagement with communities to provide information about Internet safety and details about how violent extremists are using the Internet to target and exploit communities. US attorneys throughout the country, who historically have engaged with communities on a range of public safety issues, are coordinating these federal engagement efforts at the local level, with support from other departments and agencies, such as the Department of Homeland Security, the Department of Health and Human Services (HHS), and the Department of Education. US attorneys and others involved in community engagement will seek to incorporate information about Internet radicalization to violence into their efforts, as appropriate. At the same time, the federal government will engage with state, local and tribal government and law enforcement officials to learn from their experiences in addressing online threats, including violent extremism.

As the federal government implements this effort, agencies will continue to investigate and prosecute those who use the Internet to recruit others to plan or carry out acts of violence while ensuring that they continue to uphold individual privacy and civil liberties. Preventing online radicalization to violence requires both proactive solutions to reduce the likelihood that violent extremists affect their target audiences as well as ensuring that laws are rigorously enforced.[9]

8.6 FBI Kids

An area where the FBI excels in providing education for Internet safety is that of safety for children. Considering the many dangers that lurk on the Internet from child predators to cyber bullies, from malicious software to a multitude of scams, it's imperative that young people learn the ins and outs of online safety from an early age. That is precisely why the Bureau launched the FBI Safe Online Surfing Internet Challenge in October 2012 with a dedicated new website. FBI-SOS is a free, fun, and informative program that promotes cyber citizenship by educating students in third to eighth grades on the essentials of online security. For teachers, the site provides a ready-made curriculum that meets state and federal Internet safety mandates, complete with online testing and a national competition to encourage learning and participation. A secure online system enables teachers to register their schools, manage their classes, automatically grade their students' exams, and request the test scores.

The FBI-SOS website (https://www.fbi.gov/fbi-kids) features six islands, one for each grade level, with age-appropriate games, videos, and other interactive materials in various portals. The site covers such topics as cell phone safety, the protection of personal information, password strength, instant messaging, social networking, and online gaming safety. The videos include real-life stories of kids who have faced cyber bullies and online predators.

FBI-SOS includes a monthly competition among schools across the country. There are three categories based on how many students are participating. The ten highest scores in each category are shown

Table 8.3 Students Completing SOS Program

ACADEMIC YEAR	NUMBER OF STUDENTS
2012–2013	24,475
2013–2014	75,377
2014–2015	275,656
2015–2016	497,248
Total	872,756

on the leader board each month. When possible, winning schools in each category will receive a visit from a local FBI special agent. The popularity of the SOS online cyber program has grown over the past several school years as is shown in Table 8.3.

Once a teacher's account has been verified, they receive an email with a unique URL to manage their class, along with further instructions. The link never expires, so they do not need to register for FBI-SOS every year. Once they are registered, they can create classes and an access test key for each student. The FBI does not store any information on students, so it is the responsibility of the teacher to create the test keys and keep track of which test key they assigned to each student. Students will then navigate through the various games and activities in their grade-appropriate island. When students complete the last activity, they can click the Take the Test surfboard to take the exam.

At this point, students should be certain they are ready to complete the exam, as it may only be taken once. To take the exam, students need to enter the access key that is assigned to them. The exams are automatically graded once all students in a class have finished the test and teachers have clicked the Grade Exam button. Immediately after the test is taken, a temporary web page shows each student his or her score and a list of any questions answered incorrectly. Teachers can ask students to print and save this web page, and/or they can request the exam results of each class through the class management system. The class results show the individual scores by test key.

The overall scores for each school are compared with the results of other schools nationwide with similar classroom sizes as part of a national monthly competition. Categories are determined by the number of students participating from each school: Starfish is 1–50 participants, Stingray is 51–100 participants, and Shark is 100+ participants.

The ten highest scores in each of these categories during the month can be viewed on the leader board. Other than what is displayed on the leader board, the FBI does not keep or distribute the rankings of schools nationwide. The leader board resets at the end of each month.

The top-scoring school in each participation category nationwide every month from September through May is awarded an FBI-SOS certificate. Teachers from winning schools are also provided certificates that they can fill out and distribute to each student. There are no participation certificates for non-winning schools or students. When possible, the winning school in each category every month will receive a visit from a local FBI special agent. Schools can only participate in the competition once per school year.

SOS can be visited at any time in the classroom or at home, and students can work at their own pace in completing the island activities and exam. However, bear in mind that finishing the exam more quickly produces a higher score. The activities do not need to be completed in one sitting. While the FBI-SOS website is accessible all year, the testing and competition only operate from September 1 through May 31. There is no testing during the summer months.

The goal of FBI-SOS is to promote cyber citizenship and help students learn about online safety while engaging in fun, interactive games. The program was designed to address current Internet safety threats while keeping each grade level's online usage and knowledge in mind.

There is also a countering violent extremism (CVE) FBI Awareness Program for Teens entitled Don't Be a Puppet: Pull Back the Curtain on Violent Extremism. It's the FBI's primary responsibility, working with its many partners, to protect the nation from attacks by violent extremists. One important way to do that is to keep young people from embracing violent extremist ideologies in the first place.

This website is designed to help do just that. Built by the FBI in consultation with community leaders and other partners, it uses a series of interactive materials to educate teens on the destructive nature of violent extremism and to encourage them to think critically about its messages and goals. The site emphasizes that by blindly accepting radical ideologies, teens are essentially becoming the puppets of violent extremists who simply want them to carry out their destructive mission which often includes targeting or killing innocent people (https://www.fbi.gov/cve508/teen-website).

The FBI encourages community groups, families, and high schools across the United States to use this site as part of their educational efforts. All Americans are asked to join the FBI in exposing the seductive nature of violent extremist propaganda and offering positive alternatives to violence. The site has five main sections that each teen must complete to successfully finish the program:

- What is Violent Extremism?
- Why Do People Become Violent Extremists?
- What are Known Violent Extremist Groups?
- How Do Violent Extremists Make Contact?
- Who Do Violent Extremists Affect?

After completing the first five sections, teens are asked to review a final section, Where to Get Help and then print and sign (by hand) a certificate of completion. The FBI will use the certificate link as a metric collection tool to count how many people successfully complete the program but will not track or store any user information when doing so. This program includes some general information on the freedoms guaranteed by the First Amendment to the US Constitution and the limits to these freedoms. The FBI suggests that teachers talk about this subject in more depth before they begin the program. The FBI also recommends that teachers be available to discuss the materials while teens are using the site or after they have completed the program. Other organizations can also consider incorporating the site into safety briefings and anti-bullying programs.

It is important for teachers to emphasize that the examples of violent extremism presented in the program represent fringe ideologies and should not be confused with the beliefs of any mainstream religious, ethnic, or political group. Providing appropriate context is important to ensure that no one uses material from this program as an excuse to bully or exclude others.

This website does not retain a teen's progress in the program once his or her web browser has been closed or the computer has been shut down. As a result, this program must be fully completed in one session or sitting. One section of this website contains videos that are streamed through YouTube. If an organization blocks YouTube on its computers, make sure to remove this restriction before teens begin the online program. Registration is not required to use this website. The FBI does not accept or store any names or other personally identifiable information in this site.[10]

On November 30, 2017, Acting Secretary of Homeland Security Elaine Duke announced the transition of the Office for Community Partnerships (OCP) to the Office of Terrorism Prevention Partnerships (OTPP). The mission of the OTPP is to enhance education and community awareness regarding the threat, provide resources as appropriate to terrorism prevention stakeholders, coordinate relevant DHS terrorism prevention activities, actively counter terrorist radicalization and recruitment, and promote early warning so that frontline defenders can intervene to stop attacks and help prevent individuals from going down the path to violence. The OTPP is the primary source of leadership, innovation, and support for the improved effectiveness of partners at federal, state, local, tribal, and territorial levels. It also leverages the resources and relationships of the Department of Homeland Security and applies the personal leadership of the secretary to empower leaders in both the public and private sectors to spur societal change to counter violent extremism.

The OTPP implements a full range of partnerships to support and enhance efforts by law enforcement, faith leaders, local government officials, and communities to prevent radicalization and recruitment by terrorist organizations. The OTPP also provides these stakeholders with training and technical assistance to develop CVE prevention programs in support of resilient communities. The OTPP leads the Department's CVE mission with the following objectives:

- Community engagement. The OTPP works with the Office for Civil Rights and Civil Liberties to facilitate community engagements to build awareness and promote dialogue with community partners, which includes engagements with DHS senior leadership.
- Field support expansion and training. The OTPP supports DHS field staff across the country to develop and strengthen local partnerships and to provide training opportunities.
- Grant support. The OTPP worked with the Federal Emergency Management Agency (FEMA) to provide $10

million in grants to community-based programs under the FY2016 Countering Violent Extremism Grant Program. Those projects have a period of performance that runs through July 2019.

- Philanthropic engagement. The OTPP works with the philanthropic community to maximize support for local communities, and encourage long-term partnerships;
- Tech sector engagement. The OTPP engages the tech sector to identify and amplify credible voices online and promote **counter-narratives to radicalization** and against violent extremist messaging.[11]

8.7 Conclusion

Preventing social engineering attacks from being successful requires that computer users remain aware and practice safe Internet habits. The collection of tips sheets offered up by various organizations and government agencies have certainly been helpful in reducing the number and the effectiveness of social engineering attacks for those people that have read them and follow their advice. However, millions of people around the world continue to be victimized, which clearly indicates that education efforts need to be greatly expanded and modernized.

8.8 Key Points

Key points covered in this chapter include:

- There are several different social engineering attack methods and goals that make awareness campaigns and education programs challenging to develop.
- In addition to usefulness and distribution shortcomings, most tip sheets and advice on social engineering attack prevention are bland, shallow, and less than effective.
- A one-size-fits-all approach to education and awareness building is not adequate to teach people to defend against social engineering attacks.
- Persuasion and sway campaign attacks are more complex and the social engineering is more sophisticated.

- Social engineering attacks designed toward radicalization of individuals politically, socially, or behaviorally is more effective on people who have a predisposition toward hatred, racism, anarchy, violence, and anti-social behavior in general.
- There is a need to teach voters how to identify socially engineered biased news media and social media activity in order to educate them on how to identify reliable objective information being emitted from campaign sources.
- If the United States, and, in fact, the world, is going to really make an effort to fight back against social engineering attacks, there will need to be considerably more effort put forth in the education endeavor.
- There is more than one way people learn, which means there must be multiple ways to teach the same message to effectively reach a greater number of people.
- Personalized learning refers to instruction in which the pace of learning and the instructional approach are optimized for the needs of each learner.
- In a blended learning environment, learning occurs online and in person, augmenting and supporting teacher practice. This approach often allows students to have some control over time, place, path, or pace of learning including the use of visual content.
- The most complex model of social engineering on the Internet has been the radicalization of individual citizens against their people or their government and their recruitment to violent extremism.

8.9 Seminar Discussion Topics

Discussion topics for graduate- or professional-level seminars are:

- What experience have seminar participants had in situations where they or somebody they know were victims of a social engineering attack? What did they do to recover from the attack?
- Discuss the viewpoints of participants toward the information on the Internet that advises people how to prevent social engineering attacks.

- Discuss why the participants think that the government does not invest more in educating people about the various types of social engineering attacks presented in Figure 8.1: Types of Social Engineering Attacks.

8.10 Seminar Group Project

Divide participants into multiple groups with each group taking 10 to 15 minutes to develop a list of methods to educate people about the social engineering attacks presented in Figure 8.1: Types of Social Engineering Attacks. Upon completion have groups exchange their lists of methods and taking 10 to 15 minutes to critic and synthesize lists. Meet as a class and discuss the how the groups original list may have been modified after reviewing the list from other groups.

Key Terms

Alternative master narratives: are designed to replace violent extremist narrative by offering an entire cultural, political, or social philosophy that eliminates the appeal of the extremist narrative.

Counter-messaging: is the process of matching radical extremist messages on a head-to-head basis in order to mitigate the recruitment and radicalization to violent extremism.

Counter-narrative to radicalization: is a narrative that neutralizes or invalidates the narrative designed to radicalize individuals or groups.

Credible voices: are those voices of trusted community leaders, religious leaders, and intellectuals that can provide a positive influence on a society or community.

Deceptive marketing: advertising or propaganda that misleads people regarding the true facts about a product, service, or corporate activity.

Disinformation: is false and irrelevant information made available in order to deceive.

Domestic anti-social groups: are groups of people or mini-societies that oppose the larger society in which they live and/or work.

Domestic fanatics: are radical groups that are residents or citizens of the countries in which they kill, sabotage, or spread hate and fear.

Hate messages: are social media posts that use obnoxious language to ridicule or discriminate against minority or ethnic groups.

Ideological conflict: is the conflict perpetuated by radicalized groups against mainstream society and minority groups.

Ideologically motivated violence: is violence that individuals or groups perpetrate toward targets because of their belief that those individuals or groups are inferior in some way and should be harmed or exterminated.

International fanatics: are individuals, groups of people, or mini-societies that are greatly differentiated from the world around them by a belief system that is totally disconnected from the larger realities in which they live and have a tendency to act out those differences in violent ways or in a politically or economically disruptive manner. They are members of radical groups that cross borders or influence individuals or groups in other countries to kill, sabotage, or spread hate and fear.

News feed: is a constantly updated, highly personalized list of stories, including status updates, photos, videos, links, and activities from the people and things an individual is connected to on Facebook. The goal of news feed is to show people the stories that are most relevant to them.

Political correctness: the use of non-biased non-discriminatory words, phrases, or images to communicate ideas or messages.

Positive message promotional activities: are those that promote positive social behavior and counter negative messaging.

Radicalization: is the process indoctrinating previously non-violent individuals or groups into anti-social violent ideologies and actions.

Recruiting and indoctrination: is the process of drawing people into a cause and teaching cause-related doctrine.

Social media presence: is an organization's use of social media accounts and applications to communicate to individuals or groups as well as the mention, comments, discussions, and display of any material on any social media application that relates to or depicts an organization.

Sovereign citizens: are anti-government extremists who believe that even though they physically reside in this country, they are separate or "sovereign" from the United States. As a result, they believe that they don't have to answer to any government authority, including courts, taxing entities, motor vehicle departments, or law enforcement.

Visual content: is any photo, video, or illustration added to social media posts.

References

1. Voting and Registration 2016. US Census Bureau. Accessed February 26, 2019. https://www2.census.gov/programs-surveys/demo/tables/voting/UnitedStates.xlsx
2. Reported Voting and Registration Among Native and Naturalized Citizens, by Race, Hispanic Origin, and Region of Birth: November 2016. Accessed February 26, 2019. https://www2.census.gov/programs-surveys/cps/tables/p20/580/table11.xlsx
3. 7 Tips to Strengthen Voter Education Programs. US Election Assistance Commission. July 2014. Accessed February 26, 2019. https://www.eac.gov/assets/1/28/EducatingVoters%5B3%5D-508%20Compliant.pdf
4. Online Safety. USA.gov.. Accessed February 27, 2019. https://www.usa.gov/online-safety#item-37272
5. National Education Technology Plan. US Department of Education, Office of Educational Technology (OET). Accessed February 28, 2019. https://tech.ed.gov/netp/#
6. Section 1: Engaging and Empowering Learning Through Technology. National Education Technology Plan. US Department of Education, Office of Educational Technology. Accessed February 28, 2019. https://tech.ed.gov/netp/learning/
7. Testimony of Donald Van Duyn, Deputy Assistant Director, Counterterrorism Division, Federal Bureau of Investigation Before the House Homeland Security Committee, Subcommittee on Intelligence, Information Sharing, and Terrorism Risk Assessment. Washington, DC. September 20, 2006. Accessed March 1, 2019, https://archives.fbi.gov/archives/news/testimony/islamic-radicalization
8. Terrorism. Federal Bureau of Investigation. Accessed March 1, 2019. https://www.fbi.gov/investigate/terrorism
9. Online Safety for Youth: Working to Counter Online Radicalization to Violence in the United States. Youth.gov. Accessed March 1, 2019. https://youth.gov/feature-article/online-safety-youth-working-counter-online-radicalization-violence-united-states
10. FBI Kids. Federal Bureau of Investigation. Accessed March 2, 2019. https://www.fbi.gov/fbi-kids.
11. Terrorism Prevention Partnerships. Department of Homeland Security. Accessed March 2, 2019. https://www.dhs.gov/terrorism-prevention-partnerships.

9

THE ASCENT OF CYBER DARKNESS

Humans seem to have a way of trashing and destroying everything they touch. The global environment is polluted in every way possible (e.g., people over-produce and dump waste into the water, burn coal and release toxins in the air, use open-air trash dumps). Many nations are dominated by dictators and military regimes and free press is being restricted around the world so that greedy and masochistic monsters can control wealth, people, and even thought. Racism, sexism, xenophobia, Islamophobia, homophobia, religious oppression, sexual exploitation, violence, animal cruelty, and bad manners are rampant around the globe and are even supported by many world leaders. So the habits then moved into cyberspace. Those people who have done bad deeds and evil acts in the physical world have unfortunately brought their inhumanity to cyberspace and found a place where they can thrive, virtually unhindered. Without drastic, well-directed action things in cyberspace will continue to deteriorate.

9.1 The Evolution of Cyber Threats and Vulnerabilities

Admiral Michael S. Rogers, General Counsel for the National Security Agency (NSA) in a 2017 keynote address at the Law, Ethics and National Security Conference at Duke Law School, North Carolina, summarized the state of the Internet and commented on the future of cyber threats. He observed that there had been a proliferation of high-profile intrusions against US companies, and emphasized that malicious cyber activity will forever be associated with the 2016 election cycle.

He also commented on the evolution of cyber threats and discussed the many forms that cyber vulnerability can take. It was not that long ago, he contended, that cybersecurity simply meant deleting emails from a Nigerian prince who needed your help in making a bank deposit. Beyond basic email hygiene, there are threats to entire networks. True, the network owner can take extra precautions to secure the network, but that security can be undermined by one user who connects to it with an infected device or downloads a spear phishing email is worrisome. Network threats by definition can be as serious as the criticality of the infrastructure or equipment controlled by the network or the sensitivity of the information conveyed by the network.

Admiral Rogers pointed out that a great deal of time and attention had already been spent assessing today's cyber threat. Study after study has echoed the gravity of cybersecurity vulnerability. Experts agree that the threat is so grave because barriers to entry and the risk of getting caught for mischief are extremely low while potential rewards are great. Malicious cyber tools are cheap and widely available on the Internet. One lone actor with few resources now has the power to wreak havoc on a network anonymously. Cybercrimes are notoriously hard to track and attribution can be challenging at best. These same studies typically put malicious cyber activity into one of three categories. First, there is cybercrime, in which criminals are seeking money outright or something else of value to resell, such as credit card numbers, tax IDs, and social security numbers, or in which they hold corporate data for ransom. The second category is cyber espionage, which typically involves nation-states and includes both political espionage and espionage for commercial gain, such as the theft of trade secrets for economic advantage. And third, there is general cyber mischief, which includes hacktivists who use cyber vulnerabilities to spread propaganda, like ISIS, and those who seek to disrupt services or sites.[1]

In April 2018, NSA General Counsel Glenn Gerstell presented remarks on How We Need to Prepare for a Global Cyber Pandemic at The Cipher Brief Threat Conference, at Sea Island, Georgia. He told a story that, in the early 1990s, an enterprising hot dog vendor in Russia seized upon the entrepreneurial opportunities created by the collapse of the Soviet Union to start his own catering company. He eventually grew his business and his restaurants and threw opulent banquets for Kremlin officials, earning him the nickname Putin's Cook. Yevgeny Prigozhin's company even won a contract in 2011 to deliver school lunches across Moscow, but children would not eat the food, complaining that it smelled rotten. Bad publicity ensued. Prigozhin's company responded, not by upgrading the food, but by hiring people to flood the Internet with postings praising the food and rejecting complaints. Presumably, they found it cheaper to use the Internet to write fake reviews than to fund good quality hot dogs for schoolchildren.

Then, not many years later, and perhaps building upon this experience, Prigozhin and his companies funded and largely controlled an organization, which began in 2013 or 2014, called the Internet Research Agency (IRA). In the IRA's office building in St. Petersburg, hundreds of individuals worked around the clock as Internet content producers. Although the IRA's original agenda was the online spread of pro-Russia and pro-Putin propaganda, that agenda quickly expanded westward.

With an annual budget of hundreds of millions of dollars, the IRA began to engage in a widespread and concerted campaign aimed at the United States. They socially engineered and created fictitious US personas on social media platforms that were designed to attract US audiences and sow discord regarding divisive US political and social issues. They used stolen social security numbers, home addresses, and birth dates of real US persons to open banking accounts to pay for expenses and to collect money from US citizens, and they produced and paid for political advertisements on US social media, concealing their true identity.

Mr. Gerstell further commented that the details of the story he shared were from allegations made in newspaper articles and publicly available criminal charging documents filed against some of the main players in the IRA's scheme. Prigozhin, the IRA, and several other Russian individuals and companies associated with the organization were indicted by Special Counsel Robert Mueller. The ultimate aim of this Russian Internet troll factory, according to that indictment, was to impair, obstruct, and defeat the lawful functions of the US government through fraud and deceit for the purpose of interfering with the US political and electoral processes, including the presidential election of 2016. The defendants were charged with conspiracy to defraud the US; conspiracy to commit wire and bank fraud; and aggravated identity theft. The indictment highlights the lengths to which sophisticated nation-states will rely upon cyberspace to carry out their objectives. These allegations reflect a threat beyond just routine cybercrime and mischief; indeed, if true, they represent an attempt to strategically undermine institutions critical to the functioning of a democracy, and, at their core, they underscore the vulnerabilities created by our digital lives.

Mr. Gerstell then contended that 2018 represented another year in which the intelligence community (IC) had highlighted the gravity of the cyber threat in its annual worldwide threat assessment. That assessment reported that over 30 countries were then believed to possess cyber attack capabilities. This number, which had increased almost every year since 2007, reflected the ease with which malicious cyber actors could obtain and deploy cyber weapons. Cyberspace has proven to be a relatively accessible vector in which to carry out malicious activities, and so less sophisticated nation-states and criminal actors were becoming better equipped in the use of cyber tool kits. China, Iran, North Korea, and Russia were seen as the nation-states posing the greatest cyber threat to the United States. The IC predicted that Russia, which has previously acted with impunity in this sphere, would conduct bolder and more disruptive cyber operations in the future.

Mr. Gerstell warned that the threats posed by malicious cyber activity had now combined with even greater toxicity to present unprecedented challenges across personal, professional, and political lives in the United States in a way that was hard to overstate. History and people's own experiences have taught that the gravity, and perhaps the probability, of risks can collectively be underestimated, and that, as a society, people react only after a crisis or calamity. Several governments worried about secret surveillance by perceived adversary countries have begun banning electronic products from those countries, resulting in a global technology trade war.

One conclusion Mr. Gerstell made was that a national cyber strategy would not be successful unless it facilitated engagement among the public sector, private companies, and other governments on cybersecurity. Importantly, educational efforts should be aimed at various types of audiences. For example, individual users might be most in need of tips and best practices for securing home networks and personal devices, while corporate network owners could benefit more from technical information tailored to their specific industry.

The United Kingdom had started to make great strides in this area. Recognizing the need to speak directly to different types of audiences, the UK's National Cybersecurity Centre had been issuing guidance tailored for readers of differing levels of sophistication. For example, the US's National Counterintelligence and Security Center (NCSC) had posted commonsense guidance for everyday Internet users about how to implement meaningful password protection while avoiding cybersecurity fatigue, the recently documented phenomenon in which individuals are feeling overwhelmed by the scope of the cyber threat and frustrated with complex cybersecurity guidance. On another end of the spectrum, they also recently posted information for local authorities about securing systems supporting local elections.

Mr. Gerstell's third and final point was that the federal government was a necessary, but not sufficient, participant in a unified cyber strategy. Indeed, when discussing how best to address the cyber threat, much importance had been given to the need for a whole-of-government approach. Yet, even at its most effective, the US government could not stand alone in securing the most critical systems while cyber vulnerabilities abound in other networks and systems not under government control. What was truly needed, he explained, could be more aptly described as a **whole-of-users approach**. Those users include, on one level or another, other nations, private-sector network owners, and even everyday citizen users of cyber technologies.

To date, the US government has played a leading role in defending against and responding to malicious international cyber activity, whether acting alone or in concert with close allies like the United Kingdom. The United States also employs non-cyber tools, such as sanctions, public attribution, criminal charges, and extradition, in its responses to such activity. It would be helpful if other nations recognized the global nature of the problem and took a multilateral approach to cyber threat response.

In general, the private sector is well aware of the seriousness of the cyber threat, and some industries, such as the financial and electronic sector, have invested significant time and resources into shoring up their critical components and networks. There are many individuals and small businesses, however, who might not have the resources to invest in upgrading and maintaining expensive equipment, or access to trained personnel who could provide cybersecurity services, or who might be confused by complicated cybersecurity guidance, or simply think that they are too small to be a target. However, some private network owners, including those who control critical infrastructure are too often willing to accept some security risks in their networks that would be unacceptable to the government.

In closing, Mr. Gerstell prophesized that the enormity of these challenges could not be overstated. Malefactors of cybercrime would, in all probability, be ever more successful before society would be able to blunt or negate this threat. But this very probability, the sheer foreseeability of possible and grave harm, underscores the need for society to do more to counter this almost existential threat. The chosen alternative has been to wait until one cyber incident after another forces the adoption of piecemeal solutions to what was actually an overarching issue that should be addressed through a comprehensive approach. He contended that the United States needed to own this problem that the people have created, and take aggressive steps to manage it before a calamity occurred. After all, with a tool as accessible, cost-effective, and easy to use as cyberspace, the United States just could not predict from which hot dog cart the next big attack would emerge.[2]

9.2 Nationwide Cybercrime Sweeps are Impressive but not Enough

The Department of Justice (DOJ), Federal Bureau of Investigation (FBI), Federal Trade Commission (FTC), Securities and Exchange Commission (SEC), and other law enforcement agencies have made some very impressive and dramatic takedowns of cybercrime gangs and conspiracies. Announcements of these sweeps are made with great fanfare and claims of massive success. The major problem with the drama and New Year's Eve style blowout horns is that these really do not do much to stop cybercrime and the continued ascent of darkness in cyberspace. Cybercriminals and social engineers continue to replicate themselves and do so very rapidly after gangs are rounded up in large sweeps.

In March of 2019, the DOJ announced that it had coordinated the largest-ever nationwide **elder fraud** sweep, claiming that the cases during this sweep involved more than 260 defendants from around the globe who victimized more than two million Americans, most of them elderly. The DOJ took action in every federal district across the country, through the filing of criminal or civil cases or through consumer education efforts. In each case, the offender(s) allegedly engaged in financial schemes that targeted or largely affected seniors. In total, the charged elder fraud schemes caused the alleged loss of millions of dollars. It is important to note that the charges are allegations, and the defendants are presumed innocent unless and until proven guilty beyond a reasonable doubt in a court of law, and the actual amount of fraud will take several years to determine as the defendants go through the court system. As part of the sweep, the law enforcement partners announced a tech-support fraud takedown, designed to combat an increasingly common form of elder fraud in which criminals trick victims into giving remote access to their computers under the guise of providing technical support.

At the announcement Attorney General Barr was joined by FBI Deputy Director David L. Bowdich; Executive Associate Director Derek Benner for US Immigration and Customs Enforcement's Homeland Security Investigations (HSI); FTC Chairman Joseph Simons; Louisiana Attorney General and President of the National Association of Attorneys General Jeff Landry; Director Randolph Alles of the Secret Service; Chief Postal Inspector Gary Barksdale; Barbara Stewart, CEO of the Corporation for National and Community Service; and former FBI director and CIA director Judge Webster and Lynda Webster. Since the Elder Abuse Prevention and Prosecution Act (EAPPA) became law, these departments have participated in hundreds of enforcement actions in criminal and civil cases that targeted or disproportionately affected seniors.

Many of the cases brought as part of the 2019 elder fraud sweep, including many of the technical-support fraud cases, allegedly involved transnational criminal organizations. During the sweep period, defendants in elder fraud cases were extradited from Canada, the Cayman Islands, Costa Rica, Jamaica, and Poland. In addition, there was action taken against over 600 alleged money mules working in the money mule network that facilitates foreign-based elder fraud, and Secret Service agents aided these efforts by seizing and forfeiting elder fraud proceeds in transit from victims to perpetrators.

The law enforcement partners focused the sweep's public education campaign on technical-support fraud, given the widespread harm such schemes are causing. The FTC and state attorneys general had an important role in designing and disseminating messaging material intended to warn consumers and businesses. Public education outreach is being conducted by various state and federal agencies, including Senior Corps, a national service program administered by the federal agency, the Corporation for National and Community Service, to educate seniors and prevent further victimization. The Senior Corps program engages more than 245,000 older adults in intensive service each year, who in turn, serve more than 840,000 additional seniors, including 332,000 veterans. However, there is a long way to go in this education effort.

The sweep announced benefited greatly from the work of the International Mass-Marketing Fraud Working Group (IMMFWG), a network of civil and criminal law enforcement agencies from Belgium, Canada, Europol, the Netherlands, Norway, Spain, the United Kingdom, and the United States. The IMMFWG is co-chaired by the DOJ and the FTC in the United States and law enforcement in the United Kingdom. It serves as a model for international cooperation against specific threats that endanger the financial well-being of each member country's residents. Due to the IMMFWG's network of law enforcement, simultaneous technical-support fraud consumer education campaigns are being released in Canada, the Netherlands, the United Kingdom, and the United States.[3]

9.3 The Man Who Knew About Social Engineering and Fraud

On the same day that the announcement was made on the 2019 elder fraud sweep, another story was posted on the FBI website about a man who helped bust elder fraud conspiracies. It is a great story. The heavily accented caller who promised William Webster a grand sweepstakes prize of $72 million and a new Mercedes Benz had done most of his homework on his potential fraud target. What the caller, Keniel Thomas, 29, of Jamaica, missed was possibly the most salient detail about his intended victim, who was 90 years old at the time: William Webster had served as director of both the FBI and the CIA, and so had a pretty good radar for pernicious criminal schemes; in this case, a Jamaican lottery scam.

"I know that you was [sic] a judge, you was a lawyer, you was in the US Navy," the caller told his elderly mark. "I do your background check. You are a big man."

Thomas's persistent calls in 2014 to Webster and his wife, Lynda, followed the familiar arc of scams that target the elderly: The caller promises riches but requires some form of payment to move the process forward. The caller demands more and more and then resorts to intimidation when the cooperation tapers off. In the Websters' case, the former judge was told he had to pay $50,000 to get his prize. When the money was not forthcoming, the frequent calls escalated to scary threats, which led the couple to contact the FBI.

"I don't know how the conversation turned sour," said Webster, director of the FBI for a decade beginning in 1978. "But it did. And at that point, he shifted gears. Instead of sweet talk, he began to threaten Mrs. Webster." In one expletive-filled recorded message left on the Websters' phone, Thomas threatened to kill them and burn down their house if he didn't get what he wanted. "You live at a very lonely place," he said. "And the moment you arrive, I'm gonna put a shot in your head."

Special agents from the FBI's Washington Field Office enlisted the Webster's help in nabbing the caller by recording their phone conversations to build a case and develop a clear picture of the scheme. The legwork ultimately led to Thomas' arrest in 2017. He was sentenced in 2019 by the Federal Court in Washington, DC, to nearly six years in prison. It also revealed that Thomas and his relatives in Jamaica had successfully scammed others in the United States out of hundreds of thousands of dollars.

Special Agent John Gardner, who was assigned to the case and had been investigating these types of crimes since 2011, said the perpetrators frequently prey on older people because they tend to be more trusting, financially secure, and lonely. The fraudsters buy and trade lead lists on the Internet with senior citizens' names, phone numbers, and other personal information. Then they start calling, hoping to reach receptive unwary ears. Gardner said scammers can be ruthless, squeezing money from their victims and then, when the money runs out, getting their victims to serve as middlemen in illegal transactions.

Lynda Webster, 63, said she and her husband frequently get suspicious calls, likely because of their demographic. William Webster said the entire experience of getting calls, working with the FBI, and seeing his tormentor in court is a reminder that seniors and the trusted friends and family who look after them need to be vigilant.[4]

9.4 Law Enforcement Training on Cybercrimes

The Webster case shows that the bad guys can indeed be caught and sent to prison. One problem that is very difficult if not impossible to overcome is there is not enough law enforcement personnel in the United States to investigate every complaint and every case until the criminals are caught and prosecuted. Each year, law enforcement agencies across the United States report the total number of sworn law enforcement officers and civilians in their agencies as of October 31 to the Uniform Crime Report Program. In 2017, there were 956,941 law enforcement employees of whom 670,279 were law enforcement officers.

In 2017, a total of 13,128 law enforcement agencies provided data on the number of full-time law enforcement employees (sworn officers and civilian personnel) on staff. Nationwide, the rate of sworn officers was 2.4 per 1,000 inhabitants. The rate of full-time law enforcement employees (civilian and sworn) per 1,000 inhabitants was 3.4.[5]

Cybercrime training is a special topic included in 57% of basic law enforcement training programs in state and local law enforcement training academies according to the Bureau of Justice Statistics 2013 census of academies. The academies that provided such training had an average of three hours of cybercrime training in their programs.[6]

The National Computer Forensic Institute (NCFI) is a federally funded training center dedicated to instructing state and local officials in digital evidence and cybercrime investigations. The NCFI was opened in 2008 with a mandate to provide state and local law enforcement, legal, and judicial professionals a free, comprehensive education on current cybercrime trends, investigative methods, and prosecutorial and judicial challenges. Run by the US Secret Service's Criminal Investigative Division and the Alabama Office of Prosecution Services, the training model is based upon the Secret Service's successful cyber investigative strategy, which relies on partnering with and sharing information between academia, private industry, and law enforcement/legal communities to combat the ever-evolving threat of cybercrime. The curriculum reflects current trends in the field and addresses potential technological obstacles as they are encountered in active investigations. The Social Networking Investigations (SNI) course is a five-day course, which offers investigators insight and practical experience regarding online investigations associated with social media, email, and basic networking, as well as legal issues and search and seizure procedures.[7]

The Federal Law Enforcement Training Center (FLETC) provides career-long training to law enforcement professionals to help them fulfill their responsibilities safely and proficiently. The Cyber Incident Response and Analysis (CIRA) course is 11 days of training designed to ensure evidence is located, preserved, and analyzed, with details on how to analyze evidence collected from cyber incidents. These incidents may be from simple log files on a home router to enterprise-level network witness devices. The program also focuses on the common methods used by criminals to access computer systems through phishing emails and malware, and includes scanning for vulnerabilities and the examination of network traffic. An applicant must be a law enforcement officer/agent with arrest authority in the prevention, detection, apprehension, detention, and/or investigation of felony and/or misdemeanor violations of federal, state, local, tribal, or military criminal laws. The student is expected to have attended the Seized Computer Evidence Recovery Specialist training program along with the Digital Evidence Collection in an Enterprise Environment training program and/or have experience performing forensic examinations and an understanding of network topology/traffic along with the ability to capture RAM and use various virtual machines. This program does not cover the basic uses of forensic tools, imaging computer systems, their RAM, or the collection of log files.[8]

The National Initiative for Cybersecurity Careers and Studies (NICCS) is an online resource for cybersecurity training. NICCS connects government employees, students, educators, and industry with cybersecurity training providers. The catalog lists the Certified Expert in Cyber Investigations (CECI) program offered by the McAfee Institute, which is an online self-paced course with a six-month Professional Board Certification, focused on how to conduct successful cyber investigations. This program contains over 500 video-based lectures resulting in hundreds of hours of online training, online prep review quizzes to prepare for the final exam, and, of course, the necessary study manuals to help the student along the way.[9]

9.5 Conclusions

The Internet has grown to be an integral part of society, providing numerous benefits to individuals, businesses, government, and human services. It has also ascended into a very dark place supporting criminal enterprises, racist attitudes and activities, electronic aggression, propaganda, disinformation, and misinformation. Evil has found a happy home in cyberspace. The Internet did not create this evil; the Internet just reflects the evil that exists in the hearts and minds of people.

9.6 Key Points

Key points covered in this chapter include:

- Cyber threats continue to evolve as new applications and technologies that can be exploited by deplorable people become available.
- Without intervention, the future of the Internet may be so infiltrated by crime and exploitation of various types that it will become a burden to society rather than an asset.
- Educating Internet users to identify and avoid cyber threats is essential to keeping people safe when online.
- Law enforcement agencies can coordinate efforts and successfully apprehend cybercriminals but even more cybercriminals step up to replace those prosecuted and incarcerated.
- Many of the cases brought as part of the 2019 elder fraud sweep, including many of the technical-support fraud cases, allegedly involved transnational criminal organizations.
- One obstacle to policing the Internet is that there are more victims than there are law enforcement personnel ready and able to investigate the thousands of cases of fraud and abuse.

9.7 Seminar Discussion Topics

Discussion topics for graduate- or professional-level seminars are:

- Discuss how participants view the future of the Internet and what can be done to assure that the future is a positive one.

- Discuss how law enforcement and educational outreach can be improved and who should participate in the outreach programs.
- Discuss the views of the participants toward the action or lack of action on the part of the US Congress to improve online safety.

9.8 Seminar Group Project

Participants should each interview five people outside of the seminar group to determine their views about online safety or the lack of online safety. Write up the results of the interviews in 500 words or less and discuss those results in a group setting.

Key Terms

Elder fraud: criminal activity focused on extorting or exploiting elderly people on or off the Internet.

Whole-of-users approach: refers to an organized effort of all Internet users, regardless of whether they are organizations, groups, or individuals, to participate in creating and maintaining online safety.

References

1. Confronting the Cybersecurity Challenge—Keynote Address. Admiral Michael S. Rogers, General Counsel for the National Security Agency. 2017 Law, Ethics, and National Security Conference at Duke Law School. February. 25, 2017. Accessed March 4, 2019. https://www.nsa.gov/news-features/speeches-testimonies/Article/1619236/confronting-the-cybersecurity-challenge-keynote-address/
2. How We Need to Prepare for a Global Cyber Pandemic. Glenn Gerstell, General Counsel for the National Security Agency. Remarks at The Cipher Brief Threat Conference, Sea Island, Georgia. April 9, 2018. Accessed March 5, 2019, https://www.nsa.gov/news-features/speeches-testimonies/Article/1611673/how-we-need-to-prepare-for-a-global-cyber-pandemic/
3. Justice Department Coordinates Largest-Ever Nationwide Elder Fraud Sweep. Attorney General Focuses on Threats Posed by Technical-Support Fraud. Department of Justice, Office of Public Affairs. March 7, 2019. Accessed March 9, 2019. https://www.justice.gov/opa/pr/justice-department-coordinates-largest-ever-nationwide-elder-fraud-sweep-0

4. Foiling an Elder Fraud Scam Former FBI Director Webster Assists Investigation. News Stories. Federal Bureau of Investigation. March 7, 2019. Accessed March 9, 2019. https://www.fbi.gov/news/stories/former-fbi-director-william-webster-helps-foil-fraudster-030719

5. 2017 Crime in the United States Full-Time Law Enforcement Employees. FBI Criminal Justice Information Services Division. Accessed March 9, 2019. https://ucr.fbi.gov/crime-in-the-u.s/2017/crime-in-the-u.s.-2017/tables/table-74

6. State and Local Law Enforcement Training Academies, 2013. Bureau of Justice Statistics, State, and Local Law Enforcement Training Academies, 2013 Reaves, Brian A. July 2016. Accessed March 10, 2019. https://www.bjs.gov/index.cfm?ty=pbdetail&iid=5684

7. About. National Computer Forensic Institute. Accessed March 10, 2019. https://www.ncfi.usss.gov/ncfi/pages/news.xhtml?dswid=-3042

8. Cyber Incident Response and Analysis. Federal Law Enforcement Training Centers. Accessed March 10, 2019. https://www.fletc.gov/cyber-incident-response-and-analysis/cyber-incident-response-and-analysis#

9. Certified Expert in Cyber Investigations. National Initiative for Cybersecurity Careers and Studies. Accessed March 10, 2019. https://niccs.us-cert.gov/training/search/mcafee-institute/certified-cyber-investigative-expert-ccie

Glossary

Acceptable use policy: is a document that establishes an agreement between users and the enterprise and defines for all parties the ranges of use that are approved before users can gain access to a network or the Internet.

Access control for computer systems: is a process that either allows or disallows individual users to have access to specific computer applications and computer datasets including what the user is allowed to do on the systems with their level of access.

Access control systems: are those automated and human functions that allow a properly identified person or logical entity access to an organization's facilities or computer systems.

Active measures: is the coordinated direction by a centralized authority of overt and covert techniques that propagate Russian ideas and political and military preferences, and undermine those of democratic adversaries.

Advance fee fraud: are fee schemes that require victims to advance relatively small sums of money in the hope of realizing much larger gains. Not all advance fee schemes are investment frauds. In those that are, however, victims are told that in order to have the opportunity to be an investor (in an initial offering of a promising security, investment, or commodity, etc.), the victim must first send funds to cover taxes or processing fees, etc.

Affinity fraud: perpetrators of affinity fraud take advantage of the tendency of people to trust others with whom they share similarities, such as religion or ethnic identity, to gain their trust and money.

Alternative master narratives: are designed to replace violent extremist narrative by offering an entire cultural, political, or social philosophy that eliminates the appeal of the extremist narrative.

Appropriate separation of duties: is an organization structure that prevents individual employees or agents from having access to or control of work functions in a manner that would allow them to independently misappropriate corporate assets with little chance of detection.

Authorized logical access: is the access that an insider is allowed to have to an organization's computer and communication systems that an employee may need to perform their job duties.

Authorized physical access: is the access that an insider is allowed to have to an organization's property, buildings, and areas of buildings that an employee may need to perform their job duties.

Best practices: are techniques or methodologies that, through experience and research, have reliably led to a desired or optimum result.

Civil society leaders: are individuals who hold government, business, or religious positions that enable them to influence their societies, communities, and individuals.

Comprehensive security plan: covers all security needs of an organization from the ground up and is designed to mitigate known security threats.

Computer fraud: is crime involving deliberate misrepresentation, alteration, or disclosure of data in order to obtain something of value (usually for monetary gain).

Counter-messaging: is the process of matching radical extremist messages on a head-to-head basis in order to mitigate the recruitment and radicalization to violent extremism.

Counter-narrative to radicalization: is a narrative that neutralizes or invalidates the narrative designed to radicalize individuals or groups.

Credible voices: are those voices of trusted community leaders, religious leaders, and intellectuals that can provide a positive influence on a society or community.

Criminal enterprises: the FBI defines a criminal enterprise as a group of individuals with an identified hierarchy, or comparable structure, engaged in significant criminal activity.

Criminal groups: are comprised of people who are organized for the purpose of committing criminal activity for economic gain, political clout, or dominance in a specific geographical area.

Culture of security: is an organization culture in which security pervades every aspect of daily life as well as all in all operational situations.

Cyber-stalking: is the use of the Internet, email, social media, or other electronic communication devices to stalk another person.

Deceptive marketing: advertising or propaganda that misleads people regarding the true facts about a product, service, or corporate activity.

Disaster fraud: is often committed by individuals who seek to profit via false claims of damages; there are also non-insurance-related disaster frauds as many organizations and individuals solicit contributions for the victims of the disaster. Fraud victims may be approached through unsolicited emails asking for donations to a legitimate-sounding organization. The schemer will instruct the victim to send a donation via a money transfer.

Disinformation: is false and irrelevant information made available in order to deceive.

Domestic anti-social groups: are groups of people or mini-societies that oppose the larger society in which they live and/or work.

Domestic fanatics: are radical groups made up of residents or citizens of the countries in which they kill, sabotage, or spread hate and fear.

Doxxing: is the process of gathering an individual's PII and disclosing or posting it publicly, usually for malicious purposes, such as public humiliation, stalking, identity theft, or to targeting an individual for harassment.

Effective prosecution: is the successful prosecution of intellectual crime perpetrators while simultaneously protecting trade secrets and other intellectual property of the victim organization.

Elder fraud: criminal activity focused on extorting or exploiting elderly people on or off the Internet.

Fake refund: is a socially engineered scheme where criminals contact a victim offering a refund for tech support services allegedly provided previously. The criminal requests access to the victim's device and instructs the victim to login to their online bank account to process a refund. This action provides the criminal control of the victim's device and access to their bank account.

Gaps in security: are security measures or mitigation methods that are inadequate to protect an asset or do not thoroughly protect the asset that they were deployed to protect.

Gray outlets: media properties that are established by unknown or obfuscated political, economic, or social powers to disseminate information favorable to their goals or to undermine the activities of their adversaries.

Hate messages: are social media posts that use obnoxious language to ridicule or discriminate against minority or ethnic groups.

Identity monitoring: provides alerts when personal information, such as bank account information or social security number, driver's license, passport, or medical ID number, is being used in ways that generally will not show up on a credit report.

Identity recovery services: are designed to help regain control of a name and finances after identity theft occurs.

Identity theft crimes: identity theft and identity fraud are terms used to refer to all types of crime in which someone wrongfully obtains and uses another person's personal data in some way that involves fraud or deception, typically for economic gain.

Identity theft insurance: is offered by most of the major identity theft protection services, and it generally covers out-of-pocket expenses directly associated with reclaiming an identity.

Identity theft protection: offers monitoring and recovery services that watch for signs that an identity thief may be using personal information and helps to deal with the effects of identity theft after it happens.

Ideological conflict: is the conflict perpetuated by radicalized groups against mainstream society and minority groups.

Ideologically motivated violence: is violence that individuals or groups perpetrate toward targets because of their belief that those individuals or groups are inferior in some way and should be harmed or exterminated.

Individual assessments: are designed to evaluate how well an individual employee is performing a specific task or types of tasks necessary to fulfill their job responsibilities.

Insider misconduct: conduct by an employee that is against organization policies or procedures or that can otherwise harm the employing organization.

Insider-outsider team: is two or more people that jointly conspire to act maliciously against an organization with which one of them (the insider) is employed or has privileged access.

Insider-outsider threat: is a threat that emerges as a result of a relationship between one of an organization's employees and a person working for an outside organization or who is otherwise not related to the employee's organization.

Intelligence operations: is the variety of intelligence and counter-intelligence tasks that are carried out by various intelligence organizations, and activities within the intelligence process.

International fanatics: are individuals, groups of people, or mini-societies that are greatly differentiated from the world around them by a belief system that is totally disconnected from the larger realities in which they live and have a tendency to act out those differences in violent ways or in a politically or economically disruptive manner. They are members of radical groups that cross borders or influence individuals or groups in other countries to kill, sabotage, or spread hate and fear.

Key-logging software: captures and records the keys struck on a keyboard, typically covertly, so that the person using the keyboard is unaware that their actions are being monitored. The information can be retrieved by the person who is operating or who installed the logging program.

Malicious links: are hyper links that lead users to websites that contain malicious code such as spyware, viruses, or Trojans that can infect computers that are used to visit those websites.

Malware: includes viruses, spyware, and other unwanted software that gets installed on your computer or mobile device without your consent. These programs can cause your device to crash and can be used to monitor and control your online activity.

They also can make your computer vulnerable to viruses and deliver unwanted or inappropriate ads. Criminals use malware to steal personal information, send spam, and commit fraud.

Money mules: are defined as persons who transfer money illegally on behalf of others.

News feed: is a constantly updated, highly personalized list of stories, including status updates, photos, videos, links, and activities from the people and things an individual is connected to on Facebook. The goal of news feed is to show people the stories that are most relevant to them.

Onboarding: a process that integrates the new hire into the social and cultural aspects of an organization.

Online alias: is an online identity encompassing identifiers, such as name and date of birth, differing from the employee's actual identifiers, that use a nongovernmental Internet Protocol (IP) address. An online alias may be used to monitor activity on social media websites or to engage in authorized online undercover activity.

Open organizations: tend to be more informal and not highly structured—they often lack strict hierarchal communication structures, project teams are fluid, information flows freely, and employees have extensive access to information, systems, and people.

Personal technologies: include employee-owned devices such as cell phones, tablets, laptops, and digital media that can be used to inappropriately record and remove propriety information from an employer's facilities.

Personal use: means using a service or an item for personal reasons and goals that do not have any relationship to the organization employing the individual using the item or service.

Personally Identifiable Information (PII): is information that can be used to distinguish or trace an individual's identity, either alone or when combined with other personal or identifying information that is linked or linkable to a specific individual.

Phishing: phishing is when a scammer uses fraudulent emails or texts, or copycat websites, to get you to share valuable personal information—such as account numbers, social security numbers, or your login IDs and passwords. Scammers use your information to steal your money, or your identity, or both.

Political correctness: the use of non-biased non-discriminatory words, phrases, or images to communicate ideas or messages.

Ponzi schemes: are an investment fraud that pays existing investors with funds collected from new investors. Ponzi scheme organizers often promise to invest your money and generate high returns with little or no risk. But in many Ponzi schemes, the fraudsters do not invest the money. Instead, they use it to pay those who invested earlier and may keep some for themselves.

Positive message promotional activities: are those that promote positive social behavior and counter negative messaging.

Propaganda outlets: media properties that are established by political, economic, or social powers to disseminate information favorable to their goals, or to undermine the activities of their adversaries.

Publicly available social media: covers social media applications and content that can be accessed and viewed by a general public without restrictions.

Radicalization: is the process indoctrinating previously non-violent individuals or groups into anti-social violent ideologies and actions.

Ransomware scams: employ a type of malware that infects computers and restricts users' access to their files or threatens the permanent destruction of their information unless a ransom is paid, which is often required to be paid in Bitcoin.

Re-targeting: is when a scammer who has attempted to or who has successfully exploited a user in the past makes a second attempt at exploiting that user for financial gain or access to additional information or systems.

Recruiting and indoctrination: is the process of drawing people into a cause and teaching cause-related doctrine.

Revanchism: is a policy of seeking to retaliate against political or military adversaries for diplomatic losses or to recover lost territory, reputation, influence, or power.

Sandboxing: is the use of a restricted, controlled execution environment that prevents potentially malicious software, such as mobile code, from accessing any system resources except those for which the software is authorized to limit the access and functionality of executed code.

Scareware: is socially engineered malware designed to cause shock or the perception of a threat in order to manipulate users into buying malicious software. It is type of malicious attack that can include rogue security software, ransomware, and other scams that get computer users to be concerned that their computer is infected with malicious code and often suggests that they pay a fee to fix their computer.

Security awareness: is the basic level of understanding of security and recognition of the importance of security.

Security threats: are conditions, people, or events that can jeopardize the security of a nation, organization, a facility, or any asset belonging to the threatened entity.

Security vigilance: is a constant attention given to security during day-to-day operations; it contributes to security by encouraging the reporting of security violations, and it makes suggestions on how to improve security when weaknesses are observed.

Self-promotion: in the case of social media, this means providing information or making claims that are designed to result in personal or financial gain for the individual using social media accounts.

Social media presence: is an organization's use of social media accounts and applications to communicate to individuals or groups as well as the mention, comments, discussions, and display of any material on any social media application that relates to or depicts an organization.

Soft cyber influence operations: the use of legal but perhaps sinister cyber techniques to influence or persuade target groups to adhere to a particular philosophy or perform desired behaviors.

Sovereign citizens: are anti-government extremists who believe that even though they physically reside in this country, they are separate or "sovereign" from the United States. As a result, they believe that they don't have to answer to any government authority, including courts, taxing entities, motor vehicle departments, or law enforcement.

Spear phishing: spear phishing attacks differ from regular phishing attempts because they target a specific recipient and appear to be from a trusted source.

Spoofing: is an attempt to gain access to a system by posing as an authorized user. Synonymous with impersonating, masquerading, or mimicking.

Swatting: is when people call law enforcement authorities to report a hostage situation or other critical incident at a victim's residence, when there is no emergency situation. When the police arrive, it may result in a potentially dangerous situation.

Synchronized trolling accounts: social media accounts that in unison, or in a carefully timed manner, post or convey the same, similar, or supporting messages.

Typosquatting (typosquatted): also called URL hijacking, is cybersquatting (sitting on sites under someone else's brand or copyright) that targets Internet users who incorrectly type a website address into their web browser. When users make typical typographical errors they can be sent to a website owned by a hacker, which is often designed for criminal purposes.

Visual content: is any photo, video, or illustration added to social media posts.

Watering hole attacks: are malware attacks in which the attacker determines the websites frequently visited by a victim or a particular victim group, and infects those websites with malware, which in turn infects the computer of the visiting website users, and thus can infect members of the targeted victim group.

White outlets: media properties that are established by unknown or obfuscated political, economic, or social powers that are disguised as representing one cause or perspective but may be working on behalf of other parties.

Whole-of-users approach: refers to an organized effort of all Internet users, regardless of whether they are organizations, groups, or individuals, to participate in creating and maintaining online safety.

Index